MW00454115

23 Miles and Running

23 Miles and Running

My American Journey from chopping
cotton in the Mississippi Delta to
Sleeping in the White House

Ty Pinkins

Some names and identifying details have been changed to protect the privacy of individuals.

NEW DEGREE PRESS

COPYRIGHT © 2020 TY PINKINS
All rights reserved.

23 MILES AND RUNNING

My American Journey from chopping cotton in the Mississippi Delta to Sleeping in the White House

ISBN		
	978-1-64137-417-0	*Paperback*
	978-1-64137-496-5	*Hardcover*
	978-1-64137-418-7	*Kindle Ebook*
	978-1-64137-419-4	*Ebook*

To Josephine & Edgar, Willie Mae & Freddie,
Sabrina, Joseph, and Rukiya

Contents

"A winner is a dreamer who never gives up."

-NELSON MANDELA

Preface

———

The opportunity to write this book came at the beginning of the second semester of my second year in law school. Initially, I questioned the rationale. My law school requirements were already overwhelming. After further thought and some urging from family and friends, I decided to put pen to paper and share my American journey.

This is a personal memoir. It takes a glimpse into my family history, shining a light on many of the events that made me who I am today. It is, however, by no means an exhaustive life timeline. I wrote it for two main reasons—first, to create a checkpoint for my family, generations who will come after me, and second, to share my story with others.

Mine is the story of a black kid raised among cotton fields in the Mississippi Delta, yet who somehow grew up to sleep in the White House while working for the first black President of the United States. It is a story of camaraderie and service to country. It is the story of the people who came before me and laid the groundwork to make me who I am today. It is the story of those upon whose shoulders I stand. Most of all, it is one of family, sacrifice, hard work, heartache, and redemption. It is the story of my American journey.

Introduction

———

I had been running—alone in the dark—for what seemed like forever. As I passed trees lining both sides of the road, each individual stride sent the rhythmic crunch of gravel echoing through the forest. Sweating profusely, chest heaving, and feeling more isolated and alone than ever before, I glanced nervously back over my left shoulder.

Frantically, I thought, "Am I still being chased?" My pace quickened.

Peering again back into the darkness, I couldn't tell if I was still being pursued. Every now and then, eerie yellow headlights of a passing car provided a momentary sigh of relief, temporarily illuminating the path ahead. The respite was brief—gone in an instant as each automobile's glaring red tail lights slowly diminished before vanishing altogether into the distance.

Again, I found myself running alone in the darkness, struggling to make out the path ahead. The only thing I was sure of was that I still had many miles to go until I got there, and I knew I couldn't stop—wouldn't stop. Too much was riding on this. Others had fallen behind and gotten caught. Some had even sacrificed themselves and their long-held dreams of making it so I could keep running. Knowing they had given it all up for me was a constant and heavy weight, a thought that perpetually occupied a dimly lit corner in the back of my mind. Everything depended on me getting to that twenty-third mile. Exhausted, placing one aching foot in front of the next, I kept running alone in the dark—hoping I wouldn't get caught like so many others before me.

** **

We've all heard that old saying: "Pull yourself up by your bootstraps."

Tossed around casually, it rolls off the tongue light and quick, but it catches you with a slow, heavy weight. Much like the wait we endure as we hold on to the American dream that if you just work hard, you can overcome and achieve anything.

But what happens to the person who has neither boots nor straps?

More than thirty years ago, down in the Mississippi Delta, I met a child. No older than twelve. He lived in a little, old wooden shack nestled between a cotton field and a long, narrow dirt road.

When he walked out of that shack that day, he was shoeless and wore a pair of old tattered cut-off shorts. Drooping loosely from his shoulders was a torn, light blue t-shirt with the word "SOJOMAX" emblazoned in big, bold red letters. His hair was uncombed and full of tightly curled naps, resembling a congregating colony of bumblebees. I'm sure he felt the rocks beneath his bare feet as he slowly made his way down the gravel driveway. His dog, Smokey, followed close behind. It was summer; the sweltering Mississippi sun beat down on the backs of our necks.

At the end of the driveway we crossed that narrow dirt road, his toes sinking into the dust like sand on a beach. We stopped at an old rusted mailbox, leaning as if hanging on for dear life; a slight breeze could have blown it over. He pointed beyond it to a well-worn path winding through waist-high grass down to the creek's edge.

He said excitedly, "That there creek is full of big ol' catfish. I go fishin' there sometimes." We laughed; Smokey peered up at us with a blank stare.

The door of that rusty old mailbox screeched like fingernails on a chalkboard as he yanked it open to retrieve a stack of letters and flip curiously through it. To his surprise one of the letters was addressed to him. Eyes wide, a smile spread cheek to cheek when he realized the letter was from his school. Summer break had begun some weeks earlier, so this must be his final report card.

"I just really enjoy learnin'," he looked at me and said.

He was a diligent student who rarely missed a day of school. Years of watching *Reading Rainbow*, whose host LeVar Burton explained the joy of reading, made him fall in love with books. That and Bob Ross's show, *The Joy of Painting*, held his fascination in an unbreakable grip for hours on end. Every day when he got home, he'd go straight to his room to do his homework. He lived in the middle of a cotton field; so, what else did he have to do with his time?

Standing next to that tired, rickety mailbox, he could barely contain himself. He couldn't wait to tell his parents about his final grades, how well he'd done, and that he'd be moving on to the eighth grade.

In his excitement, he dropped the rest of the letters in the dirt. They rested beside his bare, dust-covered feet; Smokey curiously sniffed each discarded envelope. He ripped open the letter, scanned his report card, and with pride read each grade out loud: "A, B, A, B . . . F?"

The expression on his face morphed from excitement to shock, confusion, and finally disappointment.

"This can't be right," he exhaled in a slow, low, barely audible whisper.

Though he'd done everything right—completed all homework assignments, passed every exam, and rarely missed a day of school—his math teacher nevertheless gave him an "F." The realization that he'd have to repeat the seventh grade began to set upon him. In the middle of that dirt road, beneath the weight of that sweltering Mississippi sun, he collapsed to his knees, and he cried, and he began to give up. Smokey plopped down beside him and rested his furry head on his lap as tears dripped down the boy's cheeks.

**

Much later, around 8:30 a.m. Monday, August 28, 2017, I found myself alone and over a thousand miles from home. The morning was beautiful, about seventy-five degrees, when I parked my black Cadillac CTS on the corner of First Street and New Jersey Avenue in Northwest Washington, DC. I sat motionless, soulful tunes by Frankie Beverly and Maze drifting from the radio. His voice conjured memories of summer barbecues, house parties, and family reunions held years ago down in Mississippi.

A miniature black, leather, African drum—gifted to me by a friend over a decade ago—dangled from my rearview mirror motionlessly, suspended in time. The early morning pitter-patter of high heels, wingtips, and running shoes rushed by outside like that little boy's fast-flowing fishing creek back in Mississippi. In the mirror's reflection, only a few blocks away, the US Capitol building gazed intently at me as I waited. Waited on what? I really didn't know; I only knew I wasn't yet ready to cross the street and enter that building. I wasn't yet ready to begin my first day.

Tilting my head back onto the black leather headrest, I gazed up at the light grey ceiling, exhaled deeply, and closed my eyes. My introverted personality and twenty-one years of military service ensured my generously early arrival in preparation for this next adventure; I was in no rush at all to get out of my car. For the time being I was content to sit there, eyes closed, tapping the steering wheel to the soothing melody of "We Are One."

I reflected on the unlikely path I'd traveled from the Delta's winding dirt roads and boundless cotton fields, a journey that ultimately took me around the world to more than twenty-three countries and four continents. Now here I was in Washington with about forty-five minutes left before crossing the street to enter that building.

I rested, needing to catch my breath. I knew when that time was up, I'd have to start running again, on perhaps my most challenging and important path.

PART ONE

DOWN IN THE MISSISSIPPI DELTA

CHAPTER ONE:

Growing Up in Poverty

He stood inside—hidden, motionless—as my grandfather Daddy-Eck paced outside under the midday sun, yelling his name. "Otha Lee! Otha Lee!" Daddy-Eck called out frantically.

Silence! He was stiff, frozen with fear, as dust particles floated through scant rays of light that crept through cracks in the wall, piercing the darkness, like Daddy-Eck's voice pierced the silence.

"Otha Lee! Otha Lee!" Daddy-Eck continuously shouted, to no avail.

**

MISSISSIPPI

Mississippi ranks near last in educational attainment. While the national graduation rate is around 85 percent, in some Mississippi school districts the graduation rate is as low as 65 percent.[1] According to the Census Bureau, the national

---

1 "NAEP State Profiles," The Nation's Report Card, accessed, 2019, nationsreportcard.gov.

poverty rate hovers around 12 percent. In some counties in the Delta, child poverty exceeds 50 percent and is as high as 60 percent.[2]

Compounding the problem, Mississippi—a state with some of the country's most fertile farmland—faces the worst food insecurity and hunger rates nationwide. In some rural areas, nearly 40 percent of children have low access to a supermarket or a grocery store.[3]

Generation after generation of Mississippians feel trapped by and stuck within this system. They are caught without a solid educational, economic, or even nutritional foothold. That age-old saying—pull yourself up by your bootstraps—doesn't work. They are trapped in a never-ending cycle of poverty that, despite being fixable, continually stifles growth.

OTHA LEE

Back in 1974, Otha Lee was a product of that same poverty-entrenched, food-insecure, and educationally bleak system that has contributed to the breakdown and desolation of so many black families, particularly those in the Mississippi Delta.

My mom was only fourteen years old when Otha Lee got her pregnant in the summer of 1973. I asked her one day, "How did you feel when you learned you were pregnant?"

Exhaling slowly, lowering her face to her hand, "Terrible," she said. She pinched the bridge of her nose, shaking her head slowly from side to side. She continued, "I was still a child myself! I was scared, confused, and I didn't know

---

2   "Income and Poverty in The United States: 2018," The United States Census Bureau, accessed, 2019, https://www.census.gov/content/dam/Census/library/publications/2019/demo/p60-266.pdf

3   "Map the Meal Gap." 2019. Feeding America.

what to do. All I knew was that I didn't want to quit school. I enjoyed learning."

During Mom's pregnancy, her relationship with Otha Lee was virtually nonexistent.

"It was a mistake," she said. "I don't even know why it happened."

When mom went into labor, my grandfather Daddy-Eck hopped in his old pickup truck, a blue 1965 Ford F-100. It resembled the truck from the popular 1970s television show *Sanford and Son*. He rushed fifteen miles down Highway 61 to the tiny town of Valley Park, where Otha Lee lived. Like his involvement in the rest of my life, Otha Lee was also absent on the day of my birth.

Daddy-Eck yelled out Otha Lee's name in desperation, "Otha Lee! Otha Lee!" There was no response. Otha Lee hid in the dark, dusty corner of a tall silver grain silo. And, just like that, the person who was supposed to be my initial and continual support system in life instead rejected me. That dream was snatched away before I'd even been born.

MOM & DAD

Back up Highway 61, miles and miles north of that grain silo and hidden among cotton fields, cattle herds, and labyrinthine dirt roads sat the small town of Rolling Fork, Mississippi. On Wednesday, January 23, 1974, Mom gave birth to me at Sharkey-Issaquena Community Hospital. I was born just feet from the same cotton fields I'd toil in, years later as a teenager. Mom was in the ninth grade and dropped out of school after my arrival. That decision always weighed heavily on me. I felt like my birth had taken something vital from her.

Aunt Lue and Aunt Rosetta, Mom's sisters, had given birth to my cousins Leon and Lenora just a couple of weeks earlier in the same hospital. The first week of January, Leon was born; Lenora came in the second week. I guess God set aside the third week for my arrival. We were called the trifecta and between us was an unbreakable bond. Leon was scared of water, I was terrified of sliced peaches, and Lenora was afraid of being hungry, so she stole both our bottles as we lay together in the same crib.

A year passed before Otha Lee first mustered the courage to visit me. When he did show up, an argument ensued as soon as he walked into my maternal grandmother Madea's house. See, Mom had met someone else. His name was Ali, and he became the most impactful and important person in my life.

When Mom was in labor, and Otha Lee was down hiding in that grain silo, Ali was at work thirty miles North driving a tractor through a cotton field. As soon as Ali heard that Mom had gone into labor, he parked that tractor, jumped right off, and hitched a ride to Rolling Fork. On his way to the hospital, with the meager money in his pocket, Ali bought my first set of clothes. By the time he arrived, I'd already arrived. Ali's was the first male face I saw, and—cradling me in his arms—he became Dad.

When Otha Lee showed up a year later at Madea's house, my relationship with Dad had already blossomed.

"This baby's mine!" Dad barked at Otha Lee. "You ain't been here. You walked out on 'em. He don't even know you. You can get on outta here if you know what's best for ya!"

At six feet, three inches tall Otha Lee towered over Dad, who was barely five foot nine. Standing in the middle of Madea's living room, Otha Lee looked past Dad and directly at Mom.

"Tiny Mae, come on outside now!" Otha Lee implored. "Come with me. I got somethin' to tell ya."

"No," Mom responded dismissively.

"I wanna marry ya," he pleaded.

Mom, always a reticent lady, retreated behind Dad.

Madea had been down the hallway in the kitchen. Like a proud mother hen—ultra-protective of her children and grandchildren—she appeared out of nowhere, a damp dishrag slung over her shoulder. Her time was so tied to her kitchen that the dishrag had become a permanent part of her attire. A short, sturdy, and beautiful black woman with both African and Native American facial features, she had the smoothest bronze coat of light brown skin you'd ever seen.

Apparently, Madea had heard enough. Standing her ground, she stared intently up at Otha Lee—whose slim frame and long, dark flowing hair draped down over his shoulders—and flatly refused to break eye contact. After several tense, silent seconds Otha Lee turned and, without another word, walked out the door.

Several years passed before Otha Lee made another appearance. When I saw him not only did I not know who he was, I was also still under the impression that Ali was my biological father. Nobody had told me otherwise; Ali was the only Dad I'd known. Otha Lee engulfed me in an awkward embrace. My favorite cartoon, *Tom and Jerry*, played on an old-fashioned, wood-trimmed floor-model television tucked back in the corner behind the tall stranger hugging me.

Eyes instinctively darting around the room, I searched for Dad a few feet away on the couch beneath the open window, curtains billowing around his face from the incoming breeze. This time Dad said nothing; he allowed our meeting to run its course.

Growing up, I didn't feel any anger toward Otha Lee. The only resentment I may have harbored rested in the fact that he clearly did not help Mom at all. However, Dad had more than made up for Otha Lee's absence.

Otha Lee and I met on only two other occasions. When we last saw each other, he asked, "How do you feel toward me? Can you forgive me?"

"I don't dislike you," I said. "As far as my feelings for you go, there's nothing there; it's just an empty space. No hatred, no anger; it's just empty."

In a weird way, I'm glad Otha Lee hid in that grain silo as Daddy-Eck yelled out his name. I'm glad Mom rejected his marriage proposal, and I'm glad Dad showed up when he did.

*

Some people call it fate. Others call it chance. I don't know what to call it, but what I do know is that Dad—along with his parents and eleven siblings (Glen, Bud, Lil' Buddy, Joe, Willie, Cleotha, Sentha, Glo, Bertha, Doll, and Sally)—had moved a few doors down from Madea only two weeks before my birth.

"Ali and Bud were on top of that old house fixing the roof," Mom later told me.

Like the other houses on Elemwood, the one they worked on was a row house resembling those found on cotton plantations.

"They peered down at us as we walked along a dusty trail through calf-high grass on our way to Mama Willie's house," Mom said. "My belly was already big; it looked like I was about to pop. Nita, thin as a twig, walked next to me.

"Ali looked at Bud, pointed and said, 'That lil' ol' red gal right yonder. I'ma get her, she gonna be my girlfriend.' Well, that lil' ol' red gal wasn't me! It was my sister Nita." Mom laughed at the recollection.

"The next day, Ali left town without saying anything to either of us. When he returned several days later..." she paused, "Bud and Nita were together."

"We started going on double dates—Nita and Bud, and me and Ali, to the Joy Theatre up in Rolling Fork. It was still segregated, so we had to enter through the side door and sit up in the balcony while the white folk sat down below in the good seats. After a few dates, we were leaving the theatre one day when Ali said, 'You wanna be my girlfriend?' I blushed and said, 'yeah!' He held my hand as I wobbled, still pregnant, out the theatre's side door."

Dad's existence altered my life's entire trajectory and set me on a path around the world to some of the best educational institutions, and ultimately to sleeping in the White House.

* *

MADEA & DADDY-ECK

We lived on a plantation called Elemwood, just outside Rolling Fork city limits. Mom and her nine siblings—Aunts Lue, Clara, Rosetta, Nita, Van, and Crissie; Uncles Mane, Preacher, and Vell—along with all their kids, lived in one house with Madea and Daddy-Eck. Madea was a giant in our family; she was the glue that held everything and everyone together. She was queen, mother hen, matriarch.

Her presence was particularly significant given that we kids were being raised in the belly of poverty. All we knew was that we had family, and we were happy with having that and not much else. Aunt Lue always said, "Poor is a state of mind." There must have been some truth to it; as children we had no idea that what we had was so much less than some others.

Madea's house was always packed with people. My cousins and I, sometimes as many as twenty of us, did everything together. We played together and ate together. Many of us even bathed together; at night we each found a spot on that dusty wooden floor and slept together. The house was old, with spaces between floor planks and gaps in the wallboards. In the summer, the heat and the mosquitoes were overwhelming; in the winter the cold was bone-chilling. Madea would cover us with as many blankets as she could find. There were so many of us we slept positioned head to toe. After lying there for a while our combined body heat toasted us warm.

Madea loved animals. She raised chickens and always planted a large garden. She made weekly town trips to Ms. Courtney's store and purchased small seed packets. Tomato seeds, cucumber seeds, watermelon seeds, potatoes, corn, okra—you name it Madea planted it. And we, of course, ate it.

Aunt Lue later said, "If nothing else, Madea knew that if she lost everything, she'd always have those chickens and that garden to feed her children and grandchildren."

Madea found an old incubator; in it she placed eggs, hatched baby chicks, and raised them into full-grown hens and roosters. She developed an intricate system that continuously produced enough chickens, ducks, and geese to provide eggs and meat for the nearly twenty people under her roof. She made a lot from a little.

Willie Mae Pinkins and Freddie "Ali" Jackson first met in January 1974, only a few weeks before I was born. Mom and Aunt Nita were walking past this house on Elemwood while Dad and Uncle Bud worked on the roof.

Taken in January 1975, this is the earliest photo of me. My mom is on the left with Aunt Nita cradling me in her arms on the right. They are standing behind Madea and Daddy-Eck's house out on Elemwood. In the distance is one of the many fields where Madea and her daughters Luella, Rosetta, and Clara picked cotton before I was born and where Mom went back to work after my arrival.

Myself in 1978 at preschool in the Ripley-Blackwell Head Start Center in Mayersville, Mississippi.

Spring of 1980, Mom, Dad, Freddie "Pee Wee" Jackson, Jr., and I took our first family photo at Sears in the Greenville Mall.

My grandparents, Josephine "Madea" Pinkins and Edgar "Daddy-Eck" Pinkins

Late 1970s, Josephine "Madea" Pinkins with her sister Jessie Mae Booker and their father Dave Booker, Sr. standing outside Madea's house on Elemwood.

1959 photo of my
Aunts Claretta,
Juanita, and Luella.
In the background
is the house
in which they
lived with their
six siblings.

Bottom row from left to right: Mom, her siblings Claretta "Clara" Hite,
Billie Pinkins, Juanita "Nita" Jackson, Rosetta Pinkins
Top row from left to right: Vanalean "Van" Dennis, Luella "Lue" Brown,
Nathanial "Preacher" Pinkins, Sylvester "Vell" Pinkins, and Claude
"Pop" Hayes.

My fraternal grandparents Mary Jackson and Colee Jackson, Sr.

Standing from left to right: Dad with his brothers Colee "Lil' Buddy" Jackson, Jr., Robert "Cleotha" Jackson, Sr., and Willie James Jackson. Kneeling from left to right: Alfred "Bud" Jackson, and youngest brother Glen Jackson.

Cousin Monicat outside Elemwood. At the end of the road beyond the
trees is Mt. Herald Missionary Baptist Church.

Getting ready to walk to Mount Herald for Sunday School.
Front row left to right: Turkessa, Pee Wee, Don, Monicat, Dean.
Back row left to right: Danika, Shawonder, Marvin, Lenora, Jent, James,
and myself (the tallest and wearing glasses).

An industrious woman, Madea woke early each morning around five and went to work in her garden, turning the soil, and preparing it for planting. Later, she'd wake all her grandchildren with the smell of bacon, eggs, and grits in the kitchen. After feeding us, off she'd head to work in white folks' homes, cleaning and caring for their children. Once home in the evenings she'd kill a chicken, pluck its feathers, grab some vegetables from her garden, and prepare dinner for her own family.

Equally as important, she taught her children—almost from birth—how to cook and help with the garden. Madea never owned a measuring cup or measuring utensils. If asked how much seasoning to add, she'd say with a smile, "Oh, just add a couple pinches of this and a handful of that."

Just as Madea passed traditions down to her children and grandchildren, so too did Daddy-Eck. He drove tractors and raised pigs. At any given time, Daddy-Eck had ten to twenty hogs in a boarded-up, wooden pen behind the house and beyond the big ol' weeping willow tree. Mamma-Willie, our great grandmother used to make us go pick our own switches from the willow when we got in trouble. She'd braid those switches together and tear our butts up, especially if we begged for too much food and didn't eat it all. She didn't believe in wasting anything. Not a day went by where we didn't hear Daddy-Eck's hogs rooting around in the back yard, or smell them when we ran around and around that house. The odor usually hit us square in the face just as we passed beneath the willow tree.

Every fall was harvesting season when Daddy-Eck, along with his sons Vell, Preacher, and Mane, slaughtered two or three hogs. It was a pretty big deal—the meat we got from those hogs, along with what was killed during deer hunting season, was prepped and stored to feed the family in winter.

The workday usually started early when we'd all gather around the hog pen out back. Daddy-Eck had prepped two or three pigs throughout the summer. He'd caged off an area and built a wooden floor to keep them off the ground and out of the mud to keep clean. To clean out their system and fatten them up, he fed them only corn for months and months. When fall came Uncle Vell and his brothers would dig a slanted hole in the ground and insert a fifty-five-gallon drum at a forty-five-degree angle. Once dead, the hog would be inserted headfirst and doused in hot water. Next, they'd scrape all hair from every inch of the body.

Madea and Daddy-Eck never wasted any part of the pig. Everything from the rooter to the tooter was cleaned. The meat would be seasoned and stored in either a freezer, a salt-box, or the smokehouse out back. They'd make their own bacon, pork chops, pork ribs, cracklings, breakfast sausages, chitterlings, hog head souse, mountain oysters, pig feet, pig ears, and pig tails. Between the garden, hogs, and deer, there was usually no reason to go to the grocery store.

To me, the most fascinating and compassionate aspect of the harvest wasn't the process itself. Just as Madea would distribute her garden's vegetables to family members, neighbors, and even strangers, Daddy-Eck did the same with his bounty.

"Back then, people gave things to each other. Everyone understood that their neighbor was struggling, too," according to Uncle Vell. "If someone was down to only one rooster, but had ten hens, we gave them a rooster. If someone didn't have enough meat for winter, we went hunting, killed a deer, and gave half of it. As a community, we took care of each other. We didn't have much, but we made sure nobody went hungry.

Madea had her entire cookbook committed to memory. She knew specific ingredients, how much seasoning to add, and how long to cook each dish—no need to check the book. She prepared huge, delicious meals from her vast mental catalog. Thanksgiving or Christmas never went by without a kitchen full of freshly baked pecan and sweet potato pies. Jelly, caramel, and lemon cakes abounded. To me, the best part of the chicken, rice, and gravy dinners were huge, fluffy homemade biscuits that paired perfectly with her homemade syrup. Neighbors far-and-wide stopped by for a meal and were never turned away.

During summer, my cousins and I would play kickball in the front yard while Madea and her daughters gathered around buckets and buckets of fruit. They'd peel plums, peaches, and pears to be boiled, preserved, and stuffed into old mason jars for the coming fall and winter.

Like a long line of baby chicks trailing a mother hen, we'd follow Madea out to her garden. While our parents worked the adjacent cotton field, we dug potatoes from the ground. For us it was a game to see which kid could find the biggest potato; Madea knew it was survival—a way to feed her family and pass on tradition.

Madea called out to us children around noon each day to gather on that old, front porch for lunch. We'd come running with a trail of dust behind us—many of us barefoot. We sat on that wooden porch with the summer sun beaming down as Madea served us bowls of pinto beans and cornbread while we watched our mothers walk by as they worked in the cotton field behind the house.

Over the years, that image has never faded for me. At that age, I didn't realize that one day—like so many of our ancestors before us—I'd also walk those rows of cotton. That said, as daunting as Mississippi Delta poverty could be, our real saving grace was the joy derived from having such a large, close-knit family. Val, Darlene, Peterman, Lenora, Leon, Pee Wee, Monicat, Niki, Marvin, Boom-Boom, Shawonder, Becky, Lil' Willie, Dean, Howard, Greg, Nay, Jeff, and Jent—we were all first cousins and had an unbreakable bond, forged under the shelter of Madea and Daddy-Eck's roof.

* *

VAL

Val, Aunt Lue's daughter, was the eldest cousin. While our parents exemplified hard work, Val took the baton and showed us how to run a different race.

One day, while we ran shoeless around and around Madea's house chasing chickens, ducks, geese, and pigs we heard Val's voice call out, "Hey, y'all, come-on round here! I'm setting up a stage. We gon' have us a talent show!" At the sound of Val's voice, immediately, the pitter-patter of our dusty little feet could be heard coming around the corner of the house.

Val and her sister Darlene, the two oldest cousins, shared a room at the back of Madea's house, next to the kitchen. Exiting their room, you'd step out onto a wooden back porch with an old tin roof. To the left was an old white washing machine that shook so hard I always thought it'd jump off the porch. On the right was an old deep freezer where Daddy-Eck stored frozen pork, deer meat, fish, and rabbit. The rest was a plain, dusty wooden porch, which would serve as our stage.

Val gathered us around the porch, under the branches of the weeping willow, and organized us into different singing groups—like Cameo, The Temptations, New Edition, The Commodores, and The Gap Band. She called a group of kids up on stage and pointed out who would be the lead singer, handing over a hairbrush to substitute as a microphone. She identified who would be backup singers and dancers, and who would play imaginary guitar. This was our first talent show, but it wouldn't be the last. We were totally thrilled and enthralled each and every time Val held a talent show featuring us.

There was only one problem. I didn't participate. I couldn't do anything—couldn't sing a lick, and my dancing was even worse. It was horrible! Zero rhythm! None! To top it all off, I wore these big ol' brown glasses, thick as a Coca-Cola bottle; I got teased a lot and was embarrassed. Eventually one day, Val called me to the back porch while the rest of my cousins were still running around playing.

She asked me, "Tyrone, you wanna be in the talent show?"

"Yeah," I replied, "but I can't do nothing! I can't sing, I can't dance, I got on these big ol' glasses, and everybody's gonna laugh at me." I wanted so badly to be part of the show, but at the same time the introvert in me was absolutely terrified!

She grabbed my hands, stood in front of me, and said, "Follow me. Do what I do."

Moving from left to right, she counted, "One-two, one-two." I followed her steps, shifting from left foot to right.

"Good," she said. "Now that's the two-step."

She then pulled out a record. Val loved music and had endless vinyl.

After some tinkering with the player she announced, "Tyrone, this is your song, and I want you to learn the words." I still remember that song like it was yesterday—"When We Get Married," by Larry Graham.

Several days later, Val yelled out, "Y'all come on 'round here. I'm setting up a stage, we gonna have a talent show!" Again, there was that familiar pitter-patter of little dusty feet racing to participate.

"Today we got a special performance," Val announced with flair, like she was Don Cornelius standing on the Soul Train stage.

"Comin' to the stage is Tyrone, and he's gonna sing 'When We Get Married,'" she yelled out to me and my cousins gathered beneath the willow.

I came to the stage. And I sang. And I two-stepped like Val taught me. I didn't care that I had those humongous brown glasses on; I didn't care that I had on a long sleeve, blue turtleneck shirt in the middle of July; I didn't care that someone might laugh at my awkwardness. All I knew was that someone was cheering and clapping like I was Teddy Pendergrass. That somebody, of course, was Val.

Just like Madea transformed an old incubator into sustenance for us, Val turned a dusty back porch full of cousins into countless hours of entertainment and enrichment. In a sense, Val was just doing what had been passed down to her. Madea had taught her how to do a lot with a little.

Val ignited something in all of us. She gave us a space that distracted from the rampant, extreme poverty all around us. She helped us forget that we sometimes didn't have shoes in the summer and sometimes didn't have enough clothes during the school year.

You see, all we knew was what our parents knew. And because of how our parents grew up, all they knew—learned from their own parents—was the value of hard work. As they made their way from one end of the cotton field to the other, they passed that sense of hard work and determination on down to us.

CHAPTER TWO:

Peaches, Plums, and Kumite

———

"Why did you drop out of school so early?" I asked.

"Stayin' in trouble all the time. I was always fightin', fightin' with them white boys," Dad chuckled, chin held high with a defiant look on his face. "They was always picking on us; my brothers always walked away, but I ain't never back down. Anytime them white boys saw me, it'd be a gang of 'em, big ole boys. They were teenagers, and they'd try to jump me, probably 'cause I was the littlest of my brothers. In school and after school I had to either fight or run, and I ain't never run."

That sounded just like Dad. Though he was one of the nicest people I knew—always smiling and willing to help anyone—he wouldn't back down from anyone or anything when he felt like he or his family was threatened.

"I was about ten years old when I almost killed one of 'em," he said. "They caught Bud up on that ol' bridge and surrounded him. When I ran up, we got to fightin' and I hit one of 'em cross the head with a pipe," he paused and, flexing his right hand, stared down at his fingers. "I just didn't like how they was treatin' us. I didn't like how they treated black folk."

The kid he'd hit with the pipe went into a coma, almost died.

"The police came and got me, took me to the jailhouse over in Greenville. I was so little they just sat me in a chair," Dad explained. "They kept me there, sitting in that chair all night long. The white man Daddy worked for came and got me out of jail the next day."

Dad's parents knew things weren't working out for him in Arcola where they lived. In fact, they feared for his life.

"Momma and Daddy was worried about me, so they sent me, only twelve years old, to Chicago with Lil' Buddy." He chuckled, "Momma and Daddy was trying to get rid of me quick 'cause they knowed I stayed in trouble."

One day Lil' Buddy picked him up from the sixth grade. Driving a blue 1963, Buick Deuce-and-a-Quarter, they headed straight to Chicago. Dad was twelve, and it was his last time to ever sit in a classroom.

"I hated being in Chicago," he said. "Whenever I went outside, someone either tried to rob me or make me join a gang. I had to fight all over again just like I'd been fightin' them white boys back down in Mississippi."

After several years in Chicago, Dad returned to Mississippi. His father, Colee Jackson, had been hired to work on a different farm, so they'd moved from Arcola to Rolling Fork. Pete Johnson, a farm agent, went around hiring black folk to work different plantations. Ironically, he was also the uncle of the little boy Dad had hit several years earlier. Still, Pete didn't realize who Dad or his family were. He told Colee about a job working on a farm owned by Mr. George Cortwright down in Rolling Fork.

Like many wealthy white farmers in Mississippi, Mr. Cortwright owned land all over the Delta. He had cotton farms out on Borderland, where the ground was very flat, and Council Bend, which was bisected by a fast-flowing creek. He also owned land located between Rolling Fork and Anguilla. As I grew older, I often wondered how much of that land had once belonged to black folk who'd been swindled out of it by greedy whites. Thankfully, Daddy-Eck had held onto the land passed down to him over generations. Still, though, reminiscent of post-Civil War exploitative land-grabbing, white folk had been trying to steal it from Daddy-Eck ever since. Though he was illiterate, Daddy-Eck held on tight.

* *

Dad moved us out of Madea's house, and for the first time I was separated from all my cousins. I couldn't believe it! They broke up the crew, the trifecta! That move, losing that cousinly closeness, was brutal. Occasionally, I got to visit Madea's house on the weekends. Each time I visited, I got lost all over again in a world filled with Madea's cooking, chasing farm animals, and the love and laughter that came with our large family.

The move took us several miles from Madea's. Our new home was a red wooden house out on bumpy, potholed Indian Creek Road. It was on Borderland, one of Mr. Cortwright's cotton plantations. The house was off the highway and across what the kids on my school bus called the "broken bridge" above a tiny creek. The middle of the bridge had the biggest hump we'd ever seen. Each day on the way home from school, the bus driver would speed across the bridge and hit that hump so hard that all the kids would go flying. It became our daily ritual to time it just right, so when the bus driver hit that hump we'd jump up as high as we could and come crashing down, in piles of gleeful laughter. I think the driver played along because the bus just so happened to speed up right before the hump.

The red wooden house was surrounded by fields; the property was flat with more endless dirt roads. It was an old house with a huge backyard containing several peach and plum trees. Plump, juicy fruit covered the backyard; I had ready-made snacks every day after school. On many days I sat on the back-porch steps as Mom hung clothes on the line to dry. Next to me would be a pile of freshly picked fruit. I'd munch the day away as peach and plum juice glistened in the sun, dripping from my chin. It seemed like not a day went by without us seeing at least one slithering snake, or others coiled away in corners inside the house. Once, we even found one lurking in the toilet.

Out beyond the clothesline, past those luscious trees, was a vast cotton field. Standing on the back porch, I'd take a bite of a freshly picked peach, look out across all that white cotton, and wonder where those long rows ended! How far out did they span? I dreamt of running through those rows to the forest, far on the other side. I felt like an adventure was waiting just beyond those trees, and I wanted to know what it was. But I was too little to go out there alone; I would've probably been run over by a tractor.

The house wasn't far off the road, so there wasn't much in terms of a front yard. The tractors, combines, and massive bean trucks had beat the snot out of that road; it looked like a war zone. To the right of the house was another cotton field, and to the left was a looming silver grain silo. Across the street was a tattered grey garage where some of Dad's coworkers repaired tractors, combine harvesters, and other farming equipment. That garage was where Dad went to work early each morning before sunrise. Sometimes I'd sneak barefoot across the road, and behind one of those enormous tractor tires, I'd hide and try to sneak up on him at work.

"I see ya back there," he'd say without turning around. "Come on out here. What are you doing over here?"

"Nothing," I'd whisper shyly, lowering my head thinking I was in trouble, though I wasn't. I'd stand there beside him, making circles in the dirt with my shoeless toes as birds fluttered around the ceiling.

"Gone on home now! I'll be there indirectly," Dad would say as he climbed onto a big, green tractor and roared off to the fields.

Oftentimes he returned home well after dark, bone-tired from a full day in the fields. He'd plop down on the couch while Mom warmed leftovers for dinner. If I was still awake, I'd run into the living room and struggle to tug dust-covered work boots off his feet. He'd look down at me, laughing. Considering Dad was the sole breadwinner, I'm amazed he alone provided for a family of four off such a meager salary. He is, indeed, an amazing man. Still today I wonder how I was so lucky he walked into my life before I even came into this world.

**

"Cortwright's a good man," Dad said. "He treats me fairly. Don't ever hate anyone. Some folks hate us cause of the color of our skin, but that don't mean you gotta hate 'em back. It'll just eat you up inside like it's eatin' them."

Although Mr. Cortwright treated Dad well, he too held on tight to certain post-Civil War norms, particularly those regarding sharecropping arrangements. Our wooden red house was owned by Mr. Cortwright, and this fact played a significant role in our time on Borderland. Like sharecropping agreements of old, Mr. Cortwright allowed us to live in the house so long as Dad worked his land harvesting cotton, beans, and wheat. If Dad ever decided he no longer wanted to work Mr. Cortwright's land, we'd be kicked out. There was no option to stay and pay rent. If Dad didn't specifically work Mr. Cortwright's land—rain, sleet, or shine—we had to get out. While I was too young to understand it back then, today, I can only imagine the pressure Dad was under trying to keep a roof over our heads.

I'll never forget that old rickety house. Despite its shabbiness and the conditions under which Dad had to work to keep it, it was home. He had found a place for us to live, a place where he could take care of his family. My little brother Pee Wee and I shared a bedroom, sandwiched between the living room and kitchen. Above our bed was a window, and right outside that window was a tree with long, skinny, finger-like branches. One of those slender branches was disproportionately longer than all the others. At night when it rained and the wind blew, that long, crooked branch rapped the window above us. I was absolutely terrified at that scraping tap, tap, tap, all night long. My imagination thought it was a yellow-eyed witch tapping our window with her long, dirty fingernails. Pee Wee would run to Mom and Dad's room to jump in bed with them.

I hated sleeping in their room, so I'd pull the blanket over my head and close my eyes tight. There in the darkness, that old witch continued tap, tap, tapping throughout the night.

When the moon was bright, it cast a long shadow on the wall, making it seem as though that witch was standing there inside our room. Mom and Dad never really understood why I wet the bed sometimes. Well, the witch wouldn't let me get to the bathroom, which was only a few feet away. Whenever Dad found wet sheets, he'd take a belt to my butt. I'd always rather take a whoppin' the next morning than face the witch in the night.

Our room also included a dingy, crumbling fireplace; surprisingly, it still worked. My older Cousin Jackie stayed with us, off and on. He'd babysit us when both Mom and Dad had to be away. One day around Halloween, Jackie and I were playing hide-and-go-seek; I was hiding, Jackie was seeking. I hid behind our bedroom door as he tiptoed through the house, making strange noises. My mind thought the noises were the witch's eerie laugh. My heart started racing, terrified at the thought of that old witch creeping through the house to find me.

Then there was silence. Out of nowhere, wearing an old Halloween mask, Jackie jumped out from the other side of the door and screamed right in my face! My eyes bulged, heart pounded, and instinctively I swung the metal poker from the fireplace at his head. I almost killed poor Cousin Jackie with the fire poker. Luckily, he ducked just in time; the poker lodged itself into the wall instead of his head. We looked at the hole in the wall, gawking at each other while he rubbed his head, and then we laughed.

Once in a while my step-sister, Niecy, came from Arcola to stay with us. She was a few years older than me and big enough to help Mom around the house. One day she was supposed to wash dishes. We didn't have hot water, so to bathe and wash dishes we'd boil water on the stove in a big grey pot.

One day Niecy was over and the pot full of boiling water was too big for her to lift and dump on her own.

"I can move it," I said, puffing out my nonexistent chest. I was scrawny as a beanstalk.

Niecy was older and taller than me, so I don't know what made me think that if she couldn't move the water, I could. Well, I tried, and failed—miserably! With a dish-towel wrapped around each of my hands, I reached up and over the stove and grabbed the two large handles. It had been boiling so long, and now so rapidly, that it bubbled up over the edge.

I'd barely lifted the pot from the stove when it tipped over, dumping all of its boiling hot water directly onto my upper body. I screamed louder than Cousin Jackie did when I almost took his head off with that fire poker. Steam curled up from my shirt; it felt like my torso was on fire. Niecy poured cup after cup of cold water on me as I writhed in agony on the floor.

Later that evening, Mom took me to Madea's house to spend the night on Elemwood. When I got there, I forgot all about my pain and played with my cousins until my heart was content. I fell asleep that evening in bed beside Madea. I woke early the next morning, ready for breakfast and another day of play with my cousins. There was only one problem, though—I couldn't get out of bed. I couldn't move at all.

Whenever I tried something seemed to yank me back. I looked down and realized the overnight effect the boiling water had had on my stomach. It caused so much damage that while I slept, the skin had decomposed and the blanket became fused to my belly. I panicked and started to scream. Madea heard me crying and ran into the room.

"It's gonna be alright, baby. Grandmama's baby gonna be alright," she said as she sat on the bed, looking down into my tear-filled eyes.

A grandmother who can calm her grandchild while peeling a blanket and skin away from his stomach is someone special. The sound of her voice alone could erase fear, pain, and anything else that was wrong. She had that effect on us all. Back then, you only went to the hospital if you were dying. After the peeling, she got a brown bottle of peroxide and a rag. She disinfected, bandaged me up and said, "Come on in the kitchen. I got some bacon, eggs, and grits for ya." That was the Madea we experienced each and every day, our everything.

Back home on Borderland, Dad had a heavy ax outback for chopping wood. He'd haul in an armload at a time to the fireplace to keep us warm in winter. I'd follow right behind him, carrying a few scrawny twigs of my own through the house. Wanting to be like him, I tried to haul as much as I could. Usually a trail of branches followed me. Mom would look at me with a sorrowful smile, shaking her head in pity. While the fireplace served us well in winter, sweltering Mississippi summers were unforgiving. We had no air conditioning and had to tough it out with only a box fan wedged into the window to keep cool. Of course, in the summer with windows thrown open we also had to contend with mosquitoes seemingly the size of pigeons.

"Don't you go out there in that ol' grain bin," Mom always told me, wagging her finger in my direction. Whenever she pointed that finger, I knew she was serious. But that just made me want to do exactly what she was warning me against.

I certainly didn't listen well, and because of it, I was often injured. Whenever my parents—or anyone else for that matter—told me not to do something, the first thing that popped into my mind was, "Why not?" followed by, "I'm doing it anyway!"

Doing it anyway, of course, always got me into trouble.

I'd walked by that silver grain bin several times prior but had never gone inside. It seemed dark and spooky, but I was nevertheless intrigued when I passed it each day to board the school bus. It sat right inside the barbed-wire horse pasture fence. There was one dark, doorless entrance and no windows. One day the bus chugged down the road and, as usual, crossed the "broken bridge." I timed the bump just right, flew high into the air, and came crashing down. The bus stopped in front of our house, and I got off, immediately fixating on that dark entrance. I heard Mom's voice as though she was an angel sitting on my shoulder. "Don't you go into that ol' grain bin," she said.

On my other shoulder sat a tiny little devil whose voice said to me, "Do it!"

I dropped my backpack in the grass next to our driveway, where Dad parked his mint green pickup truck. Walking over to the entrance of the grain bin I stopped, thinking, "This is not a good idea." I continued, though. Instead of waltzing right in, I poked my head across the threshold, into the darkness. The dust inside was thick, the air damp; it smelled like death.

In that dusty, damp, deathly, darkness, I could barely make out the shape of broken furniture. Apparently, someone had used it to store or dispose of unwanted items. There was a broken table on the right, a rickety wooden chair and ancient television to the left. Straight ahead was a plain wooden box leaning against the far wall, calling out my name. I couldn't tell where the rotting, foul stench was coming from. Maybe there was a dead rat or something. I walked the five or six feet toward the mysterious box. Flies buzzed around, likely feasting on whatever emitted that awful odor. Once fully inside, all of a sudden, WHAM! It felt like someone had hit me in the face with a baseball bat. Whatever it was, it knocked me clean off my feet. I rolled over, scrambled up, and bolted. The flies buzzed even louder and now seemed to be everywhere, on every surface and in the air. It seemed to take forever to get to the exit only a few feet away. When I finally got outside, I realized those weren't flies. They were enormous black and yellow bees. One had stung me right between my eyes, knocking me down.

I ran home screaming and dived into Mom's lap, holding my face in my hands. When she pried my hands apart, a big purple knot, the size of one of those plums I loved, had already swollen between my eyes. She went to the kitchen and got the same towel I had used when I spilled that boiling water on my stomach. She wrapped ice in the towel and pressed it against my forehead.

As I lay beside her with my head on her lap, she stared down and said sharply, "I told you not to go in there!" Through the anger in her furrowed brow and the worried look in her eyes, I could tell that it hurt her deeply to see my pain. A mother's love is unmistakable.

"A hard head makes a soft behind," she mumbled under her breath, holding me close. "You gonna learn to listen when I tell you something." She rocked me slowly until I fell asleep in her arms.

**

I have never forgotten that without Dad, my life's path would have been drastically different. Although he smiled a lot in the face of hard work, he never offered me much verbal advice. What he didn't say out loud, though, he made up for through the example he set. He taught endless, valuable life lessons. He shaped who I am today.

Dad recognized early on that I was a quiet child, introverted just like Mom. Aside from the relationship I had with my cousins, I usually kept to myself.

One Saturday afternoon, when I was around ten, I hopped into Dad's mint green pickup; we drove several miles into town, to the high school gym. I swear that was the loudest truck I'd ever heard. Dad and Pee Wee seemed to enjoy the engine's roar as we barreled down Highway 14 toward Rolling Fork. I covered my ears.

Technically still segregated, Rolling Fork had two schools. The white kids attended private Sharkey-Issaquena Academy. Rolling Fork Elementary and High were public and mostly black. Ironically, many of the white teachers at the black school sent their children to Sharkey-Issaquena Academy.

That hot summer Saturday, we parked outside the Rolling Fork High School gym. I followed Dad across the cracked, potholed parking lot, past the red brick auditorium on the left and the cafeteria on our right. He yanked open a stuck, heavy metal door.

Inside the gym, birds fluttered above. About five feet high, small, dusty glass windows lined the wall. Rays of sunlight strained their way through magnified tiny dust particles suspended in the air. The lines on the court had long faded, and the basketball nets struggled for dear life, hanging by threads.

The kids there were dressed in white martial arts uniforms. While Dad spoke to a big burly black man, I marveled at the kids as they yelled, kicked, tumbled, and jumped.

"Ty!" Dad tapped me on the shoulder. "I want you to meet someone. This is Daniel Duckworth, and he is going to be your sensei."

A military vet, Sensei Duckworth was a second-degree black belt who taught Tae Kwon Do to community kids. Sensei Duckworth stood right in front of me: "Hit me!"

"What?" said a tiny, scared voice in my head.

My heart rate quickened as I thought, "You're over six feet tall and easily more than two hundred pounds. I don't even know you, and you want me to hit you? No thanks, buddy!"

Again, he demanded in a firm voice, "Hit me, right here!" He jabbed his index finger into his abdomen.

I desperately wanted to hide my puny sixty-five-pound body behind Dad. With my index finger, I pushed my big brown glasses up the bridge of my nose. I reared back and threw a right-handed punch that bounced harmlessly off rock-hard abs. Out of nowhere, with what sounded like a scream from the far reaches of East Asia and felt like a bolt of lightning, Sensei Duckworth hit me with a swift punch to my chest.

Next thing I knew, I was on my back, sliding in slow motion across the dusty gym floor, glasses twisted awkwardly on my face. Lying on my back, I stared up at the birds. They danced above, laughing at me. I got to my feet, fixed my glasses, and stood behind Dad as they shook hands.

"Bring him back Monday after school," Duckworth declared.

"Wait, what? Bring him back after school? Bring who back after school?" the voice in my head asked hysterically.

Dad and I left the gym; as usual, he didn't say much. On the ride home, however, he broke the silence. Above the loud roar of the engine, he asked, "You wanna come back on Monday and begin Tae Kwon Do lessons?"

I don't know if I was more afraid of disappointing Dad by saying no, or that Sensei Duckworth was gonna beat the crap out of me on Monday after school. I could see in Dad's eyes that he cared deeply about me and wouldn't place me in an uncomfortable situation.

"Yes." I'd decided.

He smiled, nodded in approval, focused on the highway, and drove on. The only other sound was the roaring engine.

I quickly grew to enjoy the rigors of martial arts training. Luckily, Lil' Joe—one of my cousins on Dad's side of the family—was also in Tae Kwon Do. Lil' Joe was a year younger but had already been practicing Tae Kwon Do for at least two years, and boy was he fast. So quick and nimble, I thought he was a miniature, black Bruce Lee. Having him in the class made it easier to acclimate. Because we were similarly sized, we were regularly pitted against each other in Kumite. Class after class, we went at it pounding each other. Some days, he'd beat me. Other days, I'd get the better of him.

About a year later Dad dropped me off for practice one Saturday morning. I was scheduled that day to test for belt advancement. When I entered the gym Sensei Duckworth instructed me to move to the middle of the basketball court, face away from him, stare at the brick wall, and stay silent. My ears tuned to the sound of fluttering birds above. My mind preoccupied itself with the particles of dust drifting in the sunlight that fought its way through those dingy gym windows. To be honest, I don't even remember what color my belt was that day. What I do remember is Sensei Duckworth walking up from behind and ordering me to turn around to face him.

Before I could fully rotate to face him, two things happened. First, to my horror, I realized two additional black-belted men stood before me: Brad Craddock and Ellis Screws. Brad was a slim, redheaded, freckle-faced white guy with lightning quick speed. Ellis was a big guy, comparable to Sensei Duckworth in size and weight. Second was a familiar scream and solid punch as Sensei Duckworth rocked me with his right hand. Brad and Ellis joined in on the assault. Weighing only about seventy-five pounds myself, I was still light as a feather. Every time I kicked, one of them would whack me in the jaw. When I spun around to confront the sucker puncher, I'd get a kick to the ribs from someone else.

It was like fighting ghosts. I was punched, kicked, knocked down, and dragged across the floor. Everything became a blur. It felt like birds flew all around me, phantom punches coming from everywhere. Then I got whacked in the jaw and knocked off my feet; everything moved in slow motion. My ears rang like a giant church bell was inside my head. I landed on the floor, and my glasses flew off, the world going out of focus. Breathing heavily, my uniform hanging off my body, I was about to start crying. I wanted to quit.

I wondered, was this what Dad felt as a child when those bigger white boys tried to jump him? Or when the rain and sleet pounded down as he worked the farms day in, day out to provide for us? Was this what Daddy-Eck felt as an illiterate farmer, resisting repeated attempts to take his land? Could this be how Otha Lee felt hiding in that grain silo? Was this the feeling felt generation after generation by my ancestors, who walked those endless rows of cotton across the Delta?

As the ringing slowly dissipated, I could hear those birds fluttering. I could hear the heavy breathing and the shuffling feet of Brad, Ellis, and Duckworth behind me just waiting for me to stand up to pound on me some more. As I lay there on the floor trying to catch my breath, I pushed my glasses up the bridge of my nose with my index finger. Vision restored, I noticed someone had wiped the dirt away from one of the dusty square windows. I looked closer, and it was Dad. His eyes locked with mine; I read his lips.

"Get up!" he was saying. "Get up!"

I staggered to my feet. And I continued to fight! And I got knocked back down! And I got back up!

I knew Dad was still standing there on the other side of the window, staring. I heard his voice in my head, saying, "Get up!" And I did! And I finished the fight.

The room stopped spinning and the world became calm. All I could hear was my own breathing. Sensei Duckworth sent his two henchmen away.

"Turn away from me and stare at the wall," he said coldly.

I was tired and nervous as I pondered what Sensei Duckworth would do next. There were no fluttering birds, only quiet. I sensed Sensei Duckworth behind me. He wrapped his arms around my waist, removed my old belt, and replaced it with a brand-new color.

"Congratulations!" he said as we both bowed out of respect.

I had passed my test!

Tired and dirty, I walked out of the gym to Dad, idling in his truck. He didn't say anything as I climbed inside. We drove down Highway 61 back to the new home we'd just moved into. Dad had found another job, which of course meant another house that belonged to another plantation owner. We left behind the peach and plum trees and moved to a place out on Council Bend Road.

For the first time, the engine's roar didn't bother me. I didn't hear anything at all in that moment. In the silence as we drove, I could feel Dad was proud of me. I leaned back into the seat as he shifted gears. With my right index finger, I again pushed those big brown glasses up the bridge of my nose. I looked out the window as rows and rows of cotton passed us by.

CHAPTER THREE:

Shoot it Again

———

Wherever Dad found work, that's where we moved. We now lived on Egremont Plantation, about four miles south of Rolling Fork. The shabby grey wooden house belonged to the plantation owner, Mr. Bradley. It was basically a shack—no hot water, and without even a bathroom. A few weeks after we moved in, they knocked a hole in the wall where Pee Wee and I slept and pulled a mobile-bathroom up to the opening. Before the mobile-bathroom arrived, we'd hauled water from outside to wash up.

In front of the house was Deer Creek, and across that creek lived some of my friends from school. They had a mean little black dog, barely bigger than a squirrel. I now lived near other kids to play with, unlike out on Borderland where the only thing occupying my time was eating peaches, counting snakes, and running from bumblebees. Even better, I was now closer to my cousins again.

Right behind our house was a cotton field, beyond which was an old railroad track running adjacent to Highway 61. Immediately across Highway 61 sat Egremont Chapel—isolated and alone. Behind Egremont Chapel, about two miles up Highway 826, was Elemwood and all the people who meant so much to me. I was gleefully excited to walk those two miles to them. Though Mom knew I missed my cousins, she wasn't about to let me cross Highway 61 alone and walk two miles by myself.

"Mom, can I walk to Madea's house?" I asked. At this point I was eleven or twelve, school was out, and summer break had started.

"Boy, naw! You too little to be crossin' that highway all by yourself. It's too doggone hot out there anyhow. Don't ask me again. Now go outside and play," she said, standing at the kitchen sink washing dishes.

We had no dishwasher back then, just soap suds and dishrags. I hated when Mom passed that task off to me as one of my daily chores. I dreaded washing dishes more than anything.

Disappointed, shoulders slumped, I moped out the back door, hanging by one hinge, and plopped down on the back-porch steps. Pee Wee, a year younger and much smaller than me, sat down beside me.

"Can I go with you when you walk to Elemwood," he asked with a mouthful of fried bologna sandwich.

"No," I snapped. "Mom just told me no, and she sho' ain't gonna let me go if you're tryin' to tag along. You're too little." I felt myself echo the same words Mom had slung at me.

Each day I begged Mom to let me cross that highway alone to make the walk to Elemwood. Each time, the answer was the same. "No," she'd say, "and don't ask me again."

Of course, I'd wait until the next day and ask all over again.

Mom was quietly protective of us. We spent most of our time with her; she loved it, and so did we. If she wasn't busy doing housework, you'd usually find the three of us snuggled up together on the couch. Her love for us was unmatched, and Pee Wee and I felt it every day. The sixth of Madea's ten children, Mom had big, soft brown eyes and a gentle smile. Her eyes and her smile matched her spirit. She was one of the kindest and most giving people around. If someone asked for something and Mom knew it was her last, she'd probably give it to them anyway. If she didn't have it, she'd borrow it from someone else to give out. It angered me sometimes, though; I thought people took advantage of her kindness.

Her generosity, however, didn't extend to allowing me to cross that highway by myself. I had to figure out a way to get her to let me walk those two miles alone. Then it dawned on me! Every time I'd asked her, she was in the kitchen, cooking or washing dishes, and Pee Wee was beside me. Out the kitchen window, Mom had a clear view of Highway 61. I realized I had to ask her at a time when Pee Wee wasn't next to me, and in a location where she couldn't look up, see Highway 61, and imagine us hit by a speeding car. So, I waited.

The perfect opportunity came one day when Pee Wee was napping on the couch. Mom had just come inside, carrying an armful of laundry from the clothesline out back. She stood in her bedroom, folding a shirt.

Standing in the doorway, I thought, "This is the perfect moment."

I walked through the doorway, stood beside her, looked up with a smile and said, "Mom, can I play with my cousins?" I was careful not to mention the highway, Elemwood, or anything else.

"Sure, go ahead," she said without glancing down.

I couldn't believe it! She'd said yes.

I slid on the tattered shoes I'd worn throughout the previous school year from August to May, ten whole months of wear and tear. They barely held together.

Scurrying out the back door, I jumped off the porch and ran past the billowing white sheets draped over the clothesline. Walking along the edge of the cotton field, I came to the railroad track. Over the track was Highway 61. There I was; this was the moment of truth.

"Should I cross, or should I turn back?" I thought.

I peered back at our house, now far away across the cotton field.

"Technically, I didn't lie. I just failed to mention the highway, the two-mile walk, and Elemwood. Right?" I pondered.

I peered across Highway 61. To the left, toward Cary, the road was empty as far as my eyes could see. After all, with those big brown glasses I surely wouldn't miss anything. I looked to the right, toward Rolling Fork—no vehicles in that direction either. The only real danger, it seemed, was the risk of heatstroke from standing there, indecisive, under the burning Mississippi sun.

I dashed as fast of those tattered shoes could take me. Breathing heavily, I stopped on the other side of the highway, turned around, and to my surprise still saw no cars approaching from either direction. Success!

I spun back around. Straight ahead was a wide-open road, bordered by a sliver of gravel and knee-high grass, leading my way to Elemwood. Positioned every two to three hundred feet along the side of the road were wooden utility poles. These extended high into the air to support overhead power lines that drooped down like long, rubbery, strands of spaghetti. To my left, yet another darn endless cotton field. On my right, just off Highway 826, painted all white, was Egremont Chapel where Dad sang in a gospel group called the Rolling Fork Spiritual Aires.

** **

Dad's mother, Grandma Mary—matriarch of the Jackson family—made sure her children were deeply embedded in the black church. Dad and his sisters and brothers were a tight-knit group, and held no one in higher regard than their mother. Without hearing a word, you'd recognize her children's love and affection for her. Likewise, whenever Dad and Cleotha sang with the Spiritual Aires, her affection and love for her children were on full display.

"Momma made sure we went to Sunday school and church every week," Dad would say.

Dad was a Deacon and a member of the choir. In this capacity he met another Deacon, Malachi Washington.

"I just loved sangin' the gospel," Dad later told me. "Even when I was little, Momma and Daddy used to put me in church programs out in front of everybody. My other brothers and sisters also sang in church. Every week Momma made sure we was in Sunday school."

Malachi had already formed a group called the Gospel Bell Tones, which consisted of cousins Leroy and Charles Ray Lindsey, Bob Booker, Henry Burden Sr., Peter Lindsey, and Malachi's younger brother Jaimie Lee Washington. Dad joined the group after attending a rehearsal at Egremont Chapel. Dad's brother Cleotha soon followed. It wasn't long before they decided to change the group's name from Gospel Bell Tones to the Rolling Fork Spiritual Aires. That's when Clarence C.J. Smith and his son Precious joined as lead and bass guitar players, along with Henry Burden Jr., who played drums.

Egremont Chapel was one of those little, old wooden churches with double doors in front. When you entered, a dark, maroon-colored carpet led up the aisle, splitting the rows of brown, wooden pews left and right. Square, stained-glass windows lined the walls. Between pew and pulpit was where Dad and the Spiritual Aires sang. Directly behind that, the choir section had their seats. Every Sunday, we arrived early before the church service started. Dad would bring Pee Wee and me all the way up to the bench just right of the pulpit. I always felt like we had front row, VIP seating for one of the world's most amazing shows. And a show it was!

Each Sunday, there was so much energy packed not only into our little church, but all black churches throughout the Delta. Dad and the Spiritual Aires traveled all over—to Illinois, Texas, Florida, Tennessee, Missouri, Ohio, Kansas, and beyond. They performed as a group, but also sang backup for groups like the Gospel Keynotes, Blaire and the Violate Notes, Dorothy Norwood, and The Truthettes. They'd open for groups like Willie Banks and the Messengers, Slim and the Supreme Angels, The Jackson Southernaires, and The Canton Spirituals. All that distance and Grandma Mary made sure to follow wherever they went, every performance she could.

The cool, trickling breeze from the window-unit air conditioners was no match for the heat and energy produced by passionate singing and rhythmic swaying of black bodies in that church. Every Sunday, people not only brought their joy, pain, disappointment, and challenges from the week before, but also their prayers, hopes, dreams, wishes, and aspirations for tomorrow and beyond.

Dad and Cleotha always stood next to each other when they sang, two-stepping from left to right. I had never seen the simple two-step performed so smoothly by two people. Radiating from the congregation like bolts of spiritual energy would be a chorus of clapping, shouting, praise for Jesus, and hallelujahs—heightening the energy throughout the church.

When I asked him about it later on, Dad told me, a soft smile on his lips, "Momma would pull a lil' towel outta her purse, get up in the middle of the song, walk between the microphones and everyone else singing, and wipe the sweat from mine and Cleotha's face. That's just the way Momma was. Momma was right there. She was always there. She always took care of her children. Even though Cleotha and I were adults, we still knew that no matter how old we got, we'd always be Momma's babies."

After Leroy finished singing his signature song "Send Me, I'll Go," something interesting always happened. It never failed, no matter which church we were in. The song was "Hello Mother"; it was about a child who dreamt she'd gone to heaven. One of the first faces she saw when she got there was her own mother's face. It was one of those church songs that tugged at the heartstrings.

Dad shared another memory with me, "I remember one Sunday when we was sangin' up at Trail Lake Baptist Church, right outside Arcola. Leroy started sangin' 'Hello Mother' and folks in the pew started shouting. Some people began crying. Betty Mae Frasier, wearing a tall church hat with flowers in it, sitting about three rows back, right next to the aisle, was just rocking from left to right. All of a sudden, with a jerk, Betty Mae stood straight up and started clapping. A few seconds later, she jumped straight up in the air." He punctuated his tale by pointing his finger triumphantly at the ceiling.

"Betty Mae took off runnin' round, inside that church. I stepped out the way and kept sangin'. Everybody else was jumpin' out of her way too. She came back around and took off runnin' again, straight down the aisle toward the exit. Everybody was yelling catch her, catch her!

"Wham! Betty Mae ran smack into those wooden double doors and fell backward like a big ole tree, falling in the forest. She knocked herself clean out. The Deacons and Ushers gathered around her with cups of water and waving paper fans printed with images of Martin Luther King Jr., tryin' to wake her up, and we just kept on sangin."

Sitting there beside Pee Wee, I was always amazed at the amount of emotion and energy bottled up in black churches. To me, it always seemed to be an open, give-and-take relationship: people giving the stressful, painful energy that weighted them down while at the same time drawing positive healing energy from the pastor, choir, and in our case the Spiritual Aires.

At times the energy in the church was so thick, so powerful I'd cry. As a child, this confused me. With tears running down my cheeks, I'd think, "Why the heck am I crying?" Sweating out the stress of the week each Sunday while singing the gospel gave Dad the strength he needed to keep getting up after being knocked down.

* *

The heat inside Egremont Chapel was nothing compared to the Mississippi sun beaming down outside on my solo walk toward Elemwood.

I'd walked almost a mile, kicking rocks and the occasional can, counting each utility pole. At this point I noticed a group of kids walking straight toward me. There were about seven of them, and I smiled because I knew the only group of kids that large in the area were my cousins. Monicat, Dean, Lil' Willie, Lenora, Leon, Reggie, and Marvin were coming my way.

"Hey, where y'all goin'?" I asked, looking both ways—no cars in sight, just empty highway—before darting as fast as I could across the road.

"Yo' mama let you cross that highway and walk down here by yourself?" asked Monicat, dressed in Aunt Nita's handsewn clothes. She made all Monicat's clothes by hand.

"Yup!" I said, a proud smile on my face. However, I knew Mom would probably tell Dad when he got off work, which meant I'd get my butt tore up when I got home. Mom never whipped me. I don't think her heart could take it. That said, she had no problem at all snitching to Dad and then leaving the room as he snatched the belt from around his waist and went to my rear end.

"We goin' to Mr. Bullet's to get some watermelons and peaches," Monicat said excitedly.

Mr. Bullet—whose proper name was Roosevelt Watkins—was a Deacon at Mt. Herald Missionary Baptist Church, where we attended Sunday School. He lived down the road from Madea's house. All around his home were trees with limbs so full of sweet peaches it seemed the branches would snap off. Like many families in that area, Mr. Bullet also had a garden. He grew rows and rows of enormous green watermelons. He'd let us come over to pick up baskets of peaches from the yard and grab a watermelon from his garden. Walking back, each of us lugged a watermelon on our shoulders. Though I never really liked watermelon—and still don't today—I did enjoy hanging out with my cousins.

That's just how people were where we grew up. Everybody tried to help each other; everybody looked out for one another's kids. We could walk around that cotton field out nearly a half-mile from Madea's house, and the adults wouldn't worry that something would happen to us. What I couldn't do, as I found out later that evening, was get away with tricking Mom into letting me walk alone across Highway 61.

Apparently, Pee Wee woke while I was out picking peaches. He wandered around our house, searching for me.

"Mom, where Tyrone at?"

"He's outside playing somewhere," she answered.

"No, he ain't," Pee Wee responded, shrugging his shoulders.

He always snitched on me and seemed to enjoy doing so. I'd find myself getting into trouble because of something he said or did; this time, though, it really *was* all my fault. It didn't take Mom long to figure out what I'd done. She didn't panic and didn't come looking for me. She knew where I was. When I got home that day, she didn't say a word. Later that evening, Dad walked through the door.

"Didn't your momma tell you not to go across that highway?" he asked, unbuckling his leather belt.

I stopped mid-chew of my fried bologna sandwich. And that's all I'll say about that.

* *

That summer I became friends with the plantation owner's son, Cooper. He and I wasted the days away riding four wheelers and horses, and camping out in his dad's fields.

When it rained, we'd hop on the four wheelers and arrive home covered in mud head to toe.

"You gonna get mud all over my house!" Mom would shout. She'd have me strip naked in the front yard, and spray me down with a hose before being allowed to come inside for a bath.

One day Cooper and I went horseback riding. Cooper rode his horse Blacky while I rode Chocolate. Blacky spooked, reared up on his hind legs, and threw Cooper to the ground. I jumped off Chocolate and rushed to Cooper lying in the grass. He was gruesomely injured. His arm had completely hyperextended at the elbow; the bone nearly protruded through his skin.

Mom was the only adult around, so I loaded Cooper on the front rack of the four wheeler like a shot deer and took him to our house. Although Mom didn't drive often, she hopped right into Dad's old mint green pickup truck and drove Cooper to the same hospital where I'd been born. The hospital called Cooper's parents. They arrived later to find my mother still sitting there by Cooper's side, comforting him. They both showed gratitude for my mother's quick action and diligent care in looking after their son. This attitude, however, wouldn't last.

Pee Wee had been born very small, was often sick, and suffered from juvenile arthritis. Sometimes his limbs would just lock up, and my parents would have to rush him to the hospital. A few months after Mom had taken Cooper to the hospital Pee Wee got so sick that Dad had to take off work and rush him straight to the emergency room.

Mr. Bradley was infuriated. He couldn't believe that Dad dared to put his own family ahead of working in those fields.

Kicking his boot, he barked, "Ali, I pay you too damn much to be taking off work to take people to the doctor."

Dad stared Mr. Bradley down and called him everything except a child of God. Dad couldn't believe the same man who thanked my mother for taking Cooper to the hospital had the nerve now to devalue Pee Wee's health. I never saw Dad as upset as he was when he came home that evening. He usually wasn't the type of person to let others get to him.

Mom calmed him down, and they talked it over. They agreed Dad would work there for a little longer until he found a job elsewhere. The next morning, though, Dad woke up still pissed off. In the end he was so upset that he never went back to work on that plantation. I believe Dad would've hurt Mr. Bradley if he'd seen him again that day. Dad felt like there were some things you just had to stand up for. Though he was under immense pressure to take care of us, family and principles came first.

** **

It was November, deer hunting season. Hunting was, and still is, a tradition in our family. We grew our vegetables and killed our meat. All we needed either grew from the land or walked in the forests. That year, when I was thirteen, Dad bought me a twelve-gauge shotgun. I only weighed about seventy-five pounds, and the gun felt heavier than my own body.

Early one morning, he woke me. We hopped in the truck and headed to the woods. We turned off Highway 61 right before Cary, and he drove across a field into an opening lined by trees on both sides. He parked right in the middle of some tall, golden grass. The sky that day was a crisp, clear blue. Dad climbed up on top of the truck and sat with his .30-30 Winchester rifle resting across his lap.

He had a big black scope mounted to the top of his rifle; I always imagined he could probably see Mars with that thing. Down below, I sat on the tailgate with my shotgun also resting across my lap. Distracted, my legs dangled over the edge of the tailgate. I kicked stones in the dirt, daydreaming about everything except deer hunting. Though a bit bored then, I enjoyed few things more than being in the woods with Dad. For generation after generation, hunting ran in our family, and he was passing the tradition down to me.

"Get ready! Here he comes," Dad whispered excitedly. He could have easily killed it from up top where he was sitting, but he wanted me to shoot my first deer.

I hopped to my feet, pushed my glasses up the bridge of my nose, and searched frantically. I saw it and trained my shotgun on it. The barrel of my gun tracked the deer as it bound up and down, up and down, through the tall grass.

"Shoot!" dad whispered. I paused, gnawing on my bottom lip.

"Shoot it!" This time he was urgent, as the deer was about to disappear into the tree line.

WHAM!

Oh, my goodness! The shotgun flew one way, my glasses the other. I got knocked off my feet, across the truck, and hit the ground. Leaves and dirt flew everywhere. My ears rang. Clearly, the only thing I killed was some wheat. If the deer was dead, either I scared it to death or it ran into a tree because I surely didn't shoot it. Dad climbed down from the top of the truck, stood over me, and stared.

"Get up!" He handed me my gun. "Shoot it again!"

I pushed my glasses back up the bridge of my nose and set the stock of my shotgun gun in the socket of my shoulder. Now scared of the recoil, I pulled the trigger again; WHAM! It knocked me back a few feet; my glasses slid back down my nose. I didn't fall this time, though.

"Shoot again."

Wham! Again, and again, I shot until there were no more bullets. I fired that gun twenty-three times. I know because earlier I counted the rounds on the truck ride over, before stuffing them into the pouch on my orange hunting vest.

After I finished shooting, Dad sat beside me on the tailgate. He looked me in the eyes. "Don't ever quit. In life, you're gonna get knocked down. Don't ever give up."

I couldn't help but wonder if this hunting lesson was somehow related to his recent refusal to keep working for Mr. Bradley.

Dad moved to squat in front of me, now eye level, and said, "It's not about how hard you get hit. What is important is that you get back up and keep fighting. Remember, it ain't never over until you win, and the only way you don't win is if you quit. Always remember to get back up and shoot again."

We climbed back in the truck and drove home where Mom was packing up for us to move again. This time we didn't know exactly where we were moving to next.

CHAPTER FOUR:

That Old Rusty Bike and The Imaginary Line

———

Our little family split up. Dad, Mom, and Pee Wee moved five miles down Highway 61 with Uncle Cleotha and Aunt Rosie in Cary, Mississippi. I went back to Elemwood to live with Uncle Bud, Aunt Nita, Cousin Monicat, and her little brother, Dean. They happened to now live in a trailer next door to the house where Dad and Bud—working up on the roof—first saw Mom and Aunt Nita walk by all those years ago.

Cleotha and Rosie had lived with us for a while when we were out on Borderland. They'd even gotten married out in the yard, in the soft shadows of our peach and plum trees. After the wedding, Aunt Rosie told Uncle Cleotha, "You've got a few months to find us a house." Now, we were the ones who needed a place to stay, and Uncle Cleotha and Aunt Rosie's door was wide open.

Uncle Bud and Aunt Nita's white, brown trimmed double-wide trailer, sat right beneath the tall, switch-filled maple tree where Mama Willie's house used to sit. Behind their place and to the left a dirt road split the cotton fields and ran all the way back to a clump of trees along Deer Creek, where Mr. Bullet lived. We never knew why they nicknamed him Bullet; all we knew was he had that yard full of peach trees, and was one of the nicest people around. Deer Creek's tree-lined banks snaked along the edge of the cotton field for about a mile. Twisting around behind Mt. Herald Missionary Baptist Church and past the neatly manicured white folk's cemetery, the Creek popped out at the end of Indian Bayou Road before twisting its way on through Rolling Fork.

At the other end of Indian Bayou Road, buttressed by Highway 826, was the black folk's cemetery, where most of my family is buried. The black folk's cemetery had no neatly manicured paths; ground lumpy, grass sometimes unevenly cut—many of the tombstones were leaning or had fallen over altogether. Each Sunday, my cousins and I made the half-mile walk from the black folk's cemetery up Indian Bayou Road on our way to Sunday School. Formidable women—Wendolyn Booker, Dorothy Pearson, Betty Ross, Mattie Jones, and Rebecca Hall— taught us the bible.

One of the original founders of Mt. Herald Missionary Baptist Church was my great-great-grandfather William Pinkins, Daddy-Eck's grandfather. The church was founded in 1908, and Mr. B.S. Scott served as its first pastor. During the Civil Rights era, Mt. Herald was one of the local meeting places for many brave men and women who fought for equal rights. The Church also served as the first high school for black students in the Rolling Fork area, before Henry Weathers High School was built.

Our half-mile walks to Mount Herald started at Aunt Rosetta's house when cousin Lenora and her baby brother, Lil' Willie, would come outside. They'd make their way past Madea's house where Leon, Marvin, Val, Darlene, Boom

Boom, Nikki, and I joined the group. Across the road was Aunt Van and Uncle Poncho's house from which Shawonder emerged to join. Next up would be Monicat and Dean. Just past their house was a ditch that traversed beneath the road. On rainy days it flooded, and it was nothing for us to turn that muddy hole into our very own community swimming pool. One after another, off the side of the road, we'd jump in with a splash. Sticks, leaves, rocks, and more were at the bottom, but we didn't care. Every now and then one of us would come up limping with a bloody foot cut on glass below.

I can hear Madea's voice now, "Just put some dirt on it." Madea's remedy for nearly all open wounds was to pack them with dirt, to help the blood clot quicker.

After the bleeding stopped, we'd dive right back in. Right there, at that point in the pavement where the ditch met the road, was a slight hill. The subtle rise in the roadway was barely recognizable. That tiny little rise in the pavement turned out to be more than I bargained for one summer day.

* *

Every summer, like clockwork, my cousins Reggie and Marcus came back to Elemwood from Houston to stay at Aunt Tea's. We'd spend those summers playing kickball, dodgeball, hide-and-go-seek, and Cowboys and Indians. No one ever wanted to be a cowboy. We all wanted to be Indians because we got to make our bow and arrows out of corn cobs and sticks.

One day Reggie, Howard, and I decided to go on a bike ride up Indian Bayou Road toward Mt. Herald Missionary

Baptist Church. Dad had bought me my first bike a few Christmases prior. I named it Blacky. Like any kid worth his salt, I loved my bike and treated it like it was a brand-new car on a showroom floor. Near the tractor shed across from Madea's house, I washed it with the water hose until it sparkled. Each day I checked the tires, the seat, and the handlebar before I rode. I had such strong feelings for my bike, not because of the bike itself, but because Dad had bought it for me. On this day, Howard and Reggie rode ahead while I was forced to lag behind because my bike had a loose chain.

"Hey, Tyrone, you can't go too much faster 'cause your chain gonna jump off," Howard joked, as he and Reggie rode on.

I slowed my bike nearly to a stop right by our muddy little swimming pool.

"My chain might be loose, but even if it pops I don't even have to get off," I yelled, still sitting on my bike, leaning over to grab the chain. "All I have to do is..."

CRUNCH!

I was oblivious to my bike creeping forward down the slight decline until the middle finger on my right hand rolled between chain and teeth in the bike's sprocket. Instinctually, I snatched my finger out, leaving about an inch of it in the sprocket and a few drops of blood on Indian Bayou Road.

Those few red drops became a steady stream; my eyes grew wide and I began to holler. Howard rushed back to my scream. I hopped on the back of his bike and he peddled as fast as he could. Reggie picked up the mangled inch of finger, still in the middle of the road, and stuffed it into his pocket.

"I'm gonna die! I'm gonna die!" I screamed as Howard peddled furiously toward Madea's.

Monicat, standing on the side of the road, heard my screams. When she saw the blood, she too started crying, running, and yelling, "I'm gonna die! I'm gonna die!" Finally, at Madea's we found Mom, who wrapped my finger in a dishrag from Madea's kitchen. Madea's time-honored suggestion to "put some dirt on it" wouldn't work this time. Mom rushed me over to Sharkey-Issaquena Community Hospital and sat me and my severed finger down in a chair across from Doctor Lynch. Doc Lynch had delivered me as a baby several years earlier.

"What's he gonna do?" I was terrified, clenching my severed right finger in my left hand, holding it close to my chest.

"It's all right. It's all right," Mom said, prying my hands apart and guiding my finger to Doc Lynch. Holding my hand, he slowly unraveled the dishrag to reveal the stub. It was my first time seeing it since the road.

Something about Mom and her soft brown eyes always seemed to put me at ease. No matter what was going on or what seemed out of order, all she had to do was look at me with a smile and I'd know everything was going to be okay. Mom, however, had probably grown weary of my mishaps. The previous year I broke my arm three times in a span of four months, after which she wouldn't even let me go outside.

Next to Doc Lynch was a white cloth covering items on a silver tray. Doc Lynch retrieved a long needle from beneath the cloth.

"What's he gonna do with that?" I asked Mom in a panic, yanking my hand from Doc Lynch's lap.

"It's all right. It's all right," Mom reassured, easing my hand back over to Doc.

I didn't realize I was being tricked until it was too late. Doc Lynch and Mom were conspiring against me. While I stared into Mom's reassuring eyes, Doc Lynch jabbed that needle into my wounded finger, delivering a dose of numbing agent. My body tensed up, and my mouth flew open to scream. All I managed was a long squeal, sounding like a whistling teapot.

"It's all right. It's all right," Mom said again. My finger started to numb. While I looked into her brown eyes, she rubbed my back. Again, I became subdued.

Doc Lynch cleaned the wound, revealing uneven, jagged flesh and a one-inch segment of bone. The pain had subsided, and I was now hypnotized by the bone protruding from my finger. That is, until Doc revealed a tiny, shiny pair of wire cutters.

"What's he gonna do with that?" I asked mom, again trying to yank my hand away.

Still with a reassuring smile, mom said, "Let Doc Lynch do his work, and we'll get you some ice cream from Ashley's." Located outside the hospital, just across 4th Street, was Ashley's Drug Store. Aunt Sally worked in the pharmacy. I stared into Mom's eyes; the image of a waffle cone with a giant scoop of cookies and cream came to mind.

SNAP!

It sounded like a mousetrap slamming shut. The boney tip of my finger shot across the room, ricocheted off the cabinet, slid across the floor, and stopped next to Doc Lynch's penny loafers.

My eyes darted from Mom's eyes to that bony tip now resting on the floor, back to Mom, and then back to the tip.

"Dangit!" I thought. She'd again lulled me with those soft brown eyes and reassuring voice. While Doc Lynch wrapped my finger with thick, white gauze, Mom let out a shaky, slow exhale; the serene mask on her face slowly morphed into one of pain, fear, and uneasiness. It had all been a show. She had been putting on a calm face to keep me from panicking. "Boy, don't you ever do that to me again," she barked, pulling me close and holding me tight. Smothering me in her bosom, she slowly rocked back and forth, breathing heavily. I think the hug was now more to console her than to comfort me. By that point, I was fine. The only thing on my mind was a waffle cone and a big scoop of cookies and cream.

When we got back to Madea's house, we walked up the same steps where I had broken my arm three times the previous summer.

"Do not leave this porch!" she said sternly, worry in her eyes. She opened the screen door, disappearing inside. I plopped on a wooden chair, my legs too short to reach the floor. With what endless gauze wrapped around my right middle finger and a waffle cone with a half-eaten scoop of cookies and cream in my left hand, I stared out, ice cream smeared from cheek to cheek, at my cousins playing kickball in Madea's grassless, dusty front yard.

* *

My bike, a couple of years later, was pretty beat up; I had to scavenge for parts to rebuild it. I never found a seat but repaired it to the point where I could ride standing up. I knew my parents struggled financially, and I wanted to help. All around town, house to house, neighbor to neighbor, I rode that bike. I stopped only to ask if anyone needed help with yard work. Many in the segregated white neighborhood said no. Some looked at me with disdain. Others simply ignored me. When I got older, after my rounds, the police would follow me home from that part of town.

One day, while riding along Deer Creek on First Street, I noticed an old white man slowly walk across his lawn, struggling with the short hike to his mailbox. I stopped my bike, not daring to cross the imaginary line between the street and that white man's driveway.

"Hello," I said, maintaining my distance. "My name's Tyrone. You need any yard work done?"

"I'm Mr. Jimmy. You scared of snakes?"

"Naw, not really." I was lying. I was terrified of snakes.

"Who yo' folks is?"

"Edgar G. Pinkins is my Granddaddy," I said, referring to Daddy-Eck.

"Oh, I know Edgar!" he responded with a smile.

Turned out Madea and Daddy-Eck had also once lived on First Street, just down the road from Mr. Jimmy's. Madea used to give him vegetables from her garden behind the house where she raised her nine children. It was a small thing—one bedroom, a living room, and a kitchen. The front of the house was feet from Deer Creek. It was a shotgun house, so you could see clean from the front porch, through inside, and out the back door. There was no bathroom, only an outhouse in the backyard. Daddy-Eck, riding a tractor, hauled water from half a mile away in barrels loaded on a wagon.

Mr. Jimmy and I talked a little while longer.

"Come back tomorrow. I'll have some work for you."

"Thank you," I responded, riding off on my seatless bike.

I couldn't wait to get home to tell Mom I'd found a job. She was in the kitchen, washing dishes, when I burst through the door, out of breath from the ride.

"Mom, Mom! I got a job!"

"A job? With who? Doing what?" she questioned me, turning around and drying her hands on an old dishrag.

"Mr. Jimmy told me to come back tomorrow. Said he's gonna have some yard work for me," I explained.

"Who in the world is Mr. Jimmy?" Her brow furrowed.

"Some man over in the white folk's neighborhood. I rode my bike around, asked folks if they needed help in their yard. He was the only person to say yes," I stammered, searching for a sign of approval on her face. "He said he knows Daddy-Eck."

"Okay," she said, smiling.

"Be careful crossing that highway on that bike," she cautioned and then returned to washing dishes.

For the rest of the summer, I stopped by Mr. Jimmy's a few times each week and helped hand-till his garden. He'd sit on his back porch in a rocking chair, swatting flies with a rolled-up copy of the *Deer Creek Pilot*. Oftentimes he fell asleep there.

Every now and then, when I was on my knees, pulling weeds, I'd come across a snake.

"Get that shovel and kill it," Mr. Jimmy yelled.

Usually, I'd use the shovel to carry the snake and release it to slither off into Deer Creek. By the time I'd return, Mr. Jimmy would be snoring again—newspaper on his lap, and a fly on his nose.

End of each day, he'd hand me a ten-dollar bill. I'd spend some on a chili cheeseburger and fries over at Chuck's Dairy Bar near the softball park, or on playing Street Fighter at the arcade in the Sound Waves video rental store. I was just a kid, unaccustomed to having any money. Earning it myself, however, ignited a passion in me to work harder to help my parents.

CHAPTER FIVE:

It's Pronounced Puhkhan, Not Pecan!

March arrived, which meant spring break and a week off school. Mom, Dad, and Pee Wee were still living in Cary with Uncle Cleotha, Aunt Rosie, and cousins Shell, Cedric, Junior, and their newborn baby sister, Miriam.

The week out of school, however, wasn't the reason I was up before the break of dawn that day. I'd already been living with Aunt Nita and Uncle Bud since we'd left Egremont Plantation about five months prior. I missed Mom, Dad, and Pee Wee. I'd never been apart from them for more than a few days, when I'd had sleepover weekends at Madea's house. One of these weekends in particular stands out in my mind.

"Next Saturday is the Big Day," Mom had told me the week prior.

Well, that next Saturday finally arrived, and I was up early while Monicat and Dean still slept. The front door slammed as Uncle Bud headed out for work. I walked out onto the front porch as he pulled out the driveway.

Up the road, behind Mt. Herald Missionary Baptist Church and the white folk's cemetery, the sun peeked over the trees. My destination that morning was in the opposite direction. I was headed down by the black folk's cemetery, across the street from Aunt Tea's house and right next to Highway 826.

The five months I lived away from my parents and brother seemed like forever. When I got older, I often wondered about the pain and anguish my ancestors felt when children, even babies, were snatched from mothers, husbands stolen from wives, fathers taken from daughters. Five months was nothing compared to the forevers lost back then.

** **

Even at twelve years old, I knew we didn't have much. However, like many families in the Mississippi Delta, what we did have was each other. That was enough—enough to hold on to, like a last little thread of hope. We were always worried, though, that the social circumstances that had robbed us of so much of our history would somehow steal us away from each other too.

When the electricity bill didn't get paid, lights going off, we were in the dark together. When there wasn't enough to eat, we stretched those food stamps and sliced thin that block of USDA cheese that came in brown cardboard boxes.

At times it was hard just to make ends meet. Near the end of each month, when food got scarce, Mom worked wonders with that block of cheese. She'd make things like cheesy rice, cheesy spaghetti, macaroni and cheese, spam and cheese casserole, cheese toast, and grilled bologna and cheese sandwiches. She made those simple meals taste like gourmet dinners. We shared what little we had as evenly as we could. When we were hungry, we were hungry together.

When things really got bad—when we had to be separated—Mom and Dad reassured us that very soon, we'd all be together again.

Although Dad had only a sixth-grade education, he was one of the smartest, craftiest people I knew.

He once explained to me, "During winter months, there wasn't much field work. Plantation owners knew we were trapped between a rock and a hard place. Either we lived on their land in exchange for them profiting off our bodies, or we, along with our families, got kicked out in the cold."

Despite this, Dad always had a hustle. A plan! He seemed to always be one step ahead of the societal bear traps that continually jumped up to bite black families at the most inopportune moments.

"You see it?" Dad pulled his mint green pickup truck over to the shoulder, slowing to a stop. "Hop out and go get it!"

Pee Wee and I thought it was a game. Each time Dad stopped, we'd take turns hopping out of the truck.

He'd drive another mile or so, pull over, and point to a patch of grass about calf-high, and say, "You see it? There it is right there."

I'd jump out, race over, grab the can and toss it in the truck bed.

Around our house, around the neighbors' houses, along the side of highways, even while out hunting and fishing, Dad picked up sacks and sacks of aluminum cans. Beer cans, soda cans—any type. If it was lying around, Dad picked it up and stuffed it into a black trash bag. At the end of the week, he'd load the bags onto the back of his truck and hit Highway 1 toward Greenville. There, he'd stop at Freedmen's Salvage Yard and sell the cans for a few cents per pound.

I was always amazed by Dad's level of dedication and focus. Always, behind that gentle smile, lurked an idea to keep his family afloat. The same can be said about Uncle Bud, which is probably why they were always together. Although Uncle Bud was a year younger, they were like twins. If you saw one, it was a good chance the other was nearby.

Pecan trees—correctly pronounced "puhkhan"—were and are today scattered all over the Mississippi Delta. Some places were literally covered with them. Out in the middle of a field, behind an abandoned barn, or down on a creek bank, you'd find Dad and Uncle Bud out there, bent over, picking up pecans.

"Whenever I saw a puhkhan tree, long as it wasn't on somebody's private land, I got out and picked 'em up," Dad told me. "I reckon me and Bud picked about twenty to forty croker sacks full of puhkhans each week."

They'd stop and go knock on any country door.

"We see y'all got a lot of puhkhans in your yard. Mind if we pick 'em up?"

For them, it didn't matter if the homeowner was black or white. They were on a mission. Pecan season was fall and with winter fast approaching, the two were simply trying to earn money to provide for their families. Black folks generally didn't mind. Some white folk said, with a slammed door, "No, get off my land." Others allowed it. There were so many pecans it could be overwhelming.

"Some white folk let us pick up on half," Dad explained. "Pick up on half meant whatever we picked up, we'd give the homeowner half of 'em. Other folk let us take whatever we wanted. Me and Bud would be out there for hours. We'd clean that whole yard, front and back."

At week's end, Dad and Uncle Bud drove south to Vicksburg or north to Greenville and Indianola. "Wherever they was payin' the most per pound, that's where we went." Dad laughed at the recollection. "Big ole croker sacks stuffed full of puhkhans hanged off the side of my truck. Usually, we got around ninety cents a pound. Sometimes, they tried to cheat us, though. They didn't wanna pay us a fair price."

Dad and Uncle Bud would drag twenty to forty croker sacks of pecans inside the warehouse to be weighed. Some weighed over a hundred pounds. Sacks and sacks were scattered all over the floor.

According to Dad, "I reckon they thought we couldn't count. We didn't get mad, but we wasn't fixin' to just stand there and let 'em cheat us. Each time that guy weighed a sack and called out a weight that was a few pounds too light, he slid it to the side and drug another sack back behind the counter. While he was struggling to get that hundred-pound sack up on the scale, me and Bud slid the same sack he'd just weighed back into our pile. He unknowingly weighed it all over again."

Dad was one of the nicest people I knew; he always tried to treat people with kindness. However, when someone tried to take advantage—assuming that, because he may not have had a formal education, they could pull the wool over his eyes—he'd let them think they were taking him for a ride. All the while, he'd apply a little poetic justice of his own.

What the white pecan man behind the counter didn't realize was that, although Bud had left school in the ninth grade, he could add in his head fast as a calculator.

Dad concluded, triumphantly, "When we finished with that guy, me and Bud walked outta there with double what we woulda got if he ain't tried to cheat us. Serves 'em right for tryin' to take my puhkhans."

Through those years of driving tractors up and down cotton fields, picking up cans, and selling pecans, Dad played a figurative game of chess. He worked a long-term strategy that I was too young to comprehend. Although he always wore a gentle smile, he truly disliked living under the thumb of plantation owners. Like many black folks living on Delta plantations, he worried day in and day out that if he got fired, he'd have to pack his family up and find a new place.

For years Dad pinched pennies, saving a little bit here and a little bit there.

*

That morning, age twelve, I stood on Aunt Nita and Uncle Bud's porch, eyes closed, head tilted back, face toward the sky. I took a deep breath. The sound of one of Madea's crowing roosters echoed down the road from the direction of the black folk's cemetery. That's where I was headed.

I exhaled and descended the wooden steps Uncle Bud had built. Heck, he'd built the whole porch. When Aunt Nita said she wanted a sunroom, Uncle Bud built that, too. All this despite having dropped out of high school. Leroy Lindsey taught him carpentry, and Uncle Bud was a damn good carpenter at that! If someone needed a roof fixed or a room added, Bud was there.

I walked across the yard, stepping over Monicat's yellow banana bike. Aunt Nita's maroon and white van, a Chevrolet Astro, sat in the gravel driveway. Crickets chirped in an early morning symphony. I stood in the middle of the road, next to the maple tree where Mama Willie's house used to be. Mama Willie used to sell all sorts of sweet goodies. For fifty cents, we could get a candy bar or moon pie or a pop. We used to tease our cousins who visited from out west and up north. They didn't know what a pop was. They called it "soda." Beyond that tree was our swimming ditch and the spot in the road where I'd lost part of my finger a few years back.

From Mama Willie's house, all the way down the road to the black folk's cemetery, old houses lined the street. Cousins, uncles, aunts, and grandparents, all cobbled together their lives on Elemwood. The county had finally put a couple of lights along the road. It was empty, and I could see clean down to the black folk's cemetery as I walked.

I passed Grandma Mary's house on the left—the house where Dad and Bud had first peered down at Mom and Nita. A little further along and on the right was where Charles Ray, and his wife Tina lived. It's also where Uncle Glen fell from a Chinaberry tree as a teenager. He'd impaled his arm clean through with a branch.

"I was way up in that Chinaberry tree, and Carolyn was throwing dirt clods at me," Uncle Glen recounted to me. "I was trying to catch 'em and throw 'em back at her. The branch broke under me. I think I hit every limb on the way down."

Doctors said Uncle Glen's right arm would be paralyzed. In fact, he turned out so fine he became star player on the high school football team and earned a scholarship to Kemper Military School & College out in Boonville, Missouri.

Across the road from Charles Ray's house, Uncle Mane and Aunt Billy lived with Cousins Greg, Howard, Nay, Jeff, and Jent. Off their porch and along the side of their house was one of Madea's gardens. On the other side of that garden full of lima beans, butter beans, peas, okra, and tomatoes was Madea's house itself. Val, Darlene, Peter Man, Leon, Marvin, Boom Boom, and Nikki were likely inside, still asleep so early in the morning. Madea, though, was probably already up. She was likely in the kitchen cooking pancakes, grits, bacon, and eggs for her beloved slew of grandchildren.

Across from Madea's house, Aunt Van and Uncle Poncho lived with cousin Shawonder, Roshunda, and DeEdgar, who'd just been born. Next to Aunt Van's house was an old wooden tractor shed, held up by six thick wooden poles. Leon had jimmy-rigged a basketball goal up there. He'd found an old bike wheel, ripped out the spokes, and nailed it to one of the poles. Marvin, Leon, Boom Boom, Lil' Charles, Lil' Willie, and I played for hours in the thick dust beneath that shed.

We didn't have a basketball, so we usually played with an old kickball or even a tennis ball. Whatever we could find that was round and bounced would do. For hours and hours, under that shed, we'd battle—kicking up dust and tossing balls through the bike rim.

Tractors were also parked under the shed and piqued the interest of one of us to his detriment. Cousin Leon's younger brother Marvin was only about ten years old at that point. He was two years younger than me and got into any kind of mischief he could find. A day didn't go by without Aunt Lue yelling at Marvin about something; he'd thrown a brick and killed one of Madea's turkeys, or he'd climbed on top of the house and tossed the cat off to see if it would land on all four feet (sometimes it did, sometimes it didn't). He'd once even shot Leon in the chest with a BB gun. Marvin was a handful and it's no surprise he got more beatings than any of us.

Even at that young age, Marvin was fascinated with driving. We'd be playing over behind Madea's house; all of a sudden, Marvin would vanish. Across the road he'd go, under the shed, trying to start the tractors. Like a rock climber, he'd scale up the side of tractor after tractor, turning the ignition with no luck.

Eventually he climbed up on an old, green John Deere, turned the key, and the tractor roared to life. He sat in the driver's seat with the tractor idling, rumbling beneath him. His only problem was he didn't know how to make it move. All he could do was pull the throttle to rev the engine. So, that's what he did. He revved the engine up as loud as it could go. The noise got Daddy-Eck's attention.

Scared when he spotted Daddy-Eck coming across the road, Marvin jumped off the still rumbling tractor, ran, and hid. Daddy-Eck suspected that Marvin was the culprit but couldn't prove it. If he could've, Daddy-Eck for sure would have snatched that John Deere hat off his bald head and gone straight to Marvin's butt with its bill.

We didn't lock doors back then. All up and down our road was family; no one worried about having anything stolen from houses or cars.

Well, the very next evening Marvin climbed into the front seat of his mom's brown Chevy Nova. The keys had been left dangling from the ignition. Marvin sat himself in the driver's seat. Barely able to see over the steering wheel, he reached down, grabbed the key, and turned it. The engine fired up.

He yanked into drive, hit the gas, and peeled off.

CRASH!

Right into Daddy-Eck's blue pickup truck. The same truck Daddy-Eck had raced down Highway 61 the day I was born.

Aunt Lue's room was just inside the front door of Madea's house. She heard the crash and bolted outside. "Catch him!" she told Peter Man, Marvin's older brother.

Marvin hopped out and hauled tail around the side of the house with Peter Man right behind. Chickens and ducks leaped out of their way. Marvin knew that if he got caught, Aunt Lue would beat the living snot out of him. Around the house and across that yard they went.

Peter Man was older and faster, but Marvin small and quick. Peter Man just couldn't quite get his hands on him. Right when he got close enough to grab, Marvin dove under the house where the ducks, chickens, and geese were. He crawled deep where it was dark and dusty, and sat there for hours. Madea came home after nightfall. Only then did Marvin emerge. He knew Madea wouldn't let Aunt Lue whip him. "Leave that baby alone," Madea would say when any of our parents tried to hit us. If we were going to do something wrong, we knew to do it while Madea was home.

That tractor shed served many purposes. It even served as a gathering spot for family reunions. Many family members had left Mississippi during the Black Migration, from 1916-1970, in search of a better life up north or out west. Though gone away, they came back down each summer for family reunions.

Daddy-Eck would slaughter a goat or a cow, and Uncles Mane, Vell, and Preacher tossed it on the grill with pork ribs and chicken. Catfish—caught out at Eastprong Creek on Highway 14, Lake Washington off Highway 1, or Pluckman's Creek—was battered and deep-fried.

Madea and her daughters whipped up potato salad and coleslaw, and they cooked baked beans and macaroni and cheese. Every cake or pie imaginable crowded a wooden table, lined up beneath the shed. Those were nothing compared to the peach cobbler and dewberry dumplings. That and those hot, out of the oven, home-made biscuits were enough to make you slap yourself. To top it all off Madea would pull out her old, wooden ice cream maker. A bucket of ice dumped inside, my cousins and I took turns turning the hand crank until we had a tractor shed full of kids with ice cream all over our faces.

The "real" basketball courts were located on a grassy hill across the road from the shed. Cousins Peter Man and Bear made an entire court for themselves as teenagers. They were older and bigger, so they wouldn't let us play with them. Peter Man played high school basketball and ran track. He had a long, wet jerry curl and reminded me of a young Ronnie DeVoe from RnB group, New Edition.

Peter Man was also on the high school track team. Some evenings when he came home from school, he'd take off running down the dirt road, which led back toward Old Man Bullet's house. He'd run all the way around the cotton field. We'd be right behind him, trying to keep up; the only time he wasn't trying to beat us up was when he was running. However, the moment we stepped on that grassy basketball court to play, he'd chase us away. Behind the basketball court was Madea's second garden. Here she planted potatoes, corn, cucumbers, squash, and just about anything else that would grow. Beyond the garden was another cotton field.

The sun continued to rise, and I walked on toward the black folk's cemetery. I passed a wooden barn on the right, where Big Blue lived. He was a hound dog Daddy-Eck used for deer and rabbit hunting. When not hunting, Daddy-Eck chained him to the barn next to the tractor shed.

Big Blue and Cousin Lenora had a fraught relationship. Lenora teased him every chance she got. Sometimes the rest of us threw rocks at the side of the barn to wake Big Blue, but Lenora taunted him persistently. Her mom, Aunt Rosetta, and Cousin Lil' Willie lived further down the road next to Aunt Tea. Every time Lenora left their house to walk to Madea's, she'd stop to tease Big Blue. The dog knew what was coming whenever he saw her; he'd go crazy barking and yanking his chain, nearly ripping it from the side of the barn.

Late one evening, Lenora was walking to Madea's house, and, as usual, stopped to pester Big Blue. She threw rocks at the side of the barn to get his attention. Immediately he lunged. At first, the chain yanked him back. Lenora kept teasing; Big Blue got madder and madder.

The dog lunged again and then, CLINK!

The chain broke.

Big Blue was closer to Lenora than Lenora was to Madea's house. She couldn't run back to Aunt Rosetta's house, even further away. She was in no man's land! When Lenora took off running, all we saw was legs. She barely made it to Madea's porch in time to escape Big Blue.

I continued past Aunt Rosetta's house, stopping across the street from where Aunt Tea lived.

I'd made it to the black folk's cemetery. I sat down next to one of the barely standing tombstones. I stared across Highway 826, out beyond an unplanted cotton field.

"That's our land," I thought . . .

CHAPTER SIX:

Finally, A House We Could Call Home

That land on the other side of Highway 826 had been in our family for generations—passed down from my maternal great-great-grandmother, Sally Frasier, to my great-grandmother, Juanita Frasier. Eventually it went on to her son, my mother's father, Daddy-Eck.

Like many black landowners in the Deep South, they faced decades of attempted swindling by whites, but they always held on tight. Instead of selling, Daddy-Eck rented to white farmers—albeit at an unfair rate benefitting the farmers. Like his parents before him and grandparents before them, he'd tried to turn the land into a profit without losing it.

But Elemwood, the land all along the road I'd just walked, didn't belong to us. Ironically, it belonged to one of the white farmers Daddy-Eck was renting to. That entire row of houses—from Mama Willie's all the way down to the east side of Highway 826 where I now sat at the black folk's cemetery—belonged to a plantation owner. Those houses could be occupied by us only so long as our family worked those fields.

Out on Borderland and over on Egremont Plantation, Dad had learned it the hard way. The moment he decided he wanted a better job, the moment he tried to pull himself up, we'd have to vacate the premises. Owning your own body didn't sit well with some white folk. In the mind of many plantation owners, an old saying rang true as a bell in the middle of a dark, silent night: "You ain't got to go home, but you got to get the hell outta here."

A stone's throw away, back over on the west side of Highway 826, the land had been passed down to us. It belonged to us in name, but was rented to people who had our family's livelihood under their thumbs. Every last acre was rented to white farmers, usually at a cut-throat rate. But that was about to change.

The highway was empty; I sat motionless in the grass, still shimmering with morning dew. In the distance, about a mile away in the direction of Egremont Chapel, I thought I saw the flashing lights of an approaching vehicle. It was the only vehicle I'd seen for the last half hour. As the lights neared, I rose and pushed my glasses back up the bridge of my nose. Squinting my eyes, I inched closer to the highway. Something about the approaching vehicle commanded my attention.

It was a little white pickup truck. Attached to its hood was an orange emergency light, flashing its beacon in the not-quite morning. The truck approached and my body slowly rotated, following as it innocently drove by. A slight breeze tickled the hairs on my arm. The gravel crunched beneath my feet as I took another step closer to the highway. I was mesmerized by that flashing yellow light. It grew smaller and smaller the further and further away the truck drove. I squinted, and, again pushed my glasses back up the bridge of my nose. I figured it was nothing.

All of a sudden, WHOOSH! A gust of wind nearly knocked me off my feet. Rocks and dirt flew through the air. I stumbled away from the highway, and the unmistakable blare of an eighteen-wheeler semi-truck horn filled the air. The horn blared so loudly I thought it might wake my dead family members, buried just a few feet behind me. The wind settled; the dirt cleared. My hand moved away from shielding my now dust-covered face.

A house! The semi was pulling an entire house down the middle of the highway. I surely wasn't dreaming. The horn blared again, as the semi continued on past Indian Bayou Road and Elemwood on the right. A few seconds later, the truck's bright red brake lights lit up. The yellow left turn signal blinked.

Still in a daze, I was now transfixed on the semi. Stumbling slowly across the pavement to the west side of Highway 826, I didn't even look both ways to check for traffic. I plopped down in damp grass to watch. About three hundred yards across the field, beyond the lumpy clods of dirt, the semi-truck had turned off the highway. It slowly pulled down a narrow, bumpy, dirt road.

First, the little white truck stopped, and then the big semi pulled up behind it. Air brakes exhaling, PPPSSSHHH, it halted on the tiny acre of land that Daddy-Eck had set aside for Mom. I couldn't contain my emotions, tears tracking down my dust covered cheeks. Mom had told me today would be the "Big Day."

Mom and Dad's plan was coming to fruition right before my eyes. Like so many black families, we'd lived under the thumbs of white plantation owners since I was born, since my parents were born, since their parents were born, and since their parents' parents were born.

For about an hour I sat there, watching. I waited until the trucks pulled off. They both made a right onto the highway and disappeared back from where they came. I stood up and glanced over my shoulder, past the black folk's cemetery, back toward Madea's house on Elemwood. I turned to peer at our new home. I started walking across the lumpy, dirt clod covered field.

The house didn't even have steps yet. The bottom of the doorway was about four or five feet off the ground. I was twelve; the doorknob was too high for me to reach. I found a discarded five-gallon bucket next to the road, dragged it over, and climbed. Stretching on my tippy toes, I was just tall enough to reach. With the tips of my fingers, I struggled to turn the knob.

The door cracked open. I hauled myself over the threshold, like a diver struggling to pull his gear and body into a boat after a deep-sea dive. I nudged the door open with my head. Once inside, I rolled over on my back in the middle of the living room floor. I fell asleep with a tear-stained, dust-covered smile on my face. Soon, Mom, Dad, Pee Wee, and I would be back together again.

** **

It was a mini-migration of sorts. Each family eventually moved off Elemwood. They either crossed over west of Highway 826 to what soon became known as Pinkinsville Road or moved on to another place to live. Some decided they no longer wanted to work the fields. Uncle Vell took a job at the Department of Transportation; Uncle Poncho started working for the county. Uncle Mane went out to the Catfish Farm, and Uncle Bud went to work on a different plantation.

Like clockwork, each time one of them started their new job, trying to pull themselves up another rung on the ladder, that long-abided, unspoken rule kicked in. Those men and their families had to get off that white man's land. You couldn't simply pay rent. Similar to the ownership of our ancestors' bodies, if landowners couldn't profit off our parents' bodies, we had to go. They needed to feel they owned those black bodies to justify letting them occupy those houses. Like those tractors under that shed, our bodies were resources, a commodity, a business asset. When those bodies, those commodities, ceased to generate a profit for plantation owners, they had to be liquidated. Rent wasn't enough. They needed to own you, to drain as much as they could from your existence, or else you had to go!

**

Over the five months we'd been separated, Dad had also been searching for another job. An avid hunter and fisherman, on any given day he was out on a creek bank or in a boat catching white perch, buffalo, gar, and catfish. Mostly he'd simply give the fish away to friends, family, and neighbors. Back then, helping others was like breathing. It came naturally even when folks didn't have much to give.

"I'd just finished fishin' out at Eastprong and decided to drive out toward Mayersville on Highway 14," Dad recounted. "I turned off on Willet road and after a few more miles, I seen a tractor shed out cross the field. I drove on around and pulled up to the shed. James was out there working on some farm equipment."

James Hamlin, twenty-four years old, had recently inherited his father's land.

"Hey there! My name's Ali." Dad climbed out of his mint green truck he'd had for as long as I could remember. "How you doin'?"

"I'm James. How can I help ya?" Hamlin stood up, wiping the thick black motor oil from his palms with a rag. They shook hands.

"Need any work done around your farm?"

"Well, seein' as I'm gettin' ready for harvest, I might need some help. Can you drive a combine?" James pointed over at a bulky red combine at the far end of the shed.

"I can drive anything. Cotton picker, combine, tractor, or truck! You name it, I can drive it."

"Well, I only got part-time work right now," said James. "When can you start?

"I can start today or whenever you need me." What began as a part-time job became full-time employment, and more importantly, over thirty years of friendship.

"Out on that farm, I started driving combines, cotton pickers, tractors, and anything else with wheels," Dad told me. "A couple other guys already worked for James, but they drank too much and didn't always show up."

That was one of the things I admired in Dad. In all my years, I never saw him smoke or drink alcohol. Of course, I always thought he drank too much pop; the same was true for Mom. It likely did a job on their kidneys. With the stress to keep their heads above water, who could blame them?

"James was a nice guy," Dad recalled. "It wasn't no black or white thang neither. He treated me like a man, and I treated him like a man."

Dad was quickly promoted to foreman, managing the farm.

"James took off and was gone for days, sometimes two or three weeks. He told me I could hire folk. I'd go find people, especially black folk, who needed a job and bring 'em out to the farm. I hired family members and young guys around town who wanted to make some money," he said, shrugging his shoulders. "I once even brought my entire softball team out there to work."

James gave Dad the reins. He didn't care who he hired as long as the work got done.

"I'd started getting plenty of job offerings for more money on other farms, but I told James I was stayin' out there. We had a good relationship, and most importantly, I knew I could take care of my family," he continued, with a solemn expression.

One day James announced to his white employees, "Y'all best not be makin' them racist jokes around Ali cause he ain't gonna take it. Don't play with Ali cause he'll go off on y'all." They'd been cracking nigger jokes.

It was probably a good thing he warned them. Dad was generally a peaceful person, but that's one thing he wouldn't suffer. I seldom saw him upset, but an undercurrent of frustration must have flowed just beneath his surface. Dad had been treading water forever. Wave after wave of targeted racial animus must have affected him.

"Every time I took a step forward, they made it feel like I took two steps back," he told me. "It's hard to make it in a system built to grind you to dust and then throw you away like trash." Then he stopped talking. Like snow melts when winter yields to spring, his scowl dissolved, replaced by his unmistakable warm smile. "I ain't never want no trouble from nobody. I just wanna be treated fair. I just wanna take care of my family. That's it."

Now, instead of living on someone else's plantation, we lived on our own land. He now had much more leverage because he knew we were in a better position. He no longer had to put up with so much hatred and racism; he could demand time off if Pee Wee got sick or if another emergency arose. He had the flexibility to walk away if he so desired. Though he and Mom still struggled to make ends meet, he'd at least gotten our heads above water, given us a little bit of room to breathe. That was power! Ownership of his own body.

**

Times were still tough, though. We needed those food stamps each month. Cousin Lil' Charles called them "brownies." Paper food stamp notes came in multiple colors, depending on the denomination. Each had an image of the Liberty Bell, that iconic symbol of American independence. The one-dollar coupon was brown; along with the Liberty Bell, off to one side, was a picture of the Founders discussing the Declaration of Independence. The purple food stamp was for five-dollars. It depicted Thomas Jefferson along the edge. The ten-dollar food stamp was green with a portrait of Alexander Hamilton.

Mom had just got her food stamps for the month. She and Aunt Nita were about to drive to Greenville to "make groceries." This didn't mean one was about to head off to a factory to manufacture products or goods. Like pop is to soda, "make groceries" is one of those Southern phrases that simply means going to shop for food.

Back then, there were five grocery stores in Rolling Fork. Deer Creek flowed alongside Sunflower Grocery, the white-owned store on the corner of Locust and Walnut Street. Right across was the Sharkey County Court House and TW&L, a general appliance store. Over on East China Street, sandwiched between the Sharkey-Issaquena County Library and Denton's Clothing, was Chinese-owned Sam Sing Grocery. The moment I'd step in that store, Mr. Sam had his eyes on me. I couldn't walk down an aisle without him popping out like a ghost, hands folded behind his back.

Further down China Street and across Deer Creek was Sunlight Grocery. Across from Sunlight was a post office before the latter was relocated to Walnut Street. When the post office moved, Aunt Rosetta opened a thrift store in its place. Cousin Monicat worked there after school, sorting clothes. Brook's Grocery store, also owned by a Chinese family, was located out on Highway 61 next to the National Guard Armory. Over in the South Gate community, on the corner of Hoyt and Walnut Street, was the Food Center. Though there were five grocery stores in Rolling Fork, mom thought them all overpriced. She'd rather drive to Greenville to shop at stores like Sack-N-Save, Kroger, and Bing's.

Like many black families around the Delta, ours was large, and our parents had to stretch their food stamps thin. It was Saturday and spring break was ending, which meant I had to be back at school on Monday. "Mom, I still need shoes for school," I said. I felt bad, knowing money was tight.

"Okay," she stared out the front door, waiting for Aunt Nita to pull up in her Chevy Astro. "I just got my food stamps. Me and Nita goin' over to Greenville to make groceries. I'll get your shoes while we're there."

"Can I have a pair of Reeboks?" I knew I was pressing my luck. No way Mom could afford those shoes.

Aunt Nita's van pulled up, and the horn sounded. "Sure, I'll get you a pair," she said, rushing out the door. Like a mini

Michael Jackson, I moonwalked across the living room floor in celebration. I was elated as Aunt Nita's van disappeared in a cloud of dust. Mom was gonna get me a pair of Reeboks!

Greenville was a forty-five-minute drive up Highway 1. When she left that Saturday morning, I had plenty of time to consider why I wanted a new pair of shoes. It all started the previous week, that Friday—the last day of school before spring break.

I'd had my current pair of shoes since the beginning of the school year. Either I had grown, or the shoes had shrunk; my big toe was poking out of my left shoe. With every step, the bottom sole of my right shoe flapped like Big Blue's long, wagging tongue. Any day now, that right sole would fall off. I just knew it! I was terrified that my shoes would explode at school.

The bullying had already begun.

Burt, a wide-nosed, slender kid, slightly taller and a grade ahead of me, and Stomp, a short, round, porky kid, with a scar on his face, noticed my flapping right shoe during lunch break that Friday.

"Look, everybody!" yelled Burt. "Tyrone's shoe is talkin'."

Stomp pointed and laughed hysterically. My eyes darted, frantically searching for a safe place, a dark corner to hide, some refuge from the wave of taunts sure to follow. The school cafeteria was in the distance to my left, Mr. Russell's shop class was a little closer on my right, and the JROTC building was behind me. The safest place to hide was the shadowy seventh grade hallway straight ahead.

I hobbled quickly toward the red double doors. Those big brown glasses slid down my nose. With each painstaking step, my right sole flapped like a fish out of water, gasping for air. They followed me, laughing hysterically like a pack of yellow-eyed Hyenas. I quickened my limp as Burt and Stomp pointed and laughed out loud. Flap, flap, flap, went my right shoe with each clumsy step. I couldn't get away fast enough.

"Please don't fall off, please don't fall off," was my only thought, pleading desperately with the flapping sole. With each step, flap, flap, flap, wiggled the sole of my right shoe.

Other kids started laughing and pointing, adding fuel to Burt and Stomp's fire.

"Yo' mama so poor, she can't even buy you no shoes," Burt yelled, pointing while he doubled over in laughter. I never took too well to yo-mama jokes. Even my cousins knew not to include me in that particular game. I wasn't good at it and always got angry when someone said something about Mom.

Next to me as I limped toward the seventh-grade door, Stomp was now down on the ground conversating with my flapping shoe. "Hey, what yo' name is? I'm Stomp. Can we be friends?"

I made it to the door. "Whew! Finally," I thought. "Safety! All I need to do is open the door and enter. All the mocking and laughing will end." Most importantly, the sole hadn't entirely fallen off my shoe. Math book in my left hand, I reached out to open the door with my right.

I pulled. I pushed. In a panic, I pulled and pushed again!

The door was locked. I was trapped in the corner, between the hallway entrance, those two cackling hyenas, and the echoing laughter of all the other kids. Burt reached out, touched my shoulder, shouted, "Hey, Tyrone! Yo' mama so fat..."

Sensei Duckworth always told us to never use in anger what we had learned in Kumite. He specifically said to us that we were not to use it to fight kids at school.

It wasn't the touch on my shoulder that did it. Nor was it the toe protruding from my left shoe. It wasn't even the group ridicule of my right sole. All I heard was those four words.

"Yo. Mama. So. Fat."

WHAP! WHAP! WHAP!

I spun around and before my math book hit the ground, three well-placed punches found Burt's nose. I didn't realize I'd assumed a Kumite fighting stance learned in Tae Kwon Do. I bounced around on the tips of my toes like Bruce LeRoy in the black cult classic *The Last Dragon*. Burt lay in the dirt, nose bloodied.

During the spin the sole ripped entirely off my right shoe.

To my relief the bell rang, ending lunch. Students scurried off to their next class. Shoe sole in hand, I walked the opposite direction. Past the school cafeteria on my left and the old gym on the right, where we practiced Tae Kwon Do, I limped straight off campus. With an entire shoe on my left foot, and now half a shoe on my right, I walked the nearly two miles home. Each time the bottom of my bare foot hit the ground, I heard Burt's voice echo in my head, "Yo mama! Yo mama!" With each echoed insult, I got angrier and angrier.

Despite my introverted demeanor, the one thing that always set me off, pushed me over the edge, was someone saying something bad about Mom or Madea.

"Why ain't you at school," Mom asked, confused as I entered through the front door.

"My shoe fell apart." I held up the sole.

Now, a week later, Saturday, she'd told me I was getting a brand-new pair of Reeboks. "No more bullying," is all I could think as I awaited her return.

Several hours passed before I heard the distinct crunch of gravel as a vehicle turned off the highway. I glanced out the screen door. Aunt Nita's Chevy Astro rolled down the road, a trail of dust behind it. I was so excited, I wanted to moonwalk again. Instead, barefoot, I leaped off the porch and hurried across the yard. Grabbing an armful of groceries, my eyes scanned each bag, searching for a shoebox.

There it was, a Payless ShoeSource bag.

I rushed down the hallway, past the back entrance, and into my bedroom, slamming the door behind me. This was the moment I had been waiting for, and I didn't want to share it. Sitting on my bed, I removed the black shoebox from the white plastic bag. I opened the box, pulled out a shiny, new pair of . . . USA 900s? These were not Reeboks. These were imitations.

Surely Mom knew that wearing a pair of cheap imitations would get me teased just as badly. I knew I was being selfish; I should have been grateful for a new pair of shoes, but I was so disappointed. Thankfully, just over a month of school remained. Burt didn't bother me anymore. I guess he'd learned his lesson. Stomp snickered and pointed, but he mostly laid off as well.

That is, until the last day of school.

I was running around in the grass next to the seventh-grade hallway. I pivoted to make a sharp turn; the sole ripped off my right USA 900. Burt and Stomp were right there, and the bullying started once again.

The next day, I approached Dad.

"I want a summer job so I can buy my own clothes," I said.

He didn't say much. Dad simply looked at me and nodded, "Okay."

Several weeks later, before the sun rose, he walked into the bedroom Pee Wee and I shared and shook me awake. I pulled on the oldest pair of jeans and the raggediest long-sleeved shirt I could find. While brushing my teeth, I heard a truck's engine idling out front. The squeaky screen door moaned as we walked out. Stepping over dogs and cats asleep on our front porch, I walked down the steps in an old pair of his work boots. Dad tossed me a tattered red cap.

I crossed the lawn, still damp with dew, and climbed into the bed of a red pickup with men twice my age. Cousin Leon was there, too. With a startling jerk and a grunt, the truck rumbled off. We turned left, and after a few minutes, made another left heading west on Highway 14 toward Mayersville. We crossed Steel Bayou Bridge over Eastprong Creek. After another mile or so, we made a left onto Willett Road. The sun began to peek over the trees.

The truck rumbled to a halt. Cousin Leon and I, along with the older men, climbed out. We stood in the middle of a long dirt road, staring silently at rows and rows of freshly grown cotton. I was still short, barely a teenager, and hadn't yet hit my growth spurt. The long, green cotton stalks loomed over my head.

Chopping cotton was grueling, back-breaking work. The sun blazed hot, and those rows seemed to go on forever. In the early morning hours, the damp and leafy fields would saturate my clothes with dew. The stickiness clung to my body. Thick, wet cotton leaves scraped the top of my cap and slid across my face as I made my way down each row.

I could see only a few feet ahead. Eventually, we'd pop out the other end, clothes covered with dew and silkworms. I'd shake my body like a wet golden retriever, worms falling and wriggling all around me. One row complete, I'd turn around, choose another row, reenter the field, and trudge on back to the other end.

Today was my first time working a cotton field, and after a couple of hours the heat from the sun started to wear on me. At one point, I fell to my knees, exhausted, dehydrated, dizzy. I'd skipped breakfast, so I was starving as well. I tried, but I couldn't get up. I stayed on my knees, hearing the older men's footsteps grow faint as they walked on, not realizing I was no longer with them. Silence replaced their steps; I stared at my fingers, clenching the dirt. Cotton stalks stared down. "Get up," a voice said from above. "Get up." Someone grabbed my arm and yanked me to my feet. It's was Uncle Joe Nathan, Dad's younger brother.

"Keep moving. Don't stop." He was already walking away. I followed.

At the end of the row was an orange cooler of ice-cold water.

Uncle Joe Nathan pointed, "Drink that."

I took a few gulps, wiped the sweat from my brow, chose a new row, and trailed Uncle Joe Nathan and the older men who had already reentered the field.

For the next several summers, throughout middle and high school, I worked those cotton fields and learned that earning my own money—being able to provide for myself—was incredibly empowering. At times those cotton fields nearly broke me down. Over time, though, I realized those experiences actually built me up.

Many days some cousins were out there with me. Other times it was just me. Out there all alone, I'd listen for the sound of a vehicle traveling the perimeter of the field. Every hour or so, I'd hear the truck. Whenever I felt the vibration of the engine was close enough, I'd jump as high as I could. The red cap Dad had given me would pop up out of the cotton, just high enough for me to see over. I'd get an airborne, split-second glimpse before disappearing back into a sea of cotton stalks. Though my view didn't last long, what I saw was unmistakable. In the distance would be an old, mint green pickup truck—Dad.

He didn't talk much, but he made up for it with his actions. Like clockwork, he'd pass each cotton field I worked in. He'd given me that red cap for a reason; he made sure to look for the top of it each time I popped up. After he saw my red cap, Dad kept driving, and I kept working, just trying to get to the end of yet another row of cotton. All of this was, in the end, preparation for an incredible journey ahead.

CHAPTER SEVEN:

650 Miles from Indiana to Mississippi

Indianapolis, Indiana, is about 650 miles from Rolling Fork, Mississippi. That's where Bernie Miller was born and raised. How did a lanky, white, Midwesterner, who spent hours waiting in line to get schooled by then-future NBA great Isiah Thomas, end up 650 miles away from home and have such a lasting impact on the kids in small, mostly black, Rolling Fork?

Schoolteacher, basketball coach, and freelance photographer, Bernie grew up an only child.

Bernie was a passionate, fiery coach. His love for basketball was only surpassed by his passion for the kids he was coaching. He challenged us in ways we had never experienced. Bernie had frequented basketball courts throughout his Hoosier State city. Not surprisingly, he felt that growing up playing basketball and being out on the playgrounds was one of the best ways to teach kids how to get along in the world. According to Bernie, "There weren't any referees, parents, or coaches out there. Kids had to handle business for themselves."

Sometimes other players, often black kids, got mad when he'd win. Bernie's physical, aggressive play on the court didn't sit well with inner-city boys who watched this lanky white kid dominate them on their own playgrounds.

Bernie understood that he wasn't as naturally gifted as most of the black kids and wasn't as strong as many of them either. "Being aggressive and smart was one of the only ways I could compete as a player," he explained. "When someone on the court wanted to fight me, some of the others guys would chime in and say, 'Hey man, you're just mad cause he's whipping your ass.'"

He felt he had to earn respect and support from people by standing up for himself. Bernie learned this lesson on those courts: "If I had a disagreement with someone, even though they might have been bigger and stronger than me and I knew, and they knew, they could kick my ass—if I could make them think that while kicking my ass, I could do enough damage that they'd regret it, they may not even try me." Bernie relied on that methodology, and it became a concept he employed in coaching basketball as well.

As our coach, Bernie made us believe that even though we were one of the smallest schools in the state, we could compete with big-name schools like Murrah, Lanier, Clinton, Greenville, and Vicksburg. Though things started off slow, his methods gradually worked. We grew from a team that didn't command much respect to one that was feared when we walked into opposing gyms.

At inner-city George Washington High School, Bernie had been on a pretty good track team and was the only white player on the high school basketball team. He had been heavily recruited by Mississippi College and was offered a track and cross-country scholarship for distance running. Not prepared to move so far from home—Mississippi was a long way from Indiana—Bernie instead attended Indiana University his freshman year and watched Isiah Thomas win the 1981 NCAA tournament. Not participating in any sports while enrolled at Indiana, he longed for the days when he competed on the court and in track and cross country.

His move to Mississippi was ultimately prompted by something that happened as a teenager.

"I remember reading Harper Lee's novel *To Kill a Mockingbird* when I was fifteen," he said. "I thought that if that's what the South is like, it's not something I have encountered before, and I would like to experience it. Obviously, in the book, there were lots of bad people, and there was lots of evil. Growing up in the North, it's no secret that many people had a particular image of the South, especially during that time. The novel made it seem like some good and decent people down south were trying to do the right thing."

The South seemed a foreign country to Bernie. With *To Kill a Mockingbird* imprinted on his mind, Bernie contacted the track coach from Mississippi College and told him he was still interested in attending. He completed a few years there before enrolling at Millsaps College in the heart of Jackson.

For him, moving from Indiana was a bit of an adventure. Even though it was still the 1980s, he felt Mississippi had made some progress, however small. Bernie felt in many ways, Mississippi was less racist than a lot of places up north. He'd witnessed first-hand how racism affected his high school friends; it had a profound effect on how he viewed others who didn't look like him.

After graduating from Millsaps, Bernie interviewed for a head coaching job with Mr. Oscar Peace, the principal of Rolling Fork High School. Initially, he was offered a position to coach football for seventh graders. He wasn't interested. He returned to Indiana, taught high school biology for a year, and served as an assistant coach for the junior varsity basketball team. For some reason, he couldn't shake his memories of Mississippi.

A year later, he called up Principal Peace. The timing was perfect—the varsity basketball head coaching position was now open. After the phone call with Principal Peace, he was also offered a junior varsity head coaching job in Indiana. He turned down the Indiana position, an early indication of his character. To understand the magnitude of his decision, one must take into consideration that Indiana is the Mecca of basketball. Coaching basketball in Indiana is huge. He informed them he'd already accepted a coaching job down in Mississippi, and he intended to honor his commitment.

Principal Peace told Bernie he really wanted someone who was going to, "come in, work hard, and spend time with the kids." Peace also shared that the school system didn't really have much to work with in terms of facilities and resources. Rolling Fork was then, and is now, an underserved community in the middle of one of the nation's most poverty-stricken regions.

Things have improved over the past fifty years, but the Mississippi Delta continues to be among the most underserved regions in the United States, with counties in the Delta having poverty rates exceeding thirty percent.

"We may not have many resources," Mr. Peace explained, "but we have good kids down here who are willing to work hard. We are looking for someone who is going to get the best out of them." And so, Bernie accepted the job and relocated to Rolling Fork, Mississippi, in 1989.

The first group of kids he coached included players like Bobby Jones, a shooting guard with one of the purest jump shots I'd ever seen, Chris Boston, who could leap out of the gym, and his brother Brian who also was the starting quarterback for the high school football team. Others included Larry Lindsey and Derrick Smith, who both played guard, Darryl Owens, and my cousin Leon Brown.

Bobby was the second-youngest of nine brothers. He grew up in Mayersville, about fourteen miles west of Rolling Fork. Pinched between the east bank of the Mississippi River and Highway 1, Mayersville's population barely tops five hundred people. Although small, the Mayersville community had heart and was close-knit. Like many kids from underserved communities in the area, Bobby started working at thirteen, mowing yards for his uncle's lawn care business.

As Bobby remembers it, "I didn't get my first pair of new shoes until I was in the eleventh grade. Living with nine brothers, everything was hand-me-downs. As one of the youngest, I basically wore what my older brothers wore before me." Bobby is now a police officer and lives about forty-five miles south of Rolling Fork in the river city, Vicksburg.

He was a tenth-grader when Bernie began coaching at Rolling Fork High.

"Initially, we thought he was just another goofy white guy just passing through who didn't know much about coaching basketball. We didn't really take him seriously in the beginning." Bobby had good reasons to be concerned. We'd seen time and time again young white graduates from up north or out west, come down to teach in impoverished communities for just a couple of years. It seemed their only goal was to stay long enough for the government to pay off their student loans.

Bernie, now our Coach Miller, developed deep, personal relationships with his players—unlike many preceding him. "After we got to know him," Bobby explained, "we realized Coach was different. We saw that one, he was a brilliant basketball strategist, two, we could trust him, and three, he wasn't here just to hang around for a couple of years to get his student loans paid and then abandon us."

Like so many poor kids in the Mississippi Delta, Bobby remembered that, "going to school was tough because we did not have simple luxuries that kids have today—like air conditioning. It was hot in those classrooms. But teachers like Mrs. Smith, Mr. and Mrs. Small, Mrs. Jackson, and Mrs. Nelson cared about us and pushed us to excel. Coach Miller also challenged and motivated us to exceed our own expectations. Together, they made us feel as though we were special and that we were capable. On days when I didn't have a ride to school for practice, Coach drove all the way out to pick me up and then back to drop me off. Coach bought me clothes when I didn't have anything to wear to school."

Bobby's recollection of Coach Miller's kindness is similar to those of other kids in the community. Some shared with me that Coach paid his own money to take them not only to play basketball but also on trips to museums, simply to allow the kids exploration outside their normal circumstances. Many spoke of the spaghetti dinners and pizza-making nights Coach hosted at his house, a game film always playing.

My first interaction with Coach Miller was in 1990, my tenth-grade year. It was the beginning of the school year, and the chatter was that basketball tryouts were soon. They would last multiple days. Those of us who lived outside city limits had to make the tough decision each day to miss the school bus ride home. I'd have to walk the two miles home to attend. Although on the same campus, basketball tryouts were in a different gym than the one where Sensei Duckworth, Ellis, and Brad had beat the snot out of me years prior while birds chirped in the ceiling and Dad peeked through those dust-covered windows. H.G. Fenton P.E. Building, the new gym, was located four hundred or so feet away, on the opposite side of the cafeteria.

In contrast to the other gym's shabbiness, the interior of the new gym glistened. The walls were painted red, white, and blue—our school colors. The basketball court was a shiny sea of red. The school mascot, a Brave, was painted at center court. Beneath each hoop, from the foul line to the baseline, was glossy navy blue.

On the home side, wooden bleachers looked down on the shiny red court from above. Pull-out bleachers on wheels were on the visitor's side, eye-level with the court. Small, square windows, way up high behind the bleachers, were barely reachable; the gym often got really hot in the summer as a result. Many days they brought in huge wooden box-fans that sounded like aircraft engines.

To teenagers who wanted to be a part of the varsity basketball team, merely standing on the court was invigorating. At least that was the case for me. Again, I was introverted, a very quiet kid. Nevertheless, I desperately wanted to be a part of that team, to be a part of something bigger than myself. Neither the most talented nor the most coordinated athlete, the one thing I knew about myself was that I would outwork anybody. When I really wanted something, I never gave up. Dad taught me that.

I'd sat way up high in those brown bleachers and watched older kids run up and down the court each night to thundering ovations from our community, coming out to cheer them on. I longed for the opportunity to be a part of the team, to feel that thunder. The one obstacle—tryouts. Luckily for me, I was hardwired to view an obstacle as an opportunity.

Coach Miller had hurt his back a year earlier; you could tell by his walk. With each step, his shoulders, his entire upper torso, dipped from side to side, like an inverted pendulum. He started each season's tryout exactly the same, "All right, fellas, everyone on the baseline!"

We all lined up on the baseline at the far end of the court, backs against the wall. We faced the main exits, whose two double doors were propped open. It was late August and, before even starting, it was already blazing hot in that gym.

Coach Miller's voice echoed off the walls as he shouted, "On my whistle, you have five seconds to get to the other end of the court!" The sound of the whistle reverberated off the gym walls. The heavy thud and high-pitched squeak of sneakers commenced, lasting for the next several hours as we raced from one end of the court to the other.

Each time we reached the end of the court, bent over at the waist, tugging at the hem of our gym shorts and gasping for air, again, coach Miller's voice bounced off the walls throughout the gym. "You've now got fifteen seconds to run the length of the court three times," he barked. And off we went again, as fast as we could.

Chests heaving, legs burning, sweat dripping, we'd hear his voice ricochet off the walls again, "Five seconds to get to the other end!" We ran, no one wanting to quit, no one wanting to forfeit the opportunity to be on the team. What coach was trying to teach us in this approach was that if you really want something you can't be afraid to go after it, and you can't be scared to hang in there when you get tired, when it hurts, and when things get tough. "I was testing you all to see how serious you were," he said.

On the third day of tryouts, after several hours of line drills, Coach approached us on the far end of the court. We were panting from exhaustion, bent over at the waist, tugging our gym shorts. Each of us clearly saw the four white double doors, two on each side of the gym. They were wide open, inviting anyone without the resolve to continue to quit and leave.

We awaited another blast of the whistle to send us sprinting to the other end of the court. Instead, Coach stared at us as we dripped with sweat, the sound of heavy breathing rippling throughout the building. He didn't blow the whistle. It fell from his lips, dangling from the lanyard around his neck. He leaned slightly forward in our direction. His head bowed somewhat as he looked at us from the tops of his eyes.

Matter-of-factly, he whispered, "No one is going to stop running until at least one of you quits." I heard a few moans of despair from the group, but no one moved toward the exit. I refused to even look at those double doors. I thought, "That's one of the most psychologically cruel things to say to a group of kids who've been running for hours."

The bell had sounded to end school around 3:00 p.m. The round white clock on the wall now said it was almost 6:00. We'd already been running for nearly three hours.

"Y'all are gonna keep running until one of you quits," he repeated.

At that moment, the silence in the gym felt welcoming. No thudding shoes, no squeaking sneakers, no whistle—just the rhythmic panting of teenagers trying to catch their breath. To many of the kids there that day, I am sure the doors looked inviting.

Once again we heard, "You have fifteen seconds to run the length of the court three times." The blast from the whistle pounded our eardrums.

With heavy legs and burning lungs, we took off. There were at least fifteen of us and, to be fair, there weren't enough open spots for Coach to keep everyone. As we approached the court's edge, player after player touched the white baseline, sneakers squeaking. We each pivoted, and raced back to the other end of the court.

Andre Lindsey, though, without missing a stride, kept on running, straight out the exit. He kept on running straight across the parking lot, past the JROTC building and the seventh-grade hallway, across campus back to his home in the Blue Front projects a few streets over.

True to his word, Coach blew the whistle ending tryouts. Some players vomited from exhaustion; some of us collapsed on the shiny red floor. Others limped through the doors to the lobby, in search of the water fountain. We all felt a sense of accomplishment and togetherness for hanging in there and overcoming. We were told that the next day we all would learn who'd made the team. Then would come the first day of practice.

On the way home that evening, I took the same route the cross-country team ran for practice. I'd seen kids running that route earlier in spring and thought about joining the cross-country team as well but didn't.

The next day the bell sounded, ending school. I met up with Mike and Leon. The three of us walked into the gym around half past three to find everyone gathered around the bulletin board. Some kids were already celebrating, slapping high-fives upon learning they'd made the team.

I was one of the smallest guys there, barely a hundred and twenty pounds. I waited until the crowd cleared to check for my name. I scanned patiently, confident I had made the team, simply because I had done what was asked of me. I endured the line drills and hadn't given up. Also, I had just watched my school bus drive off, so I didn't have a ride home.

My name wasn't there.

After all that work, I didn't make the team—cut from the roster. Not because I wasn't capable but because there were too many kids vying for limited spots. With unusual gusto I barged through those white double doors, knocked on Coach Miller's office door, and confronted him. I really felt I should have made the team. I had done everything right, yet was shown that doing everything right wasn't good enough.

Sitting in his office, Coach explained to me the reasons I'd been cut. First, he didn't have enough slots for everyone who had survived the tryouts; second, he expected more than one person to quit; and third, apparently, to be on the basketball team, running cross-country was an unofficial prerequisite, a requirement of which I wasn't aware.

Coach told me he was impressed with the fact that I had enough courage to walk into his office and speak up for myself. He had been surprised to see me barging through his door. In the end, he asked me to stay on as team manager. I'd help out during practice and watch from the sidelines for the entire season. The next year, however, I was out, bright and early, on the first day of training for the upcoming cross-country season. It was the unofficial beginning of my basketball tryouts.

Guess who the cross-country coach was? You got it! Coach Miller. He used cross-country as a way to begin early conditioning for the guys he thought were going to be on his basketball team. In his view, "If you quit cross-country, there was a pretty good chance you weren't going to survive basketball tryouts in the fall."

Since I'd already survived the basketball tryouts once, I was confident about surviving the cross-country season. An added incentive to being on the cross-country team was that after practice, Coach rolled out a basketball and allowed us to play.

While he couldn't officially conduct basketball practice outside of the season, he could let us play pick-up-ball in the gym while he worked in his office. It was his ingenious way of ensuring that the previous year's team continued to exercise their basketball muscles, maintaining their endurance through off-season without breaking Mississippi High School Activities Association rules.

Cross-country practice basically consisted of distance running. I, along with other runners like my karate practice cousin Lil' Joe and Walter, who lived across the creek on Counsel Bend Road, began practice on the corner of Athletic Drive and Parkway Street each day after school. We'd make a left on Parkway Street and took off running with Deer Creek on our right, red brick homes on the left.

Coming to the old red barn in the middle of the horse pasture, we'd make a right onto Indian Bayou Road. We'd run past the spot where Madea and Daddy-Eck raised Mom and her nine siblings on the banks of Deer Creek. To the left, the white folk's cemetery. A few more strides and we'd pass Mt. Herald Missionary Baptist Church, the same church my cousins and I trekked to each Sunday morning.

A half-mile on and we'd run past Elemwood's wooden houses, where most of my family members once resided. Arriving to the black folk's cemetery—my family members buried inside—we'd hang a right onto Highway 826. We'd continue past Pinkinsville Road on one side, soybean and cotton fields on the other. When we'd reach Highway 1, it was time to head back into Rolling Fork's city limit.

Running past Mr. Quick's gas station, we'd continue down Sharkey Street through the Blue Front projects before arriving back at the high school. It was a daily ritual that spring, our three-mile cross country run. Coach would follow slowly behind our group in his green Toyota pickup to make sure none of us got hit by cars as we ran along the highways.

Basketball tryouts were the same as the year before—us running seemingly endless line drills on that shiny, red basketball court. Like before, Coach used those line drills to wear us down, but also as a tool to test the team at the beginning of the season. He was weeding out those who really weren't serious, not willing to give it their all.

"I wasn't going to kill anyone, but at some point, somebody was gonna say, 'Hey wait a minute, I don't want to do this, the game is not this important to me,'" Coach reasoned. "And, they were gonna walk out those double doors." Coach felt that if that was the case, that person didn't really need to be part of the team. "If you've got bad talent but a great attitude, I will work with you on improving your talent. Or, if you've got great ability and a bad attitude, I will work with you on trying to improve your attitude."

I fell into the former category, certainly not the most talented person he'd ever coached. That said, I never gave up. I had a never-quit attitude and appreciated the opportunity to be a part of a team. Coach's final take was, "If you've got a bad attitude and no talent, there's not much I can do for you."

Line drills, cross-country training, and everything else he put us through were to locate serious kids who were going to stick it out, and who were going to do the hard things. He believed if a kid really wanted to be good at basketball, that kid had to put a lot into it: work, time, courage, pain, suffering. You deal with failure head on; you get back up, do better. Anybody who can't look at themselves that way, can't confront themselves and say, "I can make myself do this hard work, I can do what needs doing," certainly wouldn't last on Coach Miller's basketball team.

The next three days of tryouts were filled with torturous line drills, vomiting, exhaustion, and walks home in the dark. On the third day, I watched my yellow school bus drive off. This time, I walked alone, around the cafeteria, past the JROTC building, and toward the gym. This time there was no crowd around the bulletin board. Everyone was already in the locker room, getting dressed for the first practice. I stared at the list of the names. I slowly traced down the list until I got to "Tyrone Pinkins." I made the cut. I was on the team. I walked to the locker room and joined my teammates.

CHAPTER EIGHT:

Long Road to the Coliseum

———

Our 1991-92 team consisted of brothers Leon and Marvin Brown, Michael Franklin, Chris Smith, and cousins Terry and Darrell Houzah. Others team members were James Hite, Mario Lane, Joe Davis, Frank Harris, Lamone Smith, Chris Carter, Charles Williams, Cortez Coleman, Chris Thigpen, and Fred Johnson. That season we were marginally successful. We beat some talented teams that were bigger and stronger than us, but we also suffered some tough losses. We finished the season with a 20–9 record after falling in the state playoffs to the Humphreys County High School Cowboys from Belzoni, forty miles north of Rolling Fork, just off Highway 49.

That loss to the Cowboys was heartbreaking. Little did we know, though, we would soon be tested once again in Belzoni, with everything on the line. We hadn't realized it yet, but Coach Miller had molded us into arguably one of the best basketball teams in the state.

Make no mistake, Rolling Fork High School—though small—did not lack athletic pedigree. Players like Slick Watts went on to star at Xavier University. He ultimately made it to the NBA and led the league in total assists, assists per game, total steals, steals per game, and made the NBA All-Defense First-Team. Slick was the first player to lead the NBA in assists and steals in the same season. He played six seasons before retiring due to injury. Larry Smith, also from Rolling Fork, made it to the NBA All-Rookie team.

Many of the players on our '92-93 team agreed that a lot of people in the community didn't understand Coach Miller. It's true, he yelled and threw things sometimes during practice and games. He once even kicked a sink off the wall at a Leland High School away game. All of this, though, was out of frustration because he saw what we had inside of us and knew we could play ball. He was only trying to get our best out of us.

Coach Miller not only taught basketball. He also taught life. He showed us the value of being a team player, and, more importantly, showed us that we could push ourselves beyond our imagined limits. He knew the talent we held on the court as well as our potential in class and outside of school.

Many of us came to see him as more than just a coach. "We saw him as a role model. He made us come together," recalled Michael Franklin, one of our star shooting guards. According to Lamone Smith, who played center and was among the tallest kids at school, "Coach spent a lot of time with fatherless kids on the team." Michael Davis, who played center and power forward, completes the picture, "He helped us prepare for the future, life and college—not just basketball."

Coach required us to bring our report cards to practice. We had to prove we were passing all our classes or we couldn't play. He also made us bring our books. Those struggling would receive tutoring from the players who were doing well. When one player struggled in a given class, Coach identified another player who excelled in that subject and created study groups during practice. He always went that extra mile. For Coach, it wasn't just about basketball. It was also about ensuring we would graduate. This was particularly important, given the low graduation rates in the Delta.

According to teammate Bobby Jones, "No one else was doing this for us. No one else was holding us accountable like he was."

* *

Our '92-93 season proved to be something special, not only for our team but also for the broader Rolling Fork community. We didn't have much, but what we *did* have was a good basketball team on the verge of doing something great, something that hadn't been done in our little town in over twenty years. Our school hadn't progressed to the state championship since 1972. That was the year Rolling Fork lost to Shaw in the title game.

When Coach Miller first arrived, the high school's games were sparsely attended. No one was really paying attention. Years passed and Coach began building a respectable program; attendance picked up steadily as the team improved.

"A few people would show up simply because they didn't have anything else to do," recalls Mike Franklin. "After a while, the team just started clicking on all cylinders, and people started hearing that these guys were dunking three, four, five times each game. The seats began to fill, more and more." Eventually it got to the point where people would show up an hour early just to snag a seat. Fans crowded up to the rafters, pressed against the white brick walls around the court, and spilled out into the lobby until it became nearly impossible to close the doors that once beckoned the faint of heart during tryouts. I'm sure several fire codes were broken.

We started that season ranked fifteenth in the state. We won our first three games against the Vicksburg Gators, Raymond Bulldogs, and the Leland Cubs. After that we lost two consecutive games in the Yazoo City tournament.

On Tuesday November 17, 1992 the school buzzed with excitement. The Humphreys County Cowboys were coming to town to play us in our own gym. It wasn't lost on us that several months earlier, Humphreys County had eliminated us from the playoffs in their home gym.

Now they were in *our* place. We still felt the sting from that loss; we wanted payback. Over the previous four years Humphreys County had had our number. We couldn't figure out how to beat them. They were a constant thorn in our side, and games against them were always an early test for our team. As division mates, we knew we'd have to go through them to get to state playoffs and ultimately to the Mississippi Coliseum for the Championship.

The gym was packed with energy that evening as students, teachers, parents, and community members descended on our home turf, H.G. Fenton Gym. Right after tipoff, we immediately jumped out to an 18–10 first-quarter lead. By the end of the second quarter we were up 30–22.

The wooden stalls in our locker room were painted red and blue. One of the things I remember about being in that room was Coach's chart. He'd attached it to the wall next to the door. It was a basic dry-erase board about four feet wide and three feet tall. On it were handwritten statistics about every game we'd played thus far: intricate details about whether we won the initial tip, who scored first, which team led after the first quarter, who had the edge going into half time, and which team scored first after the half. It also identified which team had the most rebounds, assists, turnovers, and steals, as well as each team's shooting percentage from the field and from the free-throw line. It was color-coded, and each line of data ended with what we would need to accomplish in order to win.

That's how seriously Coach took the game. We each passed by that dry-erase board every time we went in and out of the locker room. That one simple yet intricate component of his coaching scheme greatly impacted our understanding and approach to the game. Some days after practice, I stayed behind to study that board, fascinated at how so much could be reduced to mere numbers.

After Coach gave feedback, we headed back out to start the second half. With twenty total points from Michael Davis, seventeen from Terry Houzah, and fourteen from Michael Franklin, we defeated Humphreys County 63–56, overcoming our four-year curse. Our record improved to 5–2 overall, the start of what turned out to be a hot winning streak.

We next blasted the Leland Cubs 77–42 behind nineteen points from Michael Davis, Terry Houzah's sixteen, Lamone Smith's twelve, and Michael Franklin's ten. Leland's Alphonso Morris usually gave us problems on the court, but now had only twelve points followed by eleven from Twana Ray. Our record improved to 3–0 in division play, which is just how we wanted it.

Next up was Velma Jackson High School, about eighty miles east of us in Camden, Mississippi. We trounced them 88–67. Michael Franklin led us in scoring with twenty-three points. He was clearly one of the most naturally gifted players the school had seen. One of the advantageous things about Mike was that he was ambidextrous. In class, he wrote with his left hand, but on the court, he could dribble and shoot with either. Mike had a crazy quick first step; he could take his man left or right, and he could jump out of the gym. Rounding out our scorers against Velma Jackson, Darrell Houzah had nineteen points, Lamone Smith had twelve, and Michael Davis and Chris Carter each had ten.

We had started the season by losing two of five games. Now, because football season ended and we had a complete roster, we were at full force. The next team on our schedule was one of our significant challenges of the season. On December 18, we traveled six miles north, up Highway 61, to Anguilla, Mississippi, to face our main rival—the Anguilla Wildcats.

To put it plainly, we didn't like them and they didn't like us. The bad blood wasn't contained to basketball; it spilled over into other sports like baseball and football. No season went by without some sort of fallout between our teams, even outside of school sports. Anguilla had talented players like Isadore Phillips and Michael Hollins, both absolute beasts on the court. Michael always gave us problems as his tenacity was nearly unmatched.

The Anguilla High School gym was intimidating. Aside from all the hostility in the air, their court resembled a Roman gladiator pit. All was calm as we entered the school's main doors and approached the gym. After descending a dim, narrow corridor of steps, we emerged onto their court— blinded by the high, bright lights, deafened by the screams of wild fans, and surrounded on all sides by the bleachers that towered above.

Their mascot was the Wildcat, and we sure felt like we were in a lion's den. We always had to walk into that gym with our head on straight or get it knocked off. And even if we won, in the backs of our minds, we'd wonder, "How do we get out of here without getting hurt?" The local police always dispatched extra officers to games between our teams.

Michael Franklin, our star and leading scorer, was ice cold, coming up empty against Anguilla that night. He couldn't hit the side of a barn with a shotgun; he had never played well against them. Coach ended up sitting him for most of the second half. From the bench, he watched with me as our team struggled to keep up with the Wildcats. We trailed going into half-time.

In the second half, an unlikely hero emerged. Charles Williams, one of the friendliest guys on our team, came to life. Charles was tall, lanky, and built to play down low—probably why he and Coach got into so many arguments when Charles drifted outside the arch and hoisted up three-pointers. Usually their misunderstandings led to Coach benching him. He'd struggled in the first half with only two buckets. By the second half, though, Charles was in rare form and caught fire to the tune of twenty more points.

As the clock ticked down, the score was tied; about five seconds remained when Charles was fouled hard below the basket. Our bench jumped to its feet. The home crowd booed in disapproval of the referee's whistle. Tied at 71–71, everyone was on the edge of their seats when Charles walked to the free-throw line. He wasn't the greatest free throw shooter; he reminded me of the Chicago Bulls' Bill Cortwright with his catapult-like shot.

Coach made us shoot free throws every day at the end of practice, specifically for moments like this. Charles stepped up to the line, sank the first free throw to give us a 72–71 lead. Anguilla's home crowd booed wildly. It felt like the gym was closing in on us from above.

The Wildcats called a timeout to try to ice Charles. In the huddle, he was his usual nonchalant self. He didn't say anything as Coach barked out plays in anticipation of Charles missing the next shot. After the timeout, Charles stepped back up to the free-throw line.

Ice in his veins, his next free-throw swished through the net. The Wildcats had one last shot with five seconds remaining. They inbounded to their best player, Michael Hollins. He advanced the ball past half-court and launched a deep three, only to watch it fall short. We forgot about the hostility of the crowd, the intimidating atmosphere of that gym, and the danger of being at an away game in Anguilla; we celebrated on their home court, bathed in a chorus of boos.

After a few more months of play, the regular season neared its end. Through hard work and sheer determination, we'd achieved an impressive record: 24–5. In the process we'd defeated some strong teams from much larger schools. With two games remaining, we were now laser-focused, and anxious to begin the division tournament. First, though, we had to deal with a nearby rival—the Hollandale Simmons Blue Devils.

Like our relationship with the Wildcats, there was no love lost on the Blue Devils. They didn't like us and the feeling was mutual. That day we walked away with a 70–63 win over Simmons, improving our record to 25–5.

On February 16, we again flattened Kosciusko 77–48 in a rematch at Holmes Community College. The win got us to the division championship game against Tchula Marshall; we trounced them 73–57 to win the Division IV-3A title. Terry, Mike, and Lamone were selected to the All-Tournament team.

**

The Leflore County Tigers awaited us in the first round of the North Mississippi Class 3A playoffs. We had worked hard all year and were the top seed; Leflore County had to come to our home court. The Tigers had cruised through the season, riding a dominant inside game. Their bus rolled up to our school that evening. We watched them disembark with swagger as they made their way to the visitor's locker room. They stared back at us as if we were nothing to them.

Leflore County had a population of around thirty-seven thousand, much more than the barely seven thousand people in our Sharkey County. We felt disrespected. It seemed that they'd dismissed our little town as soon as they walked through the door.

The gym was packed, and we could hear the crowd outside as we waited in our locker room. We remembered cross-country running, line drills, and late evenings in the gym. We had not forgotten our long bus rides and tough losses. Most of all, though, we realized we had grown and evolved into a close-knit family.

In the locker room everyone was anxious: knees bouncing, players stretching, shoes being laced tight. We headed out to the hallway; a few more steps and we stood outside the now-closed double doors. The building was packed. Fans spilled out into the concession area, people stood on the stairs that led up to the bleachers, and folks were stuffed into corners near the weight room. Our school band jammed in the student section.

The Leflore County Tigers had already taken the court and were warming up. The air was electric! Our cheerleading squad consisted of Sharonda Norris, Tracey McCoy, Corrie

Coleman, Renee Pearson, Nakia Willis, Felicia Dorsey, Melanie Gentry, Shemetrice Matthews, Takeshia Shelby, Latonya Brooks, Rachel Stevens, Lashonda Lane, Christi Miles, Angela Luckett, and Lacey Stevens. On the other side of the door, pom-poms waving, they'd created a tunnel for our entrance.

Mike Franklin went first as the doors opened. We ran through a tsunami of red and blue pom-poms. Our band and home crowd exploded as we exited the tunnel and appeared on the court. It seemed like all of Rolling Fork had packed into that gym. People were even hanging off the bleachers' railing. Everyone screamed at the top of their lungs. Mike led us to the opposite end of the court to warm up—the same end of the court where Coach Miller's voice, several months earlier, bounced off the gym's walls, "You have 5-seconds to run to the other end." The same end of the court where we were bent over tugging the hem of our gym shorts, exhausted and dripping with sweat from endless line drills during tryouts. The same end of the court where I once stared stubbornly at those white double doors, refusing to quit. The same end of the court where, now, the echoing memories of Coach Miller's voice were drowned out by the roar of the crowd.

As the crowd cheered, I wondered if we would walk out victorious and advance to the next round of the playoffs—one step closer to the Coliseum—or would this be the final game of my high school career?

For us seniors this was, in fact, our last home game. Coach decided to start the five seniors as a final nod to our high school basketball career. Each of us sat anxiously on the bench, waiting on the announcer to shout our name. First, he introduced Leflore County's starters: Daniel Ross,

Randy Powell, Edward Collings, Kendrick Williams, and Mike Anderson.

Then the announcer's voice blasted through the speakers, "And now . . . for your Rolling Fork Braves! Number 12, starting at point guard, Mario Lane; at forward, Number 11, Darrell Houzah; at center, Number 44, Chris Carter; at forward, Number 32, Tyrone Pinkins." I didn't think the crowd could get any louder. The announcer paused momentarily as our fans awaited the announcement of the final starter.

Physically, Michael was arguably one of the most naturally gifted students at the school. He was popular among the student body. The announcer yelled, "At shooting guard, Number 23, Michael Franklin!" and the fans were so loud the building itself started to shake. Mike bounced onto the court, arms stretched wide, pumping his fist toward the student section as if to say, "It's game time!"

"That night was the loudest the fans had been in my four years at the school," Coach later recalled. "They'd been loud after dunks and big wins, but never for three or four minutes in a row." We made our presence felt early, as Darrell Houzah scored on a putback with only seven seconds off the clock. The crowd got warmed up when Lamone timed Chris Starks' shot attempt just right to record his first rejection of the night.

Less than two minutes later, Mike stole the ball from Edward Collings and raced down the court. I felt the air leave the building as the crowd simultaneously inhaled in anticipation as Mike rose up for a high flying, monster dunk. The slam was thunderous. The following exhale was a deafening roar from the crowd that shook the building. I wondered if the roof was about to fly off. We posted seven slams that night and five blocked shots; we thrived off the energy of the crowd, who grew louder and louder with each play.

Leflore County came back with a rejection of their own when Mike Anderson swatted Terry's shot. Lamone returned the favor just five seconds later, whacking Daniel Ross' shot attempt high into the stands on the visitor's side of the court.

We dominated early. After Frank Harris' layup with fifty-nine seconds remaining, we led by 20–8 to end the first quarter. But the Tigers fought back—tossing in eight unanswered points at the beginning of the second quarter, cutting our lead.

Off an Edward Collings layup, assisted by a bounce pass from Randy Powell, Leflore tied the game at 24–24 with less than a minute and a half left in the second quarter. We regained our focus and went on a run of our own. Lamone threw down another power jam to take us into half-time leading 32–24.

In the second half, Randy Powell came up with two big blocks against Lamone and Killa. Terry tossed in a jumper in the third quarter to give us a 38–27 lead. At six foot one and over two hundred pounds, Terry was a big guy. He had a thirty-three-inch vertical and a mid-range jumper that was nearly automatic. A few seconds later, Mike slung a laser pass to Killa for another thunderous dunk, sending the crowd into a frenzy.

Lamone and Terry broke away and rammed in booming back-to-back dunks to put us ahead 55–36 at the end of the third quarter. At the beginning of the fourth quarter, Leflore's Chris Starks tried to silence the crowd with a dunk of his own. The silence didn't last long; Lamone came up with two huge blocks, each of which led to easy baskets that brought our crowd back to life.

But Lamone wasn't finished yet. After exchanging heated words with Leflore players and being warned by the referee,

Lamone took his frustrations out with another monstrous slam, which led to a technical foul as he dangled from the rim. We outscored Leflore 29–23 in the fourth quarter for a final score of 84–61. Terry had a game-high twenty-seven points, followed by twenty from Mike.

That win set us up to face another nemesis, the Warriors from Corinth High School. They had defeated Nettleton High School the previous night. Corinth had been a thorn in our side for a long time, eliminating us from the North State tournament two of the past three seasons. And this time, they defeated us again by a score of 69–60.

Not all was lost, however. Our tournament dreams and quest to reach the Coliseum weren't yet finished. The loss to Corinth simply meant a quick turnaround to face the Holly Springs Hawks in an elimination game.

We crushed Holly Springs behind a thirty-nine-point game from Killa and twenty-one points from Terry. With that win, we punched our ticket to the Coliseum and on to a quarterfinals matchup where we defeated the defending 3A state champ Kemper County Tornados.

Now with the win over them, we had an opportunity for revenge against Corinth. On Tuesday, March 9th, 1993, we met the Corinth Warriors once again in a do-or-die matchup in the semifinals at the Mississippi Memorial Coliseum. It was a much-anticipated rematch of the game we'd lost to them several days earlier. The game was tight; we traded baskets from beginning to end. In the fourth quarter, we started to pull away and were up fourteen points with less than six minutes remaining.

The Warriors went on a run and cut our lead. After two free throws by Bobby Mayes, the score was 79–75, with under a minute remaining. Corinth's Adrian Hall drained a long three-pointer, cutting it to 79–78. Lamone was fouled and went to the free-throw line with thirty-eight seconds left on the clock. He missed the front end of a one-and-one. A few seconds later, Corinth's Ron Patterson was fouled and made one of two free throws to tie the score. Mike, one of our best players, fouled out. With eleven seconds remaining, Darrell Houzah missed the front end of a one-and-one, and tall Adrian Hall grabbed the rebound for Corinth. He kicked it to point guard, Bobby Mayes, who quickly pushed it up the court. Mays drove to the right baseline and with three seconds remaining, rose for a twelve-foot jump shot that swished through the net for the win.

The loss was one of the most painful moments I'd ever felt. However, our Coach stood tall before his players. He knew we had learned the importance of getting back up and dusting ourselves off after being knocked down. We had gone toe-to-toe and never stopped fighting until the last whistle was blown. We knew he was proud of us.

Mike, Mario, Darrell, Chris, and I graduated a few months later. Our high school basketball career was finished. Coach, however, kept going. The next season he poured the same amount of support, encouragement, and energy into the next group of kids. The result? A year later the team found itself in familiar territory. They were back in the Coliseum, this time playing in the final—the championship game. They overcame! They won! And, for the first time in more than two decades, a lanky white guy from Indiana and a small group of black kids from a tiny town tucked away among the cotton fields and dirt roads of the Mississippi Delta traveled the long road to the Coliseum and walked away as champions.

CHAPTER NINE:

Tougaloo College, Blood Banks, and Compact Discs

Dad left school in the sixth grade; Mom dropped out in tenth. Early on, they taught me the importance of graduating from high school. In light of their limited access to formal education, they made it abundantly clear that they expected even more from me. They felt it was crucial that I not only finish high school but also attend college.

"What do you want to be when you grow up?" Mom once asked me, around the time I'd been stung between the eyes.

"Ice Man!" I yelled with wide, excited eyes. "I wanna be a superhero, and my name's gonna be Ice Man. I'm gonna shoot ice from my wrists, like this, peow, peow!" I thrusted my arms into the air.

Smiling and looking into my eyes, she said, "You sure will. You can do anything."

I absolutely believed her. She always made me believe that no matter how crazy my dreams were, I could achieve anything. I also felt a strong responsibility to ensure the sacrifices they'd already made were not in vain. Dad worked long nights driving tractors up and down those cotton fields, just to make ends meet. They'd poured so much of the little bit they had into me.

I'd watched Val and Darlene head off to Mississippi Delta Community College. Val, the oldest among us and Darlene, a year younger, shared their experiences when they came home on some weekends. We'd been around each other for so long there on Elemwood that the simple act of them vanishing for five days and magically reappearing on the weekends sparked my imagination. I always thought, "Where are they going? What is going on?"

Like so many in our community, I felt an obligation to those who came before me. I understood the circumstances in which my parents grew up and what they had to endure. I also realized early on that Val and Darlene were setting an example, charting a road map. In the back of my mind, I was diagramming my own path based on their experiences.

Dad had a particular way of instilling in me the importance of a good education. I was about nine years old, in the third or fourth grade and we still lived in that old, red house out on Borderland—the one with the peach and plum trees and the snakes. After school each evening, while dinner simmered on the stove, Mom sat beside me on the living room couch. If Dad got home early from work, he'd sit on the opposite side of me. I was scared.

Mom stared at the list of words I'd brought home from school. "Spell 'education.'"

I nervously sounded out each of the four syllables before attempting to spell. Pausing between each letter, I slowly mumbled each character: "E-D-U-C-A-S-H-O-N."

I knew if I made a mistake, Dad would punish me.

"Wrong!" Mom said and then whack! Right across my thigh, Dad laid into me with his belt.

"Start over, try again," Mom continued. "Spell 'education.'" She placed emphasis on the last syllable, "TION, TION, TION."

Now with tears streaming down my cheeks and a little drizzle of snot creeping from my nostrils—watching Dad's belt out the corner of my eye—I slowly mumbled each letter, "E-D-U-C-A," I paused, T-I-O-N."

Mom smiled, "Good!"

I breathed a sigh of relief and tried to smile between tears. Wash-rinse-repeat, we continued on until I'd learned the entire list. My tears were not from physical pain, but from feeling like each time I misspelled a word I was letting Dad down. With each strike of that belt, I felt like I was a disappointment, a bad investment.

Despite going over the words on the school bus during the bumpy ride home, I still got some of them wrong; when I did, Dad was sure to let me know. I didn't realize until older that he didn't know I'd misspelled a word unless Mom said so. With each strike of that leather belt, on the one hand, I felt betrayed by Mom, her soft smile, and those loving eyes. On the other hand, I felt an immense amount of love from both of them. If I had to go back and live it again, I wouldn't change a thing. I know now that my parents were only trying to ensure I understood the importance of education. They instilled in me that lesson the best way they knew how. Even in my third grade, they saw something in me and wanted me to see it too.

Approximately ten years later, I was the first of our immediate family to graduate high school and head off to college.

During my senior year my parents gave me a white 1989 Pontiac Sunbird. My friends and I named it the White Ghost. Of course, I'd already wrecked the Ghost.

In the early morning hours, after a late night of partying with my friends, Ted and Wayne, I sideswiped Uncle Bud's black pickup truck. I was tuning the radio to 99.7 WJMI when I ripped his bumper right off. It left a gigantic gash down Ghost's passenger side. Throughout senior year, we joked about that gash while driving to clubs like The Rocking Chair in Rolling Fork on the corner of Chestnut and McLaurin Street, Tony's out in Mayersville, and Lawyer's out beyond Cary alongside Highway 61. Now, in May of 1993, in the same gym where coach Miller had tortured us during tryouts, I, along with seventy-six other students, received my high school diploma.

That August, I loaded the Ghost with my few belongings and backed out of my parents' pothole-filled driveway. At the end of our road, I turned left on Highway 826. After a few minutes, I made a right on Highway 14 and headed into Rolling Fork. With the little money I'd saved from chopping cotton over the summer, I stopped at Mr. Quick's gas station.

Fueled up, I pulled out of the parking lot, made a right on Race Street, and followed the creek as it twisted its way through town. I crossed Highway 61 and then continued on Highway 16, passing the Department of Transportation building where Uncle Vell worked and Green Chapel Baptist Church where Grandma Mary worshipped. The road wound like a snake all the way out to Delta National Forest.

* *

Dad and I had often hunted out in Delta National Forest. In his old, mint pickup truck we'd drive out early in the morning. He liked to get deep into the forest and into a tree stand before the sun started to shine.

One day when I was about thirteen, soon after he'd bought me my first shotgun, we were out there bright and early. I hated the cold but really liked following him and trying to step in his footsteps as we walked deeper and deeper into the forest.

We stopped next to a creek. It was heavily forested on our side—trees bunched close with thick underbrush. On the far side of the creek was a clearing. Dad set up his stand downwind to ensure any deer traveling the trail on the other side wouldn't pick up our scent.

Dad usually placed me next to a tree and told me where *not* to shoot, which was basically in his direction. He'd then walk off, disappearing into the brush. He'd be gone for hours, and I'd be alone in the middle of the forest; my imagination ran wild. In my mind, everything looked like an animal. I'd sit in the leaves beneath a giant oak tree and lay the shotgun on my lap. It was as though the minute Dad disappeared the forest came to life. That clump of bushes fifty yards away was for sure a turkey; the shadow seventy-five yards to my left had to be a fox or a coyote. On my right, the ruffling of leaves was most certainly a squirrel or a rabbit running by.

Then there were the imaginary deer. Every bird that flashed white or light grey feathers, flying between the trees in the distance, had to be a deer bouncing through the forest with its fluffy white tail in the air. Sounds and sightings were everywhere, all around me, and I loved it. Eventually, I'd get bored, tilt my head back, stare at the thick white clouds in the grey sky, and fall asleep next to the big oak tree.

One day, I dreamed my nose was wet and cold. Sleeping against the tree, I heard myself sniffing loudly—almost too loudly. It sounded like a snort or grunt. I thought, "Am I dreaming? What's that sound, and why is my nose so wet?"

I woke up. Slowly opening my eyes, I was met with another set of big, brown eyes, inches away from my glasses. I also saw a black, wet nose. It was sniffing and snorting while nudging my cheek.

A deer! Startled, I yelled, and the deer jumped straight up in the air. We surprised each other. It ran off, disappearing into the brush. About fifty feet away, Dad could not contain himself; he rolled in the leaves, laughing hysterically. He'd been watching from behind a tree for over half an hour as the baby deer tried to figure out what the heck I was.

"Aw, he won't gonna hurt ya," Dad said, still chuckling.

Those were some of the best early childhood memories—ones of just Dad and me, doing what he enjoyed most, which was hunting and fishing, and me doing what I enjoyed most, which was hanging out with him.

** **

These memories flooded my mind as I continued my drive through Delta National Forest in my white Pontiac Sunbird. After crossing Silver Creek and passing through Holly Bluff, I turned right onto Satartia Road.

In all my travels, I've experienced very few trips more peaceful than driving through Satartia's hilly, winding roads. The area was so sparsely populated it was felt like going back in time. A few tiny stores dotted the roadside now and then.

Many of the stores seemed closed until someone's head poked out the front door to glance at the passing car.

I drove along Lake George, which bordered Panther Swamp National Wildlife Refuge and crossed Highway 3 before disappearing again in the dense forest. An occasional deer or raccoon darted across the road as I continued winding my way along the bends and turns of Highway 433. Eventually I reached Bentonia, midway between Yazoo City and Jackson. There I made a right onto Highway 49.

After passing through a town called Pocahontas, I drove a short while longer before turning left onto West County Line Road. Fifteen minutes later my destination was in sight. There it was—an arched white gate welcoming me to Tougaloo College.

Cousin Lenora had enrolled in Tougaloo the previous year. I'd driven there in Madea's old blue Chrysler many times to pick her up for weekend trips home.

Located on the outskirts of Jackson, Tougaloo is one of five historically black universities in the state, along with Jackson State University, Alcorn State University, Mississippi Valley State University, and Rust College. I'd learned during high school that Tougaloo was visited on more than one occasion by Dr. Martin Luther King Jr. That piqued my interest. In the '60s, Tougaloo, a private, independent college, was considered a refuge from the ravages of racial injustice and violence prevalent across the Jim Crow South.

A safe place for African Americans, the college produced black activists such as the Tougaloo Nine—five male and four female students who were members of the NAACP Youth Council. They participated in Mississippi's first civil rights read-in at a whites-only library in Jackson. On Monday, March 27, 1961, those nine Tougaloo students entered the Jackson Municipal Public Library in search of materials for class assignments. After the students seated themselves, library staff called the police. Refusing orders to leave, they were arrested. Their read-in drew support from nearby Jackson College and Millsaps, a predominantly white college.

I was assigned to Renner Hall, the male dormitory. It was a huge concrete building, shaped like an elongated rectangle on stilts, a centipede with long grey legs. I lived on the second of only two floors. Although the dorm was old and the rooms tiny, I thought the living conditions were luxurious compared to some of the houses we'd lived in around the Delta. No cotton fields surrounded the campus, and the streets were paved. My first time away from home felt somewhat alien to me.

My roommate, Frizell, was one of the first people I met at Tougaloo. Also from a small town, Frizell grew up not far from Jackson in Utica. He was a sophomore; we immediately bonded and became good friends. Dreadlocks sprouted from his head and dripped over his shoulders like long, dark branches dangling from a willow tree. He drove the coolest little blue 1970 Volkswagen Beetle. He took me under his wing.

The first night he asked probing questions, many of which I had no answer to.

"So, where are you coming from?"

"Rolling Fork, between Vicksburg and Grenville."

I think he realized I was a country boy with no idea what I was doing in the world. He wasn't wrong; I was definitely lost when I first arrived at the school.

"What are you majoring in?"

I had no idea. I hadn't thought about that part. Lenora had told me I didn't have to declare a major. She said I'd be taking introductory classes in my freshman year anyway. "I don't know yet. Maybe computer science," I said.

The next day Frizell gave me a quick tour of the small campus. Even at a small school like Tougaloo, with a minuscule enrollment of barely one thousand students, I was in awe. The school's size represented nearly a quarter of the population of my entire home town. We walked over to Holmes Hall, where I would finish registering for classes. Coleman Library was next door, where I'd eventually often fall asleep reading. Just across the yard was Warren Hall, the cafeteria, where I couldn't afford to eat because I wasn't on a meal plan.

On the Sundays when I didn't drive back to Rolling Fork, Frizell and I jumped in his Volkswagen Beetle. We'd drive out to Ross Barnett Reservoir, jamming all the way, old school tunes competing with the Volkswagen's noisy engine.

My drives home became fewer as the weeks and semesters passed. Mostly I enjoyed my time at Tougaloo, but I always felt something was pulling at me. Something just didn't feel right. I attended my classes and made decent grades, but I felt something calling me. I wanted to see the world; I wanted to be further away from home. I wanted to be further away from Mississippi.

One weekend, I drove home to visit Mom and Dad. My sister Dee Dee and our youngest brother Twan had been born by then. There was a pretty big age gap between us, so I asked Mom, "Why did you wait twenty years after having Pee Wee to have two more children?"

"Well, actually I wanted you to be a girl," she laughed. "I always wanted a girl, and I got Dee Dee. When Twan came, I said, 'I've got enough children.'"

I drove out to the farm in Grace where Dad was working. He climbed down from his tractor, "You wanna drive the tractor? It'll be fun."

I never told Dad about the promise I'd made myself. I appreciated and respected how he had, for so long, worked hard in those cotton fields to provide for our family. But long ago, standing in the middle of one of those fields myself, working from sunup in the blazing heat to sundown, I'd decided I would never learn to drive a tractor. I was terrified that if I learned I'd be stuck in those cotton fields forever.

So I joked and said, "I don't want to wreck it like I did the Pontiac."

He smiled. "You're probably right."

We laughed, but he knew me better than I knew myself. I had a sneaking suspicion that he knew why I didn't want to learn to drive a tractor.

During my sophomore year at Tougaloo things became difficult for me. My parents weren't able to give me money; they simply didn't have any to offer. They were now taking care of Pee Wee, Dee Dee, and Twan. I didn't have a job. So, I resorted to hocking my compact disc at the local record shop.

Now closed since 2011, Be-Bop Record Shop was a staple in the Jackson community. Its doors opened in 1974, the year I was born. Kathy Morrison, a Jackson native, along with Drake Elder and Wayne Harrison, opened the store on Fondren Street, next to the old Capri Theater.

Frizell and I visited Be-Bop pretty much every other weekend. We'd browse vinyl collections from old-school greats like ConFunkShun, Marvin Gaye, Curtis Mayfield, and Parliament. Later in the day, I'd return alone to the music shop to sell my compact discs for two or three dollars so I could afford lunch.

A couple of times a week I walked to the local grocery store with only a few dollars remaining. I'd buy a pack of bologna and a tube of mustard. While other students enjoyed dinner in Warren Hall, I was in my dorm room spreading mustard on bologna, rolling it like a fruit roll-up and eating it with no bread. I washed it down with water from the bathroom faucet.

As miserable as that was, I knew I couldn't give up. I couldn't go back home. So, I found other ways to make money. Twice a week—between classes—I took the bus across town to the local blood bank where they stabbed a needle into the thickest vein they could find. The lady at the front desk told me I could only donate twice a week; sometimes I'd sneak back in and give a third donation after she ended her shift. In exchange for the plasma, I got twenty-five dollars, some cookies, and a glass of juice so I wouldn't pass out.

I soon realized that living as a human pin cushion at the local blood bank just wasn't cutting the mustard, so to speak. I found a job working at a local newspaper printing factory across town. During the day I attended classes; at night I sorted and stacked newspapers. At the printing press I met a retired Marine Corp Sergeant, Danny Jackson. Danny was short and muscular. Everything about him said he was a Marine. He carried his Eagle, Globe, and Anchor in his pocket and had another tattooed on his bicep. During breaks, Danny and I sat and talked. He told me about his life in the military and about Parris Island boot camp. I was utterly fascinated by his travels around the world.

"Once a Marine always a Marine," he said to me one night while we were on break.

"How long did you serve?"

Danny had done twenty years before retiring for medical reasons.

"After boot camp, they shipped me to Camp Butler on the island of Okinawa, Japan. That tiny island is one of the military's best-kept secrets. Crystal blue waters, clean sandy beaches, and just a relaxing way of life." His eyes gleamed like he was still lying on one of those beaches.

I immediately wanted to go!

Each night at the printing press, the stories he shared drew me in. His traveling stories—Europe, Asia, and South America!—had my imagination going wild. When I returned to campus each night, I thought about how vastly different the world he described was from the cotton fields I'd grown up in.

One night he asked me, "Are you happy?"

"Well, I'm in college, but I feel like something is pulling me away. I feel like I am not where I am supposed to be at this point in my life. Sometimes, I want to get as far away as possible."

He interrupted, "Kill two birds with one stone."

"What do you mean?"

"Join the military, and you can serve your country and travel the world. And get this, not only will the military pay for it, they'll pay for you to complete your degree while you're serving," Danny said excitedly.

A few days later I walked into Pemberton Square Mall in Vicksburg. Sitting in the waiting area of the recruiting station, I watched shoppers walk by on the other side of the glass. An Army Staff Sergeant approached me and guided me over to his desk.

"My name is Staff Sergeant Matthew Nagel," he said, offering a handshake.

Matthew was a short, kind, soft-spoken, white guy.

"Can you tell me about serving in the Army?" I asked.

"Why don't you tell me what your goals are? What do you want to do?"

I told him I was enrolled in college; I enjoyed school but felt like I wasn't doing what I really wanted to do.

"I want to travel the world. I want to experience different cultures," I finished.

He explained the travel opportunities the Army could provide. He also told me the Army would pay for me to finish earning my degree when I was ready to start school again. He didn't have to say much more than that.

Mom found out that I had joined the Army only a few days before I was scheduled to ship off to basic training. It was around noon on a Sunday—June 23, 1996. A blue minivan pulled into our driveway, disappearing into a cloud of dust and parking right in the middle of one of our potholes.

I walked over, looked out the screen door, and said, "Mom, I gotta go." I couldn't even look in her eyes.

Dad was at work. I'd missed him that morning before he left the house and I didn't get a chance to tell him goodbye. Confused by emotions of farewell, I gave Mom a quick hug. I picked up a small, black tote bag containing everything I owned—a couple of pairs of jeans, mix-matched socks, and a few t-shirts—and walked out the door.

I made my way around the sleeping cats and dogs and down the steps. My old bike, rusted beyond repair and still seatless, leaned against the tin siding Dad had hammered around the house to keep out the cold wind during winter.

I was off to see the world, maybe even the serene island of Okinawa. I wasn't sure. Somewhere beyond the dirt roads, cotton fields, and plantations; the peaches, plums, and snakes; the cousins, aunts, and uncles; the stinging bees, soleless shoes, and seatless bikes; the gospel groups, talent shows, and slam dunks; the swimming hole, weeping willow, and wild forest; the pecans, bologna roll-ups, and blood banks; the teachers, coaches, and friends—everything I'd known, everything I'd loved… Mississippi memories swirled all around me. I was leaving the comfort of home, alone, acutely unaware of what lay ahead but enchanted with the possibilities.

I hopped into the van and tossed my bag on the back seat. Staff Sergeant Nagel honked the horn once, shifted the van into reverse, and backed out of the driveway. As we pulled off, I watched Mom, now standing on the porch, disappear in a cloud of dust. I started to miss her before we even made it to the end of the dirt road.

I closed my eyes and imagined the softness in hers when she'd told me at nine years old that I could be Ice Man. I immediately regretted not hugging her longer.

PART TWO

THIRTEEN YEARS
IN EUROPE

CHAPTER TEN:

New Orleans, Weeping Willows, and the Weird Eye Doctor

——

When the van accelerated on Highway 826, I could not help but notice Elemwood passing. I saw myself as a child running around Madea's house barefoot, chasing chickens. As we flew by the black folk's cemetery, I reminisced on the long walks to Mt. Herald Baptist Church each Sunday morning with my cousins. I smiled at the realization that even though poverty was all around us as children we hadn't had a care in the world. Our parents had done a hell of a job shielding us from the harsh realities of our situation with constant love and affection.

Still staring out the window, I noticed cotton fields in the distance—the same fields I'd watched my mother work while I sat on Madea's porch with a mouth full of pinto beans and cornbread. My cousins and I ran through those same fields shoeless and playing hide-and-seek between long rows of fluffy, white cotton. They were the same fields I had worked myself as a teenager. They were the same cotton fields Dad *still* labored in from sunup to sundown.

Generation after generation of my ancestors had toiled in those fields. They'd shed blood, sweat, tears, and sacrificed even more in those fields. Many of them had been robbed: their land stolen, property snatched away, their very bodies seized and turned into a profit. At that moment I felt like my ancestors were standing there between those long dusty rows, staring intently, focused on me, as the van continued driving down the empty highway.

At the fork in the road next to Egremont Chapel, we made a right onto Highway 61. We drove through the small town of Cary, where Aunt Rosie and Uncle Cleotha still resided and passed through Valley Park, where Otha Lee once lived. I tried to imagine the day I was born, visualizing him hiding in the grain silo's dusty darkness while Daddy-Eck yelled. Otha Lee quickly faded from my thoughts as I gazed out the window with each passing row of cotton staring back at me. We drove all the way to the New Orleans Military Entrance Processing Station, where I was sworn into the Army.

My stay in New Orleans was short, less than twenty-four hours. However, in that brief time, one of the weirdest things happened.

Years earlier I'd purchased my first pair of contact lenses. I'd finally shed those big ol' brown glasses my fourth-grade teacher, Mrs. Culpepper, had forced upon me without my parents' approval. Now that I'd joined the Army, I had to undergo another eye exam. My secret horrible vision was once again revealed! At the MEPS office a young medic, who wore a pair of brown glasses almost as thick as mine, handed me a small yellow piece of paper. On it was scribbled an address.

"A yellow taxi will pick you up on this corner in about ten minutes," he said.

It was late morning, already hot outside, when the taxi arrived. It was my first time in a cab. I hopped in and didn't say a word as I handed the driver the piece of paper and sat back, mesmerized as we drove through New Orleans. We must have driven for twenty minutes, long enough for me to be sufficiently lost. When the taxi stopped at an old house, surrounded by weeping willow trees, I realized I didn't have any money to pay. He looked at me and must have recognized what was going through my mind.

"Don't worry about it," he said impatiently. "The Army done already paid for it." He pointed me in the direction of the old house and drove off.

I sauntered up the driveway. Dead leaves were scattered everywhere. It seemed like there hadn't been a visitor in a while. The steps moaned as I mounted the flimsy wooden porch. On the porch was a rocking chair in the corner; beside the chair was a small wooden coffee table with an awkwardly bent leg. The leg resembled a dying wildebeest, struggling to escape the jaws of a crocodile. To the left, swinging from the ceiling by two long, thin chains, was a wooden bench long enough to seat at least three. Startled, I thought a spider was crawling on the back of my neck until I realized it was just a string dangling from the porch light.

I knocked on the flimsy wooden screen door. The main door was already open, allowing me to see inside. No one answered. I knocked again, my face now only inches from the screen as I strained to see what was on the other side of the door.

"Hold on! I'm commin'!" I heard someone groan from deep within the house.

The footsteps sounded slow and reluctant, almost as if the occupant's legs didn't want to work. Clomp, clomp, clomp, I heard the steps. What slowly appeared was a short white man.

"You Tyrone?" he asked.

"Yes, sir," I replied, immediately having second thoughts about entering.

"Is this some sort of trick?" I thought. I'd heard New Orleans was known for voodoo. "What if I go into this house and never come out?"

He unhitched the inner metal clasp and pushed the screen door open.

"Well, come on in!" he said in a slow Southern drawl with a hint of impatience.

I am sure we were walking, but it seemed as though I was floating. Through the living room, I drifted. Along a narrow hallway, mounted on the walls, were old pictures of people I assumed were his relatives. Or, my imagination said, maybe they were victims.

We passed the kitchen on the left. Something, perhaps lunch, bubbled in a pot on the stove as steam drifted toward the ceiling. On the right was a small dining room. A doctor's chair sat in the corner beneath an open window as the sheer curtains danced in the slight breeze. Beyond the window was another weeping willow tree.

"Sit in that chair," he said. His speech reminded me of how tired the weeping willow trees looked.

I sat in the chair, watching as he disappeared into the kitchen, curtains dancing around my shoulders. I heard water running from a faucet. He appeared again, drying his hands on a brown towel.

"Put your head back," he said.

There was no explanation of what was happening. All instructions were direct and in that same slow, willow-like drawl. Adjusting ancient optometrist equipment, he began to check my vision.

"Don't blink," he said, pinching my eyelids open with his thumb and index finger.

He squirted a drop into one eye and then the other. I blinked as the liquid coated my eyeballs. Several seconds later everything blurred. Although I wanted to keep my eyes open, they slammed themselves shut. I wasn't sleepy, but my eyes were ultra-sensitive to the light shining through those sheer curtains.

"Here ya' go," he said, placing a small piece of paper in my hand. "This way." He grabbed my forearm and guided me up from the seat. Still blinking rapidly, I realized we were back in the narrow hallway. I tried to focus on the pictures as he ushered me through the house. The images now looked grotesque, distorted, eerily disfigured.

The sound of the boiling pot seemed to be magnified; the smell of cooked pork drifted through the air. Still blurry-eyed, I winced at the light shining through the screen door as I walked on awkwardly with my hands out in front of me. I pushed the door open and stumbled down the steps. The rays of sunlight pierced like daggers. I closed my eyes tight as I felt my way down the walkway.

Finally, on the sidewalk, I heard cars passing.

"Wait here," he said. "A taxi's gonna come get you." He shoved something into my pant pocket. "Give this to the driver." He headed back up his walkway. I could hear the crunch of dry leaves, the sound of his footsteps fading.

"What in the hell just happened?" I thought as the screen door slammed in the distance.

I'd had my eyes dilated before, but not like this. This experience had been straight-up weird. Blind on the sidewalk, about to get into whatever car pulled up next to me, I was just happy to be out of that house.

I stood there for what seemed like forever, listening to the sound of engines passing by. My eyes were still clamped shut; I heard a car pull up. It stopped!

"Get in," a voice said.

I forced my eyes open for a millisecond to confirm the vehicle was yellow. I slid into the back. Hiding from bright daggers of sunlight, I lay down on the seat. By the time we arrived back at the MEPS, the dilation had worn off.

Hours later I was on a bus loaded with new recruits, headed for the Louis Armstrong New Orleans International Airport—my first time on a plane. As we lifted off and banked right, I saw the waters of Lake Pontchartrain out the window. Flying over the Delta, I was fascinated by the vastness of the cotton fields below. As the plane climbed I felt as though I'd left a piece of me behind.

*

June 24, 1996. Basic training, Fort Jackson, South Carolina.

The nonstop flight landed in Atlanta, just as the sun began to dip below the horizon. After four hours driving along I-20, we finally arrived in the night to Fort Jackson.

The bus doors opened. "Everybody off," a voice commanded from the front.

The arrival wasn't quite what I expected. While instructions were straightforward and direct, there was not as much yelling and screaming as I'd anticipated. I was assigned to the 1st Basic Combat Training Brigade.

We went through several days of initial in-processing at the reception battalion. This included completing mountains of paperwork and establishing a bank account with the local credit union if recruits didn't already have one.

On one of these days two medics stood in the front of the line of recruits. We shuffled forward one at a time for each shoulder to be punctured and then injected—immunization vaccines. Many of the vaccines I knew I'd already received when I was a child; the medics didn't seem to care.

"Keep moving," the person in charge of us instructed as we trod on like a herd of cattle ushered toward their own slaughter.

The next day I plopped down into a barber's chair. His callused hands were as big as baseball gloves. His thumb and middle finger clamped my temple in a vice-grip while his palm smashed my nose against my face. I swear it took him under sixty seconds to shave my head clean.

That day they marched us to another facility. It was a huge, warehouse-like building with neatly arranged assembly lines inside. Rows and rows of military gear were lined up behind wooden, waist-high countertops. Bright yellow safety lines crisscrossed the concrete floor. Silhouettes of left and right footprints, painted black, were stenciled on the floor in front of each counter.

Sunlight streamed in through large, square windows high on the back wall; in the distance stenciled in bold white letters on a field of green was the Army's then-motto: "BE ALL YOU CAN BE."

I was second in line. Ahead of me stood a scrawny white kid with bushy blond eyebrows.

"Small, medium, or large," asked the short middle-aged black man without looking up.

"What?" asked the scrawny white kid.

"What size are you?" the middle-aged black man blurted impatiently. "Small, medium, or large?"

"Oh! Small," the kid said, clearly nervous and finding it difficult to focus while holding open and thrusting forward his green duffle bag.

The counter guy held up a pair of camouflaged pants that were clearly too short for the white kid. I was six feet tall, and he was nearly as tall as me. Nevertheless, he stuffed the undersized pants into his duffle bag and slid to the left, aligning his shoes atop the next set of stenciled black feet.

"Small, medium, or large," the middle-aged black man said to me, again without looking up.

I took JROTC in high school, so I knew the sizing scale for military uniforms.

"Medium-Long." I held my duffle bag open like a Halloween trick-or-treater.

He glanced up perplexed before slowly dropping the camouflage treat into my bag. I slid left to the next station.

We scooted down the line, station to station, as strangers across the counter dropped items into our bags; a camouflaged jacket here, a winter coat there, two pairs of black boots. A couple of canteens, each with a silver cup, were tossed in as well. A mosquito net and a shelter-half with wooden poles were handed over, along with an odd-looking collapsible shovel. A hat, some olive-green socks, brown t-shirts, brown tighty-whiteys, and more got tossed in. By the time we'd reached the end of the line, I was lugging two full duffle bags.

The next day an olive-green bus idled near the curb. We filed on and took a seat. It was hot and crowded, especially since we had our bags on laps. We'd spent the past several days at the reception battalion; now it was time to depart to our basic training unit, Echo Company, 4th Battalion 13th Infantry Regiment.

"Put your head down, close your eyes, and don't look up," a voice from the front of the bus said. "When my bus stops, I'll give you further instructions."

I put my head down; the bus began to creep forward. Between my fingers I peered out the window at trees and buildings passing by. We drove for at least ten minutes. My legs began to ache from the weight on my lap. The lawns outside were perfectly manicured. Aside from the slight discomfort, I thought things were going pretty smoothly. Everything had been pleasant and calm thus far.

The brakes squealed as the bus jerked to a stop. The sound of the door swinging open resonated down the aisle as we awaited approval to raise our heads. No approval came.

Then everything changed.

"You've got forty-five seconds to move your nasty body and all your shit off my bus!" the voice yelled from the front of the bus.

From the back all I could see was momentary glimpses of a round, brown Drill Sergeant hat levitating atop a set of fiery eyes. Those eyes looked like they belonged to Satan himself.

"Get off my fuckin' bus! Move! Move! Move!"

I immediately regretted sitting at the back of the bus. It was surely gonna take a lot longer than a minute to get to the exit.

"Hurry up!" Satan shouted from the front of the bus. "You are moving too damn slow!"

Forty-five seconds had already passed, the recruits near the back of the bus hadn't moved an inch and red-faced Satan, brown hat covering his horns, was getting louder and angrier!

"Goddammit! Why are you moving so SLOW?" He bellowed at the recruits struggling to lug their duffle bags and suitcases through the narrow bus aisle.

By the time we started moving, I'd slung my black bag across my chest, slipped one of my duffels on like a backpack, and balanced the other one on top. The blond white kid with the bushy eyebrows struggled in front of me. Satan picked up on the scent of fear, zeroed in on the kid, and ratcheted his anger up another notch.

"Whyyyyyyyy are you heeere?" He was screaming now. "You're not gonna make it!" he blurted sharply. "Pick the bags up and stop dragging your ass!"

The kid couldn't pick up the bags. First, he didn't have the strength; second, he didn't have the room to maneuver within the bus's tight confines. Despite this, he tried all the way along the aisle. He fell down the steps, out the door, and landed on the curb. One of his duffle bags landed on top of him. I thought he'd broken something. The Drill Sergeant thought he was hurt as well.

"Are you okay? Are you injured?" Drill Sergeant yelled, his voice a few decibels lower, leaning over blondie. "Are you okay?"

"Yes, sir," the kid responded.

"Don't call me, sir!" the brown-billed demon exploded again. "I ain't no officer! I work for a living. Get off your ass and get up that hill!"

I was still standing in the doorway, last off the bus.

"We are waiting on you, Private! Get off the damn bus! You're dead last, and everybody's waiting on you!" As I tried to exit, the duffle bag straddling my shoulders became wedged in the doorway. "Move! Get off the bus! Hurry up! What are you waiting on?"

Now the Drill Sergeant stood directly in front of me. Each time I lunged forward, attempting to dislodge my duffle from the door frame, he lunged forward to scream at me. It was like a see-saw, back and forth. The bill of his hat repeatedly poked me on the nose, knocking my glasses awkwardly about my face.

I finally freed myself. Before me was a well-trampled hill, our group trekking up it with bags in hand. It looked like a war zone. Someone's suitcase had exploded. Scattered socks, underwear, and t-shirts led the way up the hill to the all-out hell the rest of the recruits were experiencing.

When I reached the top fire-breathing, profanity-spewing Drill Sergeants were everywhere. By the time they finished with us, we were psychologically overwhelmed, physically exhausted, and covered in dirt. We stood in formation, breathing heavily as the Drill Sergeants stood before us.

"I'm yo' mama and yo' daddy," one said. "You eat when I say eat! You sleep when I say sleep. You move when I say move, and when I give you an order, the only words that will come out of your mouth are: 'Yes, Drill Sergeant.' Do you understand!"

In unison we replied, "Yes, Drill Sergeant."

Then he yelled a question to no one particular.

"What makes the green grass grow!"

Silence! We didn't know how to respond. I thought, "The obvious answer is sunshine and rain," but none of us said anything.

"What makes the green grass grow!" he repeated.

Still, silence; everyone stared straight ahead.

He turned to another Drill Sergeant and asked, "Battle buddy, what makes the green grass grow?"

The second Drill Sergeant tilted his face up toward the sky. Arms spread wide, fingers extended, chest protruding, he took a deep breath and bellowed, "BLOOD! BLOOD MAKES THE GREEN GRASS GROW!"

The first Drill Sergeant looked back at us and again yelled, "What makes the green grass grow!"

In unison, we screamed, "BLOOD! BLOOD MAKES THE GREEN GRASS GROW!"

And just like that, we all agreed that blood, instead of sunlight and water, makes grass grow. The indoctrination had begun.

CHAPTER ELEVEN:

Over There

———

After ten weeks of hell—Drill Sergeants yelling and stark isolation—I'd survived basic training. Mom, Dad, Twan, and Dee Dee drove seven hundred miles from Mississippi to South Carolina to attend my graduation ceremony. I was overjoyed to see my family again. The only other communication I'd had with them was through letters and packages Mom had sent me, which sometimes included contraband in the form of candy and cookies. I stashed the goodies away inside my mattress and shared them with the soldier on the bunk above me to keep him from snitching. While basic training was challenging, it paled in comparison to the blistered hands, aching back, and sunburnt skin that came along with chopping cotton back in Mississippi.

After basic, I spent the next few months doing Advanced Individual Training at Fort Gordon in Georgia. December arrived; my AIT class graduated and we all prepared to go our separate ways. I'd become friends with James LeClear, a soldier from Lubbock, Texas. The night after graduation, we went out to dinner.

"Can I hitch a ride with you back to Mississippi as you head home?" I asked.

"Sure," he said. "But it's gonna be tight 'cause I got my wife and kids with me."

James had nearly an eighteen-hour drive ahead of him. Most of it was due west on I-20, which passed straight through Vicksburg, Mississippi. We stuffed duffle bags, suitcases, and people into every crevice of his little white Chevrolet Cavalier and hit the road. About eight hours later, he let me out at a gas station at the intersection of I-20 and Highway 61 in Vicksburg. Mom and Dad were waiting there in the parking lot.

After a couple of weeks at home, it was time to leave again. The Army offered to pay for a flight, but I chose to take the bus. Late on the evening of December 31, 1996, as the bus idled, a stranger boarded. He settled into the seat next to me as the Greyhound pulled away. After a few minutes on the road, he was snoring loudly. Without permission, he'd turned my shoulder into his own personal pillow. The Mississippi Delta's barren winter fields slowly disappeared. Rows and rows of unplanted land gave way to the bright lights of Memphis, Tennessee, and St. Louis, Missouri. I gazed out the window. Fireworks lit up the midnight sky as the Greyhound barreled across the Midwest. Destination? Fort Riley, Kansas—my first duty station.

The sudden stop and loud hiss from the brakes jarred me awake. The sun had risen. It was the beginning of a new year: January 1, 1997. I was in Junction City, Kansas. The stranger was gone, and my shoulder was sore. We never said a word to each other. I stepped off the bus, face-first into the harshest cold weather I'd ever experienced. As hard as I tried, I could not think of a time during my childhood comparable to what now seemed to rob my body of every ounce of heat.

A yellow cab pulled up. I couldn't get in fast enough! The cab driver wove through Junction City and turned onto Trooper Drive, which took us up to Fort Riley's famous Custer Hill. After several days of mandatory in-processing I was assigned to the 4th Battalion 1st Field Artillery Regiment. Within a few weeks, I found myself in a soft-shell Humvee on a retrans mission out in the middle of nowhere.

Specialist Sanchez, a sandy-haired Puerto Rican guy, had been in the unit longer than I had. He was soft-spoken with freckled cheeks, always smiling in spite of whatever challenges we faced. About a week into that mission Sanchez and I became stuck. I mean literally stuck! The wheels on our Humvee wouldn't move. The mud, previously wet and mushy, had frozen around the tires. Several other vehicles had been frozen to the ground as well.

The only thing we could do was huddle close and share the truck's air vent in a desperate attempt to stay warm. Miserable would be an understatement. The doors and windows of the Humvee were made of plastic; cold air whipped through the cracks around the zippered edges as we tried to keep warm for the next two days.

When we finally returned to civilization, I met the first of many significant and influential mentors in my career. Staff Sergeant Michael Kinsey was from Tampa, Florida. He'd already served for more than fifteen years. Mike was an absolutely brilliant thinker. Although he felt the Army had mistreated him, and he was preparing to separate, he nevertheless decided to take me under his wing.

Staff Sergeant Kinsey drove a purple 1985 Cadillac Seville. He carried himself with such professionalism and confidence you'd never know he'd grown frustrated with military life.

One afternoon, though, after lunch, he said to me, "You know, Private Pinkins, you're the only reason I come to work each day."

Staff Sergeant Kinsey had climbed the ranks quickly. He advanced so fast the Army had to slow his ascent. This frustrated him. He had met every standard and completed all the requirements for promotion to Sergeant First Class. Still, it just wasn't happening fast enough for him. When I met him, he was preparing to say goodbye to the military.

"The Army failed me," he said as we munched on chicken wings at the pizza joint across the street from my barracks. "I'm only here to lift you up and show you the way before I walk out the door." He paused for a moment to slurp his soda. "Pinkins, what are your plans? What do you want to do with your life?"

It was my first time being so far away from home. I missed Mississippi but didn't know exactly why. Was it my family? My high school girlfriend? It definitely wasn't the cotton fields.

"I'm going home after I serve out this contract," I told him. The contract I signed in New Orleans was for four years. I figured I'd travel a bit, complete my obligation, and then return to Tougaloo College to finish my degree. I told Kinsey as much.

Lifting his head slowly, brows furrowed, he responded, "Pinkins, I see so much potential in you! Don't you have dreams?"

I paused for a moment, sipping my soda, and contemplating how silly it would sound if I shared what I really desired. Other than Danny, the Marine Sergeant at the printing press back in Jackson, I'd never shared with anyone what I really wanted to do—travel.

Breaking eye contact nervously, I said, "I want to travel the world."

"Was that a question or a statement?" he asked sarcastically. "Do you really want to travel?"

"I want to get lost in different cultures, learn different languages. I want to vanish in the hustle and bustle of crowded foreign cities and take in all there is to see."

He smiled. "Well, there you go."

"Don't just be alive," he said. "You have to actually live. If you want to do something, then do it. Why don't you request to be stationed overseas?"

He told me about his time in South Korea, Germany, and Italy, and all the traveling he had done while stationed in foreign countries. He sounded a lot like Danny.

Staff Sergeant Kinsey and I had several conversations throughout my short time at Fort Riley. The summer flew by. Thank God it did because I didn't believe a place could get as hot as the Delta until I experienced July at Fort Riley. I couldn't decide if I'd rather endure the dry heat of Kansas or the Delta's humidity. What I did know, however, was that nothing I'd experienced thus far in the military compared to the difficulty of chopping cotton.

Months later on a snowy day in December 1997, Staff Sergeant Kinsey handed me a piece of paper. He walked away with a satisfied smile on his face. They were my reassignment orders. I was surprised! Shocked! The Army was ordering me to Germany. Although he denies it to this day, I believe Staff Sergeant Kinsey somehow orchestrated my reassignment. I think his goal was to get me out of Fort Riley and overseas. He'd already said he didn't think it was time for me to go back to Mississippi.

Four months later on a foggy Tuesday morning—April 14, 1998, nearly five thousand miles away from the Delta's cotton fields—I landed in Germany. I could barely contain myself as I walked through Frankfurt International Airport. The unfamiliar languages being spoken all around me were fascinating. As per my Southern upbringing, whenever someone made eye contact, I'd flash a huge Mississippi smile and say, "Hey, how you doin'?" The awkward glances I received in return piqued my interest even further.

Maybe someone else would have been stressed at the thought of being lost and wandering aimlessly around a large international airport. For me it was the total opposite. My curiosity was in overdrive and I hadn't even yet stepped outside. I listened to the chatter of German, Italian, and Turkish people speaking their native languages. I smelled unfamiliar foods and couldn't wait to taste them. It was a dam cracked and then burst apart as I was flooded with new culture.

"Hey, soldier!" someone barked from several feet away. "Get over here!"

A freckle-faced, skinny white guy in glasses commanded my attention. He waved me over to join a group of people huddled near the airport exit. The directness in which he ordered me to join him certainly didn't fit his physicality. He had bushy red hair and oversized glasses that dominated his freckled face. An ill-fitting military uniform hung on his frail frame. He wore a black armband, stenciled with the number 64 in white letters and wrapped around his scrawny left bicep.

He reminded me of the blond kid with the bushy eyebrows from basic training. According to the insignia on his uniform collar, he outranked me. This wasn't difficult. I was only a Private First Class, barely a gnat's ass above the lowest rung of the military totem pole. I begrudgingly followed his orders, ended my personal tour of the airport, and joined the group.

After a few minutes he ushered us outside into the cold, damp German air and onto what looked like a WWII-era bus. We drove around the airport to the 64th Replacement Company. The 64th greeted military families and individual soldiers at Frankfurt International Airport. They also planned and executed the logistics to get soldiers and their families to the bases throughout Germany. Destinations included places like Wiesbaden, Mannheim, Gießen, Darmstadt, Baumholder, Vilseck, Wurzburg, Heidelberg, Bamberg, Hanau, and more. My destination that day was Ray Barracks in Friedberg, about thirty-eight kilometers north of Frankfurt. Elvis had been stationed there in the late '50s.

I'd had heard there was no speed limit on the Autobahn, yet our bus seemed to creep down the highway; other cars zipped past us as if we were standing still. I peeked over the bus driver's shoulder. I was shocked to realize he was doing a steady 120 kilometers per hour (about 75 mph). After a short stopover at Gießen Army Depot, a couple of soldiers from my new platoon arrived to transport me onward to Friedberg.

The sun had set. It was dark when we drove through the main gate of Ray Barracks. We drove across the base and stopped at the headquarters building. A disinterested sergeant tossed me a room key and pointed out the window toward the three-story red brick barracks next door. The building was in the shape of a U. Behind it was a quarter-mile running track and beyond that was a baseball field.

Carrying two army-green duffle bags, I climbed the stairs to my barracks room. I inserted my key, but the door was already unlocked. Walking in, I found a young white guy, no more than eighteen or nineteen years old, sitting in the dark on the bed against the far wall. Silhouetted by the light shining through the window from the track out back, I could see his shoulders were slumped. He was crying softly. I left the light off and placed my bags on the bed near the opposite wall.

"Hey, I'm Private Pinkins. You okay?"

He didn't respond. His sobbing just intensified.

"What's wrong?" I asked. His tears progressed to all-out bawling.

"I miss my family," he said. "I can't take this! I wanna go home!"

He was new, just like me. This was only his second night in Germany. He'd been married to his high school sweetheart just before deployment.

"I wanna go home!" he yelled. "I can't take this!"

I didn't know what to tell him; I certainly didn't feel the same way. On the contrary, I was excited to be there. Going home was the furthest thing from my mind. I sat with him in the dark for a while.

"It'll be alright," I told him. "This is my first day as well."

I felt terrible for the guy. I went back downstairs and across the parking lot to the headquarters building.

"I don't think my roommate is gonna make it," I told the key-tossing sergeant.

"What are you talking about, Private?" he said with a sigh.

"My roommate. He's upstairs crying in the dark, talking about how he wants to go home."

Clearly annoyed, the sergeant looked up from his meal. "He'll be okay."

He then spun around in his chair, kicked his feet up onto the coffee table, and continued watching the Armed Forces Network on the television.

It was my first night in Germany and I didn't want to go back to my room and spend the rest of the night listening to someone cry. I left the headquarters building and walked back toward the main gate we'd entered a couple of hours before.

"What are you doing?" said a voice in my head.

I knew exactly what I was doing. I was beginning a practice that I'd repeat time and time again throughout my thirteen years in Europe. I didn't know all the rules because no one had explained them to me yet, so I made up my own rules. Apparently, for safety reasons, we were supposed to take a buddy with us whenever we left the base. The only person available was my roommate, but he was crying in the barracks. I walked alone toward the main gate.

Two soldiers stood in the guard shack on the left. Their job was to check the identification of people entering the base. As I walked past the guard shack, they looked at me. I looked at them. True to my Southern upbringing, as soon as we made eye contact, I blurted out, "Hey, how you doin'?"

Neither responded. They simply broke eye contact and continued with whatever had previously occupied their attention. I kept walking straight out the gate.

I stood for a moment on the corner of Frankfurter Straße across from *Grüner Weg Straße*. A steady stream of cars passed by heading into Friedberg. I looked left and then turned right to begin walking in the direction of traffic. As I walked, I could vaguely make out, on the opposite side of the street, the imposing silhouette of the Wasserturm Auf dem Wartburg. It was a water tower built in 1923 and served as a memorial for German soldiers who had fought and died in WWI and WWII.

After several minutes of wandering down the dimly lit street, I ducked inside a bar. It wasn't very crowded. A soccer game was broadcast on a television in the corner of the room. A few people dabbled at the pool table as I took a seat on a tall, round, wooden stool. I was presumably the only American and clearly the only black guy in the bar.

Appearing out of nowhere, the bartender said, "Hallo!"

"Hi," I replied.

"Was möchten Sie trinken?" he asked.

Embarrassed, I responded, "Uh, I don't speak German."

Sitting next to me was a German lady in her early twenties. She leaned over and whispered, "He is asking, 'What would you like to drink?'"

I hadn't even thought about drinking that night and had no idea what to order.

"What do you recommend?" I asked her.

She looked at the bartender and said, "Eine großes Hefeweizen, bitte." A memory flashed: while I was stationed at Fort Riley, Staff Sergeant Kinsey mentioned that Hefeweizen was a popular German beer.

Seconds later the bartender slid me the tallest glass of beer I'd ever seen. My eyes bulged. The woman and bartender laughed. I wasn't a big drinker and, to be honest, hated beer.

At that moment, I said to myself, "What the hell? What do I gotta lose?" I took a big gulp and forced it down.

"Are you stationed on Ray Barracks?" the woman asked.

"Yes. I just got here today."

"What's your name?" she asked.

"How do I say in German, 'My name is Tyrone?'"

She laughed, "Ich heiße Tyrone."

"Ich heiße Tyrone," I repeated. The goofiest smile crept across my face. I have always been a nerd and proud of it— speaking my first German words delighted me.

We sat there for a while as she taught me simple German phrases. Eventually I realized I needed to get back to base. I had to be up early for formation the next morning.

I finished most of the Hefeweizen, left the bar, and found my way back to the main gate. The same two soldiers were still there. When they looked up, I flashed my military ID and walked back to my barracks. My roommate was asleep fully clothed, curled in the fetal position. The next day he was gone. I never saw him again.

The Capri Club was the base party joint. A few nights later I went there with Private Daniel Villarreal. Private Villarreal was a baby-faced Mexican-American kid who grew up a stone's throw from the US-Mexico border in Mission, Texas. Trying to protect him from the Mexican Cartel, which heavily recruited along the border, Villarreal's parents had signed a waiver for him to join the Army when he was only seventeen. He'd also gone through basic training at Fort Jackson. We worked in the same shop and became instant friends.

"You wanna go to the Capri?" Private Villarreal asked.

"Capri? What's that?"

"It's the base club, and tonight's R-n-B night!" he explained.

The Capri Club was a tiny place, tucked away in the corner of the base behind the post office. It had a low ceiling and a dance floor. Soldiers crammed into that little place to pre-game before heading out to off-base spots like the Central Studio Club in downtown Friedberg, the Woodland Club in Gießen, the Park Café in Wiesbaden, or the Pioneer Club in Hanau. The great thing about Capri Club was that the base commander allowed German women to come on base to party there.

We hadn't been in the club long before I heard a familiar voice behind me say, "Tyrone?"

It was Jessica, the German lady from the bar. She ran over to give me an enthusiastic hug that I wasn't prepared for.

"Let's dance," she said, dragging me onto the dance floor.

Little did she know I was not then, and still am not today, the best dancer. The most she could get from me was a two-step with an occasional dip here or there. Luckily for me the dance floor was overcrowded, so no one noticed my awkwardness.

After a short while, she said, "You want to go for a ride? I can show you around the city."

"Sure," I said.

We walked off base and hopped in her Volkswagen parked down the street.

After a few minutes of driving, we were on Autobahn 5. Passing by Bad Homburg, we exited onto Highway 661. This whisked us through Kalbach-Riedberg until we were finally on Autobahn 3 headed toward Frankfurt.

"Where are we?" I asked as a steady stream of cars zoomed past and throngs of pedestrians trampled by on the sidewalk. We'd found a parking space along the street.

"Germany," she said sarcastically. "There is a place I want to take you. I think you will like it."

We walked a few blocks until we came to the corner of Bleichstraße and Eschenheimer Tor. On that busy street corner was Kontiki, a tiny, dimly lit Thai restaurant. The hostess seated us near a long window.

Excited, I asked Jessica, "How do I order?"

Laughing again at my interest in her language, she said, "You say 'Ich möchte' followed by what you want." She pointed to a list of items on the menu. "End your sentence with 'bitte,' which means please."

I practiced what she taught me by trying to pronounce random items on the menu. She laughed out loud at my mistakes. The introverted nerd in me was fully awake. She seemed to find it very interesting that I was so intrigued by learning and that I wasn't embarrassed to make a fool of myself. I explained that since childhood I'd dreamed of traveling the world and getting lost in foreign cultures. At that moment, in that dim light, I was living a dream borne out of stories I'd heard LeVar Burton tell on *Reading Rainbow*.

The waiter returned. "Was möchten Sie trinken?"

I paused to formulate my response. Jessica looked at me with anticipation as I tried to organize the words.

"Ich möchte Thai Ice Tea, bitte," I said.

She clapped and squealed with excitement; both of us broke out into laughter. We spent the next hour or so talking about German culture, her life, and mine. We finished dinner and walked out into the hustle and bustle. Next to Kontiki was the Turmpalast, a movie theatre initially built in 1929. Damaged during WWII, it was rebuilt in 1950. The theatre began playing English-language films in 1980.

"Do you want to go inside?" Jessica asked.

"Ask me in your language!" I was on a roll.

She replied in German, we purchased two tickets and enjoyed a movie. Afterward, we walked around Frankfurt, popping in and out of random bars into the early hours. By the time we returned to Ray Barracks, it was around six in the morning. She dropped me off at the main gate, and I hopped out and waved goodbye. I rushed to my barracks, ran upstairs, brushed my teeth, threw on my uniform, and got outside just as my bus was about to pull off. I climbed on, boots unpolished, laces untied, uniform halfway unbuttoned. It was definitely not a good look for my first day. The bus pulled off with me and a load of new soldiers, headed to Gießen Army Depot for new soldier orientation.

On the drive many soldiers talked about their new roommates, the base, and the Capri Club. I leaned back and took a nap, reminiscing about the Kontiki bar, Thai Iced Tea, the Turmpalast, and my tour of Frankfurt the night before.

The experience with Jessica that night fueled my curiosity. It led to me frequently visiting foreign cities: Berlin, Nuremberg, London, Vienna, Austria, Lago di Garda, and so many more. When driving around I'd often take a random exit off the Autobahn, one I'd never taken. I'd park on a random corner, write the name of the cross street on a piece of paper, and stuff it into my pocket.

For hours in these cities, I'd walk and explore, meeting people from all over the world. I was often invited to dinner by people I'd met earlier in the day. I once found myself at the dinner table of a random Polish family. We enjoyed *golabki*, which reminded me of Mom's cabbage rolls. Another time I found myself in an Ethiopian restaurant using my fingers as utensils; I chowed down on berbere spiced chicken and egg stew. I shared conversations with Africans who'd migrated from places like Ghana, Kenya, Ethiopia, and Morocco.

* *

Linc McCoy was born in Brooklyn, New York. His parents divorced when he was five years old. He remained with his mom, a colonel in the Army Reserves, and visited his dad on weekends. Her service to the country may provide some insight into why Linc joined. He'd seen how much his mom had sacrificed for him and his siblings and decided to join the Army after high school.

"I wanted to fend for myself," he told me in Germany. "I wanted to be able to pay my mom back for all the things she had done for me. I figured the Army was a way for me to pay for college, travel the world, and make a living while serving my country."

After completing basic training at Fort Knox, Kentucky in 1995, Linc graduated at the top of his class at Fort Gordon. The Army shipped him off to Suwon Rock Army Base in South Korea. After fifteen months in South Korea, Linc moved back to the United States and spent a year at Fort Hood in Texas before being sent back overseas again—this time to Friedberg, Germany.

I'd already been stationed in Friedberg for several months before Linc arrived in October of 1998. We first met one night at the Central Studio Club, a local discotheque dating back to 1968. Nestled in the heart of the small town, the Central Studio was easy to miss. Just off Elvis-Presley-Platz, on Wolfengasse, the club was engulfed in the shadows of the spectacularly imposing town church, the Stadtkirche Unsere Lieben Frau. Many soldiers frequented the Central Studio Club because it was within walking distance. It was also larger and livelier than the Capri Club. Central Studio also offered easier access for Germans who wanted to party with US soldiers.

It was cold outside that night and I wore a three-quarter-length black leather coat. I walked through the club door and handed the lady behind the counter the Deutsche Mark equivalent of five US dollars. The carpet at the entrance was bright red and led to a steep set of stairs. At the top of the stairs the heavy thump and thud from the speakers nearly sent me tumbling back down.

The doors opened to a medium-sized dance floor and disco ball above. To the left was a row of seats and a bar with tall stools. Beyond the bar were bathrooms where many soldiers went to puke after they'd consumed too much. Up above, beyond the second-floor balcony, were pool tables and more seating. A night didn't go by without me peering over the balcony to see some GI being berated by a European girl because he'd been caught cheating.

Linc and I had seen each other in passing on base but had never stopped to talk. He was assigned to the 1st Brigade Headquarters and I worked at the 2nd Battalion 37th Armored Regiment. One night we inadvertently collided in the club. Over the loud music, we introduced ourselves, chatted for a while, and went our separate ways. Occasionally, we ran into each other again at other random clubs. The Park Café was my favorite for its live band. Located right off Wilhelmstraße, the Park Café was definitely the place to be on a Sunday night.

Aside from random encounters every now and then, Linc and I never developed a bond while stationed in Friedberg. He had his group of friends, and I had mine. My two-year tour ended in the Spring of 2000 and the Army shipped me back to the states. Little did we know, though, that those brief encounters would evolve into a friendship that spanned more than twenty years.

A few years later, in January of 2002, across the Atlantic Ocean and nearly 7,500 miles from Friedberg, I walked into a classroom on Fort Benning Army Base in Columbus, Georgia. I scanned the room searching for the most comfortable place to sit. To my surprise, there, seated in the middle of the room, was Linc. We embraced and laughed at the randomness of meeting up again so far away from our initial contact. We were both there for the Basic Noncommissioned Officer Course in preparation for promotion to Staff Sergeant.

We spent the next few weeks hanging out together at Fort Benning. We then transitioned to Fort Gordon for the second phase of our training. There we were roommates for the next four months. After graduating from the course, Linc transitioned from enlisted soldier to Warrant Officer. He headed off to Fort Hood, Texas. I remained enlisted and the Army shipped me back to Germany.

CHAPTER TWELVE:

Promises Made

___

After a short stint back in the states the Army shipped me back to Europe. I was glad for the new assignment. I missed exploring foreign cities and getting lost in new cultures. Walking through Frankfurt, I popped into Raffaello's, just off Berliner Straße on Neue Kräme, for one of the most delicious pasta dishes I've ever tasted outside of Italy. I sat for a while at Paulsplatz, people-watching and eavesdropping, as locals came and went. I continued my walk through the Römerberg, where festivals took place in spring and summer and Christmas Markets were held in winter. I passed the Justitiabrunnen. A small group of tourists huddled around the enormous bronze statue of a woman holding a sword in her right hand and balancing the scales of justice in her left.

The dim yellow lamps illuminated the surrounding shops and buildings as well as the cobblestones below. I continued down a narrow street, passing through the shadow of the Junges Museum and then that of the Frankfurt City Museum. Scurrying across Mainkai Straße, I stopped at a little booth and purchased a ticket for a boat ride. I watched the Frankfurt skyline sparkle to life from the Main river. When I'd hop on a boat—whether in Frankfurt or Wiesbaden—I usually had no idea where it was headed. The destination really didn't matter; I was getting lost on purpose.

As the bright lights of Frankfurt reflected off the water, I sailed past the towering Dreikönigskirche, which had originated as a Gothic hospital chapel back in the 1300s. The chapel dominated the Frankfurt skyline as the boat drifted along. We sailed past the Sachsenhausen district where years prior I'd hung out with Gentry, Villarreal, and Hall—all people I'd worked with in the shop at Ray Barracks.

Gentry lived in the small town of Bad Nauheim, where the three of us met up early one Friday night after my return for a few drinks.

"Let's go out somewhere," Hall said. "Let's go to Sachsenhausen!"

"What's a Sachsenhausen?" I asked, already tipsy. I hadn't been in Germany very long, maybe a few weeks.

They stared at each other, bewildered at me not knowing what or where Sachsenhausen was. Gentry called a taxi. We stumbled out of his apartment and down the stairs, laughing as we piled into the cab idling by the curb.

"I'm hungry," I moaned as the taxi headed south on Autobahn 5 toward Frankfurt.

They all laughed but not at the fact that I was hungry. What amused them was the particular way I said it. I moaned again, like a mooing cow, "I'm huuuuuuuungry." Something was clearly wrong. Either I'd already had too much to drink or something extra had been added to my cup. Throughout the drive I constantly moaned, "I'm huuuuuuungry!"

We tumbled out of the taxi onto Schweizer Straße, a few blocks north of the Frankfurt Südbahnhof. Tired of my complaining, our group found its way into one of the many restaurants lining the street.

"What do you wanna eat, Pinkins?" Gentry asked.

"Hamburger and French fries," I slurred, barely comprehensible as the waitress scribbled down our order and walked away.

"I think she likes me," I mumbled, eyes half shut.

"She don't like you, Pinkins," Villarreal blurted. "Dude, you're drunk."

The waitress returned with our food. They'd ordered me water to try to sober me up a bit. When I reached out to grab a French fry, I had to do a double-take. Blinking intensely, I closed and opened my eyes. Something was wrong. I stared at my hands, rotating them from back to palm. I slowly flexed my fingers, curling them into a fist and then opening them again. I looked back at the plate of fries and couldn't believe what I was seeing.

My French fries had stood themselves up like little stick figures and were running around the plate. Each time I tried to grab a fry, I missed. The fries laughed at me.

"Hey, guys, y'all see this? My French fries! They won't be still!" I said, still trying to catch a fleeing fry.

The group and the fries burst into laughter.

I gave up on the fries and grabbed my burger. I took a bite. However, as I chewed there was nothing in my mouth, only air. When I looked at the burger, it had transformed into a red, green, and yellow smiling mouth. The burger-mouth laughed at me with the fries. I rubbed my face and lay my head on the table. The next day, I found out I had, in fact, been drugged. I didn't do drugs and hadn't even smoked marijuana. At that point in my life I probably couldn't tell you what weed or any other drug even looked like. Thankfully, God showed me grace.

Still on my boat ride, I continued sailing past the Sachsen-hausen district, and under the many bridges along the river Main. When I hopped off the boat, I continued exploring the city until sufficiently lost, just like I'd done many other times. Eventually I flagged down a taxi and told the driver where I'd parked; he drove me back to my car.

Soon, however, my European excursions would be put on hold.

**

Raised by a single mom with three other siblings, David Lee McCallum was born right across the Alabama line just off Highway 80 in small town Meridian, Mississippi. His mom and his siblings called him David Lee.

"Life was hard back then," David Lee told me. "Mama raised us off a maid's salary from her job at the Day's Inn. When I got out of school and on the weekends, I worked in the cotton fields. Sometimes I got a job spraying trees."

When David Lee was in the ninth grade, his mom moved out to California. He moved in with his grandmother—Big Mama—and eventually graduated from East Kemper High School in 1982.

"Big Mama didn't have no car, and most of the time, I didn't have no shoes," he said. "So, when we needed something from the store, I walked barefoot all the way."

When David Lee was around seven, having no shoes almost cost him his life.

"Big Mama called out to me one day, 'David Lee, come go to the store for me with your cousin Ray-Ray,'" he recalled. It had rained for days before David Lee and his cousin's walk to the store. "We got on the dirt road. We cut through the woods, and started walking down a hill. There was water running in the ditch along the side of the road."

Little David Lee had a phobia of standing or walking in water outside. If the water wasn't clear and he couldn't see the ground, he was terrified. That day Ray-Ray, his cousin, tried to force him to get over his fear of water.

"Now, you gotta walk all the way down yonder to the end of the ditch," Ray-Ray instructed David Lee. David Lee was already scared. When Ray-Ray took off, leaving him behind, David Lee just started walking in the water like he'd been instructed. He hadn't walked very far when it felt like he'd stepped on some glass and cut his foot.

When David Lee lifted his foot from the muddy water, a giant water moccasin was wrapped around his ankle. It had bitten his foot. By the time Ray-Ray had rushed back to David Lee, the snake had detached. Ray-Ray snatched David Lee up like a sack of potatoes, slung him over his shoulder, and ran up the road to the country store.

"A lil' ol' white lady owned the store," David Lee said. "When Ray-Ray told her I'd been bitten, they put me in her car and drove me down to Kemper County Hospital."

David Lee almost died that day.

"Doctor said if that moccasin had hit an artery in my foot, it could have taken my life," he explained. "Although I still don't like snakes, after that I wasn't afraid of water no more. I don't know why, but I just wasn't."

Several years later, age twenty, David Lee joined the Army.

"By the time my brothers found out, I was already on the Greyhound bus pulling out of the station. As the bus barreled down the highway, I looked out the window. My brothers were driving along side, begging me to get off. I waved goodbye and leaned back in the seat."

** **

In May of 2002, after my short stint at Fort Benning, the Army stationed me at Gießen Army Depot with the 2nd Battalion 3rd Field Artillery Regiment (2/3 FA). That August, a couple of months before David Lee arrived, I got promoted to Staff Sergeant. When we met, he was a Master Sergeant. Everyone affectionately called him Master Blaster.

While Master Blaster was short and slim, he wielded a big stick. Everyone respected him, partly because of the amount of time he'd served—over two decades. This included combat tours in Desert Storm, Panama, and Afghanistan. That respect, however, was also due to his intelligence, his character, and the way he treated people.

"As soon as I walked into the Battalion Headquarters, Command Sergeant Major Covington called me into his office," Master Blaster recalled. "The first thing CSM Covington told me was, "I got complaints about the commo guys."

"I'm leaving it up to you," CSM Covington told Master Blaster. "But, you need to make some moves in the commo platoon, and you need to make them soon."

I was in Alpha Battery at the time. I didn't have any soldiers. I was a one-man shop, which was fine with me. I came to work and did my job how I wanted without really worrying much about anything else. Anything, that is, except my ornery supervisor. For the previous eight months, First Sergeant Wiseman had continuously blocked my attempts to enroll in free college courses offered on base. He never provided a reason. He simply denied each request.

I really wanted to finish my degree, and because I was a one-man shop, I felt it was the perfect time to re-enroll. I also wanted to take German language courses. I didn't think

PROMISES MADE · 191

it made any sense for me to be in a foreign country and not at least try to learn the language. But Wiseman consistently blocked my requests. Even worse, he smiled in my face with each denial.

Dad had taught me something powerful from a very young age. He had told me, "When people are tryin' to be mean to you, don't take the bait. Be patient. If you react with anger, you done given up all your power. Your opportunity will come, everything happens when it is supposed to happen."

In late February, Master Blaster called me over to his office at the Battalion Headquarters. I had no idea what he wanted.

"What do you think about the platoon?" he asked.

I'd been down in Alpha Battery since I arrived in Gießen, so I really didn't have a strong relationship with the signal guys up in Headquarters Battery. I knew their names, but wasn't part of the commo platoon.

"I need you to be in charge of soldiers," Master Blaster said. "You're the new commo platoon sergeant.

In the back of my mind, I heard Dad's voice whisper, "Everything happens when it's supposed to happen."

The drums of war were beating loudly. The country had been convinced by the Bush administration that Saddam Hussein possessed weapons of mass destruction. A few weeks passed and, in late March, President Bush's shock and awe campaign began. We already knew we'd be deploying several weeks later in May.

That night, I sat alone in my barracks and stared at the wall, contemplating what I would say to my soldiers. How could I motivate them? What experiences could I draw from to encourage myself as I confronted a wholly unfamiliar situation? The sudden realization that I had never been in charge of a platoon racked my nerves.

On Thursday, May 1, 2003, I stood outside Battalion Headquarters, in front of twenty soldiers. They ranged in age from right-out-of-high-school teenagers to forty-year-old seasoned vets. They all patiently awaited the next words of a young staff sergeant, barely known to them, who was to lead them in a war being fought nearly three thousand miles away in Baghdad, Iraq.

Standing before them, I glanced confidently at each face while a fierce internal battle raged inside me. My introverted personality was in direct conflict with my driven spirit. Plus, I barely had any leadership experience. I'd been a squad leader way back in basic training at Fort Jackson. I'd also been a squad leader when I was stationed at Fort Benning, but that was it.

Yet there I was, standing in the parking lot outside our Battalion Headquarters, before our commo platoon. I was suddenly responsible for the lives of American citizens: sons, brothers, husbands, and fathers. I saw all of their faces, looked into all of their eyes. The weight of the moment was immediate. It was as if someone had dropped a ton of bricks on my shoulders.

That moment, standing there before those men, was a transformative and defining experience that began to shape me into the person I am today. Those soldiers ignited a fire in me.

Spring 2003 in Gießen, Germany, prior to my first deployment.
Out front, MSG "Master Blaster" McCallum
Bottom Row, from left to right: SGT Gibson, SPC Taylor, SPC Gilbert,
SPC Smith, PV2 Davis, SSG Pinkins
Second Row, from left to right: SGT Wolfer, SPC Hano, PV2 Commisso,
PFC Bryant, SPC Marzette
Back Row, from left to right: SPC Batchelder, SPC Loftis, PFC White,
SPC Schaeffer, PV2 Abke, and SSG Toppin

Several weeks later in Baghdad, Iraq

That day, I made three promises to them: "One, I will always lead from the front and be first through every breach. Two, I will never leave you behind, outside of the perimeter, no matter how badly you're wounded or how difficult and dangerous the situation might become. And three, I'll be the last to leave Iraq at the completion of our tour, and I'll make sure everyone returns home to their family."

Knowing many of those guys were fresh out of high school was particularly sobering. The understanding that I was now responsible for other people's lives was constantly on my mind throughout our deployment.

A few days after our first meeting we flew out of Ramstein Air Base. After a brief stop at Camp Arifjan, Kuwait, we prepared to begin the nearly seven-hundred-mile trek north across the desert to Baghdad. The next fifteen months in war-torn Iraq fueled my passion for helping others realize their true, unyielding potential. It also taught me things about myself that I never knew existed.

Our convoy was separated into chalks (the grouping of vehicles based on type, weight, unit, etc.). With vehicle caravan lined up and ready to go, we got word over the radio for our chalk to roll out. Just as we began moving, a voice blasted from the RT-1523 radio mounted to my Humvee's dashboard. It said, "HQ Five-Four, HQ Five-Four, this is Gunner One-Zero-November, over."

Gunner One-Zero-November was Master Blaster's call sign. HQ Five-Four was the bumper number on my Humvee. It was what I was referred to since I didn't have a call sign. I'd thought it was bullshit that our platoon didn't have a name like some of the other platoons. However, that would be soon rectified.

"Gunner One-Zero-November, this is HQ Five-Four, over," I responded as my vehicle slowly bounced along in the cloud of dust that trailed the line of trucks ahead.

"HQ Five-Four, this is Gunner One-Zero-November. Meet me on a secure internal channel, over," Master Blaster's voice instructed.

"Gunner One-Zero-November, this is HQ Five-Four, roger, out!"

I changed my radio's channel and met Master Blaster on a different station, one the rest of the convoy couldn't hear.

"Smitty left his medicine behind," were the first words out of Master Blaster's mouth.

Specialist Smith from North Carolina almost didn't deploy with us. He was a commo soldier and had the same Military Occupation Specialty—31U—as many other members in our platoon. Our platoon was almost evenly split with 31U and 31L.

Back in Gießen Smitty had worked in the mailroom. His office was located behind the Central Issue Facility, a huge warehouse-type building where desert camouflage gear was handed out like candy in preparation for deployment. He wasn't attached to our platoon at the time, and the plan was to leave him back in Gießen because he required regular vitamin B-12 injections. He was anemic.

We hadn't even realized Smitty was a commo soldier. He'd been tucked away over in the mailroom before Master Blaster and I had even arrived to Gießen.

A few weeks before deployment Smitty and Sergeant Hall walked into Master Blaster's office.

"I'm SPC Smith. I've been in the mailroom," Smitty said. "I know you don't want to hear this, but I wanna go."

"Go where?" Master Blaster asked, surprised.

"I wanna deploy with the platoon."

"Whoa, whoa, whoa." Master Blaster raised his hands as though he'd been stopped by the police. "Specialist Smith! You have to take those shots. That shit has to be on ice; it has to stay refrigerated. We're going to the desert, guy! Hot weather. Heat."

The first issue he explained to Smitty was that the flight to Kuwait was long. Second, this was the early stages of a war and we didn't know if there would be refrigeration options available. At that point, we didn't even know about the nearly seven-hundred-mile convoy across the desert.

"Do you realize if I let you go and we can't keep that medication cold, you could die? I can't have that," Master Blaster declared.

"I wanna go, Master Blaster," Smitty insisted. "I'll do anything! I'll buy an insulated cooler, keep my medicine on ice. I'll ask the medics if they can help me store it in the aid station. I promise you, it won't be a problem." Smitty desperately wanted to go. He didn't want to stay back in Gießen on rear detachment, watching the rest of the platoon leave him behind.

With Smitty and SGT Hall still standing there in the office, Master Blaster picked up the phone and called upstairs. On the other end of the line, CSM Covington said the same thing, "Let's leave him behind. It's too risky. He'll stay in Gießen."

Master Blaster explained to CSM Covington that Smitty proposed to keep his medication on ice and would work with the medics to help him keep it cold. After a few minutes, Master Blaster hung up the phone.

"SGT Hall, go over to the mailroom and let them know that the CSM Covington said Smitty is coming back to the commo platoon." Master Blaster then looked over at Smitty and said, "Pack your shit! You're coming with us."

By the time I heard Master Blaster's voice across the radio, our convoy had already traveled a mile or so into the desert. "Get out of the convoy, go back, and get Smitty's medicine," Master Blaster said over the radio.

The convoy was long as hell. Lines and lines of vehicles stretched across the sand. All the Humvees looked alike except for unique numbers stenciled on the corner of each vehicle's front and rear bumpers.

"Turn the Humvee around," I instructed SPC Taylor. Taylor, an aspiring rapper, was from Richmond, Virginia. He popped the Humvee out of line, made a quick U-turn, and sped back. We zipped our way back to the aid station on the base in Kuwait. When we stopped, the only thing I could see from the convoy was a distant cloud of dust. The long line of military vehicles moved further and further away.

I hopped out, ran inside, and grabbed the medicine. "SPC Taylor, let's go!" I shouted once back inside the Humvee. There was no speed limit as we raced to catch up with the convoy; we gunned it. When we finally caught up, we managed to find our original position among the long line of vehicles.

The drive from Kuwait to Baghdad was rough. I felt terrible for the guys who had to ride in the back of the cargo trucks. Not only was the trip long and bumpy, it was hot as hell too. We arrived, late afternoon, on the outskirts of Baghdad. There, we were to be met by members of the 3rd Infantry Division out of Fort Stewart, Georgia. They'd been in Baghdad since the early stages of the war. We were essentially there to relieve them, and I'm sure they were eager to turn the mission over to us so they could move on.

We twisted our way through war-torn streets—over-turned vehicles and ruined buildings on all sides—eventually arriving in the Adhamiya neighborhood in Baghdad's north-west quadrant. A small contingent of 3ID combat vehicles escorted our larger convoy to the bombed-out Azimiya Palace which was once owned by Saddam Hussein's son, Uday. We were on the banks of the Tigris River.

**

Our first few nights in Baghdad we slept under the stars. The contrast between the serene beauty of the star-filled sky and the chaotic sound of machine-gun fire, of bombs exploding all around, could not have been more stark. After several days, the 3ID handed the mission over to 1AD. Azimiya Palace became our Battalion Headquarters. We referred to it as Gunner Main. Because we were a commo platoon, I assumed communications would be our primary mission. We immediately got to work setting up the Battalion's comms systems, strengthening the network 3ID had left behind.

SGT Gibson was a quick-witted car fanatic from Grenada, Mississippi. SPC Batchelder, from New Hampshire, was a politically conscious and outspoken critic of the war. Together they were our computer gurus. They worked on the unit's network infrastructure and brought our computer systems online.

Our 31Ls—line dogs—were SGT Mack from Georgia, SGT Wolfer from Chicago, and SSG Toppin from Barbados. They—along with the rest of the line dogs, SPC Loftis from Oklahoma, SPC Taylor from Virginia, and Private White from DC—all started laying wire around the base to connect the TA-312 telephones. They also began setting up and programming Satellite Communications equipment.

For the next few days, the rest of the platoon—SGT Hall from Texas, SPC Hano from West Virginia, SPC Marzette from Ohio, PVT Bryant from Virginia, PVT Davis from Iowa, PVT Commisso from New York, PVT Abke from Michigan, PVT Edwards from Utah, SPC Schaeffer, and Smitty—reprogrammed and troubleshot radio systems in the unit's vehicles. They set up communications systems in Gunner Main and installed OE-254 antenna systems throughout the compound.

While all that was going on, Master Blaster attended senior leader meetings. He was gathering vital information that would alter the posture of our platoon. What he told me one day created a bond between the members of our platoon that few people ever experience.

"I need to talk to you." Master Blaster had found me sitting on the edge of my green cot. "Come walk with me."

We walked out of the Battery Headquarters building and across the lawn toward Gunner Main.

"I know y'all are a commo platoon, but you need to prepare the guys to do combat missions." We walked across uneven ground, dusty patches of grass here and there. "Once y'all get all the Battalion's comms up and running, your primary mission is gonna be Combat Patrols, Combat Escorts, raids of enemy compounds, and Quick Reaction Force missions."

Master Blaster stopped in his tracks and stared at me. He was sizing me up, trying to see if I was shaken by what he'd just said. After a moment he continued, "Just like the scout platoon and the survey platoon, the commo platoon is gonna be outside the wire daily. That's why I put you in charge." He yanked open the side door to Gunner Main and entered alone, leaving me to process. Combat Patrols, Combat Escorts, raids of enemy compounds, and QRF missions echoed through my mind as I walked back across the cratered ground.

We'd had training on conducting patrols and escorts back in Germany. We'd also practiced conducting raids on enemy compounds; however, I knew we needed more drilling. If one thing had me concerned, it was the thought of clearing a building. I worried that one of our guys would get shot on entry. Worse, I was concerned that we'd accidentally shoot each other.

SGT Gilbert wasn't in the platoon, but he was still a commo soldier. Gilbert was in Service Battery down by the entrance gates, near the dining area where the cooks were. He'd previously completed Ranger School at Fort Benning in Georgia, so I knew he'd been exposed to room-clearing procedures. I went to him.

"I need you to walk the guys through techniques for clearing rooms," I said. "We don't have long."

Amidst a clump of trees next to the Tigris River, we drilled for hours and hours over the next few days. Over and over again, step by step, we practiced. SGTs Hall, Mack, Wolfer, and Gibson were each a squad leader; they rotated their teams until the drills and movements became second nature.

For many of us, it wasn't about being for or against the war. It was about survival. For me, the most important thing was getting those guys back home to their families. I'd made three promises and intended to keep them, even if I pushed the guys to the point of disliking me. My bet was that their animosity toward me would force them to gel as a team, watch each other's backs, and protect one another.

Whenever one soldier did something wrong, I punished the entire platoon: push-ups behind the building in the middle of the night and running circles inside the compound until their tongues hung out. I nitpicked every little thing they did; my annoyances were constant and intentional. When they started complaining to squad leaders that I was being too hard and that I was an asshole, I knew we were making progress. Their complaints transformed into calling each other out and holding one another accountable to prevent me from inflicting more mass punishment.

And then they gelled, starting to click like a well-oiled machine.

On any given day, one of our squads would have Quick Reaction Force duty. QRF duty lasted twenty-four hours and rotated daily from squad to squad. The purpose was to have a dedicated team ready at all times to respond if another platoon or unit got attacked or pinned down outside the wire.

Sixteen guys would sleep in one cramped room. Green Army cots were sandwiched close together along the walls. During a QRF rotation, one of the squads slept fully clothed, dressed in case a mission came down in the middle of the night. Right outside their room I hammered ten nails in the wall; on those nails they hung their gear. Just outside the doorway our Humvees were lined up against a tall, tan brick wall. The vehicles were intentionally pointed west toward the Tigris. That way we wouldn't have to waste time turning them around.

We rehearsed our QRF movements endlessly. It was vital. Every second meant life or death if someone was pinned down outside the compound, waiting on us to arrive. In the middle of the night, I'd yell "QRF!" waking each squad from a dead sleep to rehearse. It didn't take long before our QRF response was smooth like butter. We got it down to a science.

One night I heard the radio operator sound the alarm. I sprang up off my cot, threw on my gear, grabbed my Kevlar and weapon, and rushed next door to Gunner Main. As I walked across the lawn, I listened for the sound of engines starting. In under a minute the group was fully geared up, weapons mounted, and engines started. Three Humvees rolled around the corner to meet me at Gunner Main.

I walked into the side door of Gunner Main, received grid coordinates and a quick Situation Report, and then kept walking straight out the main exit. Our three Humvees—fully manned with weapons mounted—were already waiting in the middle of the street. From a dead sleep, our squads could respond to a QRF alert in the night and roll out the gate on the far end of the compound in under three minutes.

When a squad wasn't on QRF shift, they'd be executing multiple combat patrols all day. We conducted foot patrols and vehicle-mounted patrols throughout Adhamiya. Either that, or we'd be busy conducting combat escorts all over Baghdad. Between QRF duty, combat patrols, and combat escorts, our platoon was always stretched thin. That stretch brought us even closer together.

The only thing we were missing was a name. When we went out on missions, we were simply referred to by the stenciled number on the front and rear bumpers of our Humvees. I called a platoon meeting.

"We need a name," I said as the guys gathered around. "What do we want to be called?"

Ideas were thrown out. I don't know who, but someone shouted, "RuffRyders!"

The entire platoon voted. We didn't ask the First Sergeant, Battery Commander, nor anyone else for permission.

"You know they gonna shut this down over at Gunner Main," SGT Gibson said smirking.

"We'll see," I responded with a defiant smile.

I had already come up with an idea. My plan would unfold later that very evening.

The sun had set; we were scheduled for a night patrol. Like usual, the guys geared up and mounted our three patrol vehicles.

"Meet me over at the Battalion Headquarters," I instructed, walking toward Gunner Main.

While I was inside getting an intel brief on the area we'd be patrolling that night, the guys pulled up outside in our Humvees. Although I had indeed come to get intel before our mission, I was also there to see who was monitoring the RT-1523 radios that night. After receiving a quick intel brief and taking a glance at the map of Adhamiya plastered on the wall, I walked out the door. I hopped into the command seat of the lead vehicle. We headed toward the main gate on the far end of the base.

Usually, when we'd depart the gate, I'd radio back to Gunner Main, identifying myself as HQ Five-Four. But not this time. Before we exited, I told the driver to stop. We could hear cars honking and see traffic passing along the street outside the gate.

"Gunner Main, Gunner Main, this is RuffRyder One-Zero, start point time now, over," I barked into the hand mic attached to the green RT-1523 radio mounted to the dashboard.

There was no response. Silence.

"Gunner Main, Gunner Main, this is RuffRyder One-Zero, SP time now, over," I repeated.

Then came a response.

"RuffRyder One-Zero, RuffRyder One-Zero, this is Gunner Main, identify yourself, over!" The radio operator barked back on the other end.

The radio operator knew who I was. He'd just seen me walk out of Gunner Main, and he knew we were about to begin our mission. He knew I would call and report our departure. He was just shocked I'd decided, all on my own, to implement a new call sign.

I am sure I broke several protocols, but at that point I really didn't care. A unique call sign, our own name, was the final ingredient to bring our platoon together in the middle of a war zone.

I responded, "Gunner Main, Gunner Main, this is RuffRyder One-Zero, formerly known as HQ Five-Four. RuffRyder One-Zero, out!"

I looked at my driver and pointed toward the exit gate. "Let's go!"

He hit the accelerator. Our three vehicles rolled out to conduct night patrol.

After patrolling for over an hour, we returned to base. As we entered that gate, I called the Battalion Headquarters to inform them we'd made it back safely.

"Gunner Main, Gunner Main, the is RuffRyder One-Zero, over."

"RuffRyder One-Zero this is Gunner Main, over," came the response.

"Gunner Main, this is RuffRyder One-Zero, mission complete, over."

"RuffRyder One-Zero, this is Gunner Main. Roger, out!"

And just like that, our platoon became known as the RuffRyders.

Of course, there was some consternation the next day. A few people up at Gunner Main were upset about the breach of protocol. Our little lieutenant crumbled and folded like a chair at the first sign of opposition. Luckily, Master Blaster was there.

"The other platoons have a name. RuffRyders is the name my commo guys want, and that's the name they gonna keep," Master Blaster said, matter-of-fact.

That decided that. The RuffRyders were born.

Our Operation Tempo was already high. On any given day, we had one squad out conducting patrols, another team running combat escorts throughout Baghdad, and another pulling QRF missions. The last squad was stretched between guarding the gate and preparing to rotate to one of the aforementioned duties the next day. We rotated like clockwork, conducting missions day after day, week after week.

Months went by. Units all around us, throughout the Division, were losing guys to mortar fire, roadside bombs, rocket-propelled grenades, improvised explosive devices, and sniper fire.

With the addition of SGT Prado and PVT Rodriguez, both from Puerto Rico, and SPC Ellerbee from Georgia, our platoon was complete. Our OPTEMPO increased even more. Nevertheless, we continued to excel; up to that point we'd suffered zero losses despite constant enemy contact. Whispers of the RuffRyders' success spread rapidly throughout the brigade, all the way up to Division.

"You guys were going outside the wire more than most other platoons," Master Blaster later recalled. "The command was expecting the RuffRyders to lose someone at any moment, but it just wasn't happening. Day in and day out, night after night, you guys were successfully completing your missions and coming back to base safely. They just couldn't understand it, especially because they saw you guys as an insignificant commo platoon. The realization they were struggling to grapple with was, how did this little platoon of commo guys get to the point where they were now outside the wire conducting infantry-like missions? How did we get to the point of using special forces tactics to raid enemy-occupied buildings?"

They started calling us the lucky platoon.

I never thought it was luck. We worked hard, we watched each other's backs, and we looked out for one another. Before long, we began receiving requests from all the way up at Division to provide combat escorts. In the Army the reward for doing dangerous work well was always more dangerous work.

According to Master Blaster, "A mission came down to escort the Division Commander, General Sanchez. But when word of the mission request got down to the Battalion, some at Gunner Main wanted to give the mission to another platoon."

The scouts were the Battalions' favorite child. 19Ds, Armored Reconnaissance Specialists, were supposed to have been more suited to perform those missions. They were one of three platoons, including commo and survey, that regularly performed missions outside the wire. Everybody knew scouts were the Command's favorite. However, what they couldn't understand was why the RuffRyders—a little commo platoon—were receiving direct requests to provide escorts all the way from Division.

Again, our lieutenant folded like a napkin. Not only did he fold, but in the next breath he offered the RuffRyders up to take extra patrols so the scouts could transition to performing combat escorts up at Division.

We were already stretched to our limit.

"If y'all not gonna let the RuffRyders complete the escort missions from Division, you're not gonna punish them with extra patrols," Master Blaster said to our lieutenant. "You're trying to punish them for excelling!" Master Blaster couldn't understand why there was so much pushback on the RuffRyders doing such a high priority mission for which the platoon was directly requested.

One of the senior officers in the room said, "Well, we have to get the scouts some notoriety."

"It ain't about notoriety," Master Blaster shot back. "It's about who can perform the mission and who was requested to do it in the first place. Fine, let the scouts have the mission. But, when another request comes down, don't look my way. You're not gonna just trample over my guys."

Up at Division, they did also realize we were just a commo platoon. However, they wanted to see how we were able to pull so many missions without losing anybody while units throughout the Division suffered losses.

CHAPTER THIRTEEN:

Promises Kept

———

There were four green Army cots lined up side by side across the room I shared with three of my four squad leaders—SGTs Hall, Mack, and Prado. SGT Gibson shared an area across the yard with Master Blaster and the lieutenant. There was barely enough space in our room to walk between the cots. Our area was sandwiched between the orderly room and another room where the additional sixteen members of the RuffRyder platoon were squeezed in even tighter than we were.

Across our room, above SGT Prado's cot, a dusty, square window overlooked the Tigris River. On one of the nails lining the wall near the window hung a small rucksack with a RT-1523 radio stuffed inside. A short whip antenna protruded from a hole in the top of the bag. Hanging next to the rucksack were a couple of camouflaged Kevlar helmets and a pair of black leather gloves.

It was August 14, 2003, early evening, still blazing hot outside. Our platoon had conducted several missions earlier that day, and I was dog tired. We'd just returned from a long combat patrol out in Adhamiya.

I laid my weapon on the chair next to my cot. After removing my sweaty Kevlar, I ripped my body armor off and hung everything on the nails staggered along the wall. I plopped down on the edge of my cot and stared down at my sweat-soaked boots.

It always amazed me that after we'd been out for a while the sweat from my body had streamed down my legs, leaving a dry crusty coat of salt on my boots. I didn't have time to take the boots off that day. None of the platoon members had much time to relax. We had another mission later that evening.

I lay back and stared at the little table next to my head. On the table, I'd been saving assorted candies like Skittles and Tootsie Rolls from the MREs I ate each day. When we were out on patrol, I'd toss the candy to Iraqi kids that we often came into contact with. I felt terrible for them. Most of the time, it seemed like that candy was all they had. When I'd toss it from the window, they'd run quickly to grab some. They didn't laugh like kids typically reaching for candy from a passing parade or into a basket of treats on a cold October day. This was something different. This seemed like it was the only meal they'd get that day. It made me think of my childhood in Mississippi; it pained me knowing these children had so much less.

I closed my eyes and tried to steal a quick power nap. I must have been asleep for about an hour when I felt someone nudge my boot. Then there was a tap on my shoulder.

"SSG Pinkins, wake up," the voice said.

My eyes opened, and I immediately reached for my M-16. I thought it was time to head out on our next mission. My weapon was no longer on the chair. While I slept, somebody had taken it.

"Come with me. We need to talk." Master Blaster stood over me.

I hadn't spoken to anyone in my family for several weeks. Usually, we used a satellite telephone or paid one of the Iraqi vendors to make a call back to the states. Things had gotten really busy for us, though. No one stateside had heard from me in a while.

I stood up and followed Master Blaster into the orderly room next door. I was mentally preparing to receive an intel brief before we headed out on the next mission. I didn't realize that Master Blaster was the one who'd taken my weapon from the chair while I slept.

When we walked in, First Sergeant King was standing in the middle of the room. The next words that First Sergeant King uttered are forever imprinted on my mind.

"Did you know your grandmother was sick?" King said, fast as lightning.

"Sick?" I thought.

Before I could respond, King followed up dryly, "She's dead."

My legs turned liquid and I collapsed to the floor. The only thing I could do was scream.

Tears streaming down my face, I screamed until I couldn't breathe. Then I screamed some more. My entire body went limp. I lay face down on the hard floor. The pain in my heart was so sudden, so profound, and so deep I wanted it to stop beating.

Every image I had of Madea flashed before my eyes. They vanished, one by one, like a picture dissolving. I tried to hold on to each memory in my mind. Still, they kept vanishing, disappearing before my tear-flooded eyes. It was terrifying, I kept screaming, and the tears flowed. I couldn't stand up as Master Blaster and other RuffRyders tried to console me.

My body had been damaged before. I'd been in difficult situations before. I'd witnessed loss before. But I had never felt such deep, sustained, aching pain in my life. And I haven't since that day.

Prado, Hall, Marzette, Smitty, Davis, and other platoon members ran into the building at the sound of my screams.

"We got you, Sarge," one of them said.

"Come on, SSG Pinkins," Hall said. "Stand up! We got you!"

"Anything you need," Prado said, "We got you!"

Master Blaster said, "Pinkins, come on now! Your soldiers are beginning to worry about you. We got you."

"I gotta go home," I wept. "I need to talk to the Battalion Commander! Today! Right now! I gotta go!"

Master Blaster understood what Madea meant to me. While I was asleep, he'd told the Battery Commander and First Sergeant that I was not going to take the news well.

"Alright, let's go see the Battalion Commander," Master Blaster conceded.

Lieutenant Colonel Rabena's hooch was further down the road, near the other end of the compound by the dining facility.

When we reached the Battalion Commander's place, Master Blaster stopped.

"Wait out here. I'll go inside and talk to LTC Rabena and CSM Covington."

I sat on the sidewalk and put my face in my hands; the tears continued to flow. I thought about how my cousins and I used to comb Madea's hair when she'd gotten old. She sat there in that living room in a chair. Throughout the day, as the sun shined through the window, one of us would grab a comb and walk up behind her to scratch and grease her scalp. We'd rub her feet and give her hugs all day long to make her smile. I gave her kisses on her cheek for no other reason than to let her know how much she meant to me. Madea was everything. She was the glue that held all of us together.

I could not believe it, and my brain would not accept that she was gone. The memories of her kept dissolving and reappearing before my eyes. I couldn't make it stop.

"SSG Pinkins," Master Blaster called out as he returned. "Commander said he can't afford to let you go home."

Surprisingly, their decision didn't upset me. My mind was already made up.

I removed my hands from my tear-stained face, looked up at Master Blaster, and said, "Actually, I was just asking them out of respect, courtesy." I stood. "It don't matter what they say. I'm leaving this compound. I'm gonna find a plane, get on it, and I'm going back to Mississippi."

"Wait a minute. Let me go talk to them again," Master Blaster said.

He knew I was serious. More importantly, he realized that if I didn't get to attend Madea's funeral I would be worthless out there.

I figured if the unit could send soldiers home or back to Europe for a week or two for a mid-tour Rest and Recuperation, surely, my loss was significant enough to let me go home and say goodbye to Madea.

Master Blaster came back out and looked at me, "We will get you out of here within the next twenty-four hours."

The next day I was on a flight headed to Frankfurt. By the weekend I was back in Mississippi. A few days later, on Tuesday, August 19, 2003—right there in the black folk's cemetery next to Highway 826—we laid Madea to rest.

As they lowered her casket into the ground, I didn't want to leave. I didn't want to let go. However, I knew I'd signed a contract. The US government, for the time being, had a lease on my body. A few days later, I flew out of Jackson and again stopped over in Germany. The Army had me on the first thing smoking back to Baghdad.

After about two weeks away, I arrived back on the base early one Friday afternoon. Our Humvee pulled up beside the Battery Headquarters. I spotted SGT Hall walking to meet me.

"Welcome back, Sarge," he said. "We need to talk."

From the look on his face, I knew something was wrong. Hall was a straight shooter. He didn't cut corners and was always honest.

"I'm sorry to drop this on you as soon as you get back," he said.

Apparently, while I was gone our out-of-control lieutenant had lost his damn mind. The word was that he'd been placing the guys in unnecessarily dangerous situations outside the wire. Things had gotten so bad that the platoon was on the brink of mutiny.

"The guys say they're not going back outside the gate with the lieutenant unless you go too," he said. "Basically, they ain't going back outside the gate without you."

I walked across the yard and entered Master Blaster's hooch.

"Welcome back, Pinkins," he said with a smile. We embraced. "Have a seat. How you feeling?" He was, of course, checking on me to see if I was okay after the funeral. I don't blame him. The last time he'd seen me I was a wreck.

"I'm good," I responded. "Family is good. I'm good. Just ready to get back in the fight and get these next months over with."

He smiled and was about to say something but was interrupted by the lieutenant.

"We got a patrol in about an hour," the lieutenant informed.

"Yeah, there's a patrol, but they ain't going with you!" Master Blaster rebuffed. "Those guys say they're not going out that gate with you, and I'm not gonna force them to."

When I walked back outside, the guys were lounging around the vehicles. They clearly did not intend on going out on the mission.

"Sarge, we can't go out with that guy. He's gonna get one of us killed," Smitty told me while the other guys mumbled and nodded. "We ain't going if you ain't going."

"Let me get my gear. I'm back and I'm going out," I said.

We started gearing up and preparing to go. The hostility between the lieutenant and the rest of the platoon was thick. The RuffRyders clearly didn't trust nor like the guy. And because they trusted my leadership more than his, he despised me.

Later that evening, I saw firsthand why they were so upset with him.

When we got in the vehicles, the lieutenant looked at me and said, "You sit in the back seat. I'm a lieutenant. I'm sitting in the command seat."

Not only did he not know Sector 18 as well as I did, he also didn't know it as well as many of the RuffRyders. He was right, though. He was a lieutenant and I was a staff sergeant. He outranked me, so I hopped in the back seat.

The funny thing I've found is that when folk's ego gets the best of them, they make bad decisions.

"Where are we?" I asked after forty-five minutes of patrolling.

Silence. The lieutenant didn't say a word. The driver, PVT Commisso, just glanced nervously ahead as the Humvee crept up an unfamiliar street.

"Lieutenant, are you lost?" I asked.

The lieutenant said nothing. He just sat in the front seat, map on his lap, fiddling with a handheld global positioning unit.

"Stop, the Humvee," I told the driver. I turned to the lieutenant. "Sir, we need to talk."

Lost in war-torn Baghdad, in the glare of the Humvee's headlights, he and I had it out in the middle of the street. When we finally made it back to the base late that night, I told Master Blaster what happened. Of course, the lieutenant threatened to punish me for insubordination, but nothing ever came of it. He realized that being out front doesn't necessarily mean you're leading, especially if no one is following.

For the rest of the tour, we had a tense dynamic. We eventually came to a mutual agreement that he'd simply do his job, and I'd do mine. And my job was to do everything in my power to ensure our guys returned to Germany safely once the deployment was complete.

* *

October 31, 2003—Halloween night in Baghdad. I and four other RuffRyders hid in the darkness beneath a raised residential home. We were out in Adhamiya on a surveillance mission. As we lay in the dirt beneath that house, the nighttime was eerily calm. We heard the occasional orchestra of machine-gun fire explosions in the distance. Every now and then we heard the steps and saw the feet of an Iraqi walking along the edge of the house.

The aroma of beef grilling at a food stand beneath the amber glow of a street light competed with the dry, musky dirt beneath us. A few feet from our position and seemingly in tune with music drifting from a nearby window, two dogs frolicked on the sidewalk. They meandered over to investigate our motionless bodies in the darkness.

Suddenly, the distinct sound of a mortar round leaving its tube echoed from a few streets over. Seconds later, we heard another round. It was the moment we had been waiting for!

Voices filled my earpiece as team leaders I'd positioned nearby began to report their status.

"Alpha team, up!" barked one team leader.

"Bravo team, up!" reported another.

I responded with my own call sign, "RuffRyder One-Zero up! All teams converge on target located approximately one hundred meters north of my position. Move!"

We scrambled from beneath the house. The dogs barked; the amber streetlamps brought our images into view. Alarmed by our sudden appearance, the food stand owner began pointing and yelling in Arabic. We quickly advanced up the street.

Humvee headlights emerged from the darkened garage of an abandoned building several meters ahead. I hopped in the command seat. PFC Bryant, an eighteen-year-old from Suffolk, Virginia, manned the gunner's turret with an M-249 machine gun. SPC Hano, the same age but from Augusta, West Virginia, drove and floored the accelerator as soon as my rear hit the seat.

Rounding the corner, I saw Alpha and Bravo teams advancing on the adjacent street. Just ahead, I noticed two Iraqi soldiers running down the middle of the road lugging a mortar tube and an AK-47. Bryant attempted to engage them with the M-249, but the weapon jammed. It wouldn't fire! Our Humvee was nearing the end of a dead-end street. The Iraqi soldiers made a right turn and ran down an alley flanked by residences.

Before the Humvee came to a complete stop, I leaped from the vehicle and took off on foot. I gained ground as the Iraqi soldiers jumped a grey brick wall into a residential yard. I scaled the wall and, to everyone's surprise, landed on top of them when I fell over. One of them was injured. After a quick struggle, the other was apprehended. We tossed them both into the back of the Humvee and headed back to base.

While we were chasing the combatants, medics back at base were performing lifesaving medical procedures on a RuffRyder platoon member, a soldier I had promised to bring home alive.

SGT Stephen Hall was born and raised in Fort Worth, Texas. While we were out on our surveillance mission, he'd just returned to Baghdad from his mid-tour Rest & Recuperation.

Not long after returning to base, SGT Hall volunteered to go out with the commander on a quick escort mission in place of a new soldier who had no experience.

"The new soldier looked terrified, so Hall volunteered to take his place that night."

Our platoon had conducted tons of escort missions. Hall knew the area and the many dangers that came along with moving through Baghdad.

When SGT Hall and the escort team returned to base, our team still hadn't made it back from the surveillance mission. He didn't know where we were, and we didn't know that he had returned from R&R. SGT Hall walked over to Master Blaster's quarters and poked his head in the door.

"Hey, Master Blaster, I'm back," he said. "I'm gonna smoke a cigarette. I'll be back over to talk to you in a minute."

"Come on in," Master Blaster said with a smile. "You can smoke your cigarette over here. I'll be with you soon."

SGT Hall didn't want to smoke in Master Blaster's room. He walked out the door and over to where a couple of other soldiers were standing. He only made it a few yards before that same mortar round we'd heard exiting the tube a few blocks over landed on the compound.

The first round landed right beside SGT Hall, blowing him back several feet.

Another round landed; the smoke and dust from the blast became even thicker.

As the mortar rounds kept exploding, Master Blaster's room filled with dust. He grabbed his Kevlar and headed for the door. Blocking the doorway, SGT Gibson said, "You can't go out there right now. Rounds are still falling!"

In the darkness, smoke, and dust, nobody knew SGT Hall had been hit.

After a few minutes, Master Blaster finally made his way outside and found SGT Hall lying on the ground.

"MEDAC! MEDAC!" Master Blaster yelled. "Somebody bring a litter!"

Soon, our RuffRyder Humvees rolled through the front gate. When I hopped out of my Humvee, Master Blaster met me.

"SGT Hall's been hit," he said. "We need an escort to the Green Zone."

I pointed over at our Humvees lined against the wall. "We're ready. Let's go!"

We escorted SGT Hall to the hospital that night. They wanted to amputate his leg, but he begged Master Blaster not to let them take it.

"Can you save his leg? When can you get him out of here and over to Landstuhl?" Master Blaster asked the Doc.

"Whether we can save his leg depends on how fast we can get him out of here," Doc responded. "We have a transport leaving at 0700, and there's one spot left. We can get him on that flight."

As the Doc began to rush away, Master Blaster stopped him.

"Doc! There's one other thing. Can his platoon members come in and see him?"

Later, after the shrapnel had been removed, we all gathered around SGT Hall's bed. He was barely conscious but awake enough to pull the sheets from around his legs to see that, for now, he still had both. After a brief visit, the rest of the platoon left the room.

Standing next to SGT Hall's bed that night, I reflected on the promises I had made before we left Gießen.

"We got'em," I said. "We got the guys that did this to you."

SGT Hall looked up at me.

"I guess I got a trick and a treat," he said jokingly before drifting out of consciousness.

Early the next morning, he was on a plane headed to Landstuhl Regional Medical Center in Germany. On November 14, 2003, SGT Hall received the Purple Heart for the injuries he received in Iraq.

**

Spring arrived. It was early April and time for us to head back to Germany. The platoon had been preparing our equipment for weeks in anticipation of our departure. We'd completed twelve months in combat; it was time to go home.

LTC Rabena called all the leaders into Gunner Palace. The RuffRyders were ready for the drive back to Kuwait and, ultimately, to reunite with their families waiting for them in Germany. However, in that blown-out palace, LTC Rabena stood before us and announced that we would not yet be leaving.

Our tour had been extended. Instead of going home, we were ordered about a hundred miles south to the city of An-Najaf, where we'd be attached to the 2nd Armored Cavalry Regiment from Fort Polk, Louisiana.

I walked out of Gunner Palace. Members of the RuffRyder platoon were gathered around our Humvees, waiting. They knew something was up. I sent someone to get the rest of the platoon. They had given all they had over the past twelve months and I was about to deliver terrible news to them. I wanted to make sure I only had to say it once. We were a group of commo soldiers who had been converted into an infantry platoon. From May 2003 to April 2004, the RuffRyders had conducted over a hundred combat patrols and escorts, nearly as many raids of enemy compounds, and several QRF missions.

"We've been extended. We're not going home."

I'd be lying if I said I wasn't ready to go home. I knew they were too. Yet it seemed like the news didn't faze any of them. We all soldiered on. We'd grown that close.

Before heading south to An-Najaf, we transitioned to Camp Victory for only a few days. I woke up there early one morning and went on a short run. Afterward, I walked over to the mess hall to grab some breakfast. After filling my tray, I scanned the room for a place to sit. Right away, I recognized

Linc McCoy. I thought as we both started laughing, "What
are the chances that we'd bump into each other again, in
the middle of a war zone nearly two years after we'd been
roommates at Fort Gordon, Georgia?"

Linc had recently arrived in Baghdad with the 1st Cavalry
Regiment—the unit replacing our 1st Armored Division. We
sat in the dining facility and caught up on old times over
breakfast. He had recently been promoted to Chief Warrant
Officer Two.

"You should apply to be a Warrant Officer," he told me.

"Man, I'm actually thinking about getting out of the
Army," I said. "My enlistment contract expired in the middle of this tour. The reenlistment NCO has been bugging
the hell out of me for months about signing a new contract."

Linc seemed surprised, but I'd already given the Army
ten years and was strongly considering moving on.

"What do you want to do when you get out?" Linc asked.

"Actually, I want to go to law school," I told him.

I had been thinking about going back to school for quite
some time. I was conflicted, though. I thoroughly enjoyed
traveling around the world. The cultural experiences were
well worth the first two contracts I'd signed with the Army.
Now that I had the GI Bill, I wanted to put it to good use.

"If you decide to stay in, and you want to go Warrant, let
me know. I'll take a look at your application," he said.

I knew if I reenlisted again, I would stay for the entire
twenty years. To me, it made no sense to go past the
ten-year mark without going all-in and completing the
whole twenty.

"Ok," I said. We embraced and again went our separate
ways. Linc remained in Baghdad with 1st CAV. I headed
north to An-Najaf with 1AD.

I spent the next couple of months in An-Najaf. Then, on July 9, 2004, I found myself on a flight back to Germany. My first tour in Iraq was complete.

I settled into my seat, closed my eyes, tilted my head back, and exhaled. Each seat on the plane was occupied by combat-clad, battle-weary soldiers who'd spent the last several months—and for many, including myself, more than a year—in battle. The rest of the RuffRyder platoon was already back in Germany. I'd kept my promise to them. I'd watched them all leave alive, and I was the last. Aside from the hum of the aircraft's engines, all was quiet.

About an hour into the flight, I stood up. A few rows ahead, I spotted Sergeant First Class Joe Zapata, the reenlistment NCO.

I tapped him on the shoulder.

"Let's do this," I said.

SFC Zapata was perhaps one of the kindest and most professional reenlistment NCOs I ever encountered. He wore a pair of black glasses and seemed to always be prepared to help a reenlisting soldier. Not surprisingly, Zapata had an American flag available. He also had the necessary paperwork to complete my contract during the flight.

We grabbed a couple of soldiers to hold the flag. Our Battery Commander, Captain Mark Manno, called the plane's passengers to attention. He read the oath of enlistment, and I repeated the words after him:

I, Tyrone Cortez Pinkins, do solemnly swear that I will support and defend the constitution of the United States against all enemies, foreign and domestic; that I will bear true faith and allegiance to the same; and that I will obey the orders of the President of the United States and the orders of the Officers

appointed over me, according to regulations and the uniform
code of military justice. So help me God!

And just like that, mid-flight, I'd signed up for another
six years.

Finishing college and going to law school was one of my
goals, but I knew I wasn't ready to leave the Army. I enjoyed
the friendships I was building with my fellow soldiers, and I
appreciated the opportunity to lead troops. And, because we
had not yet landed in Germany, the $20,000, tax-free bonus
didn't hurt either.

When I finally got back to Gießen, SGT Hall, now able to
stand, was there with the rest of the RuffRyders. A few days
later, I stood in the parking lot outside the Battalion Headquarters—the same building where Master Blaster had promoted me to Platoon Sergeant over a year earlier. It was also
the same building where Smitty had begged Master Blaster
to let him deploy with the platoon.

That day, in the parking lot, I was awarded the Bronze
Star for exceptionally meritorious service in a combat zone.
I was the only Staff Sergeant in the Battalion to receive it.

Being awarded the Bronze Star didn't matter to me. The
number of missions we'd conducted didn't matter to me.
The only thing that mattered was that I'd kept the promises
I'd made fifteen months prior. All the RuffRyders made
it home.

CHAPTER FOURTEEN:

Finally, I Smiled Again

——

A year had passed since I'd returned from my first tour in Iraq. Each day, Madea still tiptoed through my mind. Her death was a constant gravity, an unshakeable, heavy weight. I rented a tiny apartment, not far from Gießen, in the small town of Butzbach. It was a cozy place on Am Ballhaus Straße, right around the corner from a bakery, a few small restaurants, and some gift shops. Many mornings I woke to the smell of warm bread drifting through my window. On some evenings I walked around the corner, cut through a little alley, and sat down for dinner at a random restaurant where I'd watch people as they walked by.

But this morning was different. I didn't have much, so packing my things was relatively easy. In only about an hour, I had stuffed everything I owned into my little white convertible BMW. Packing everything up and relocating every two or three years was typical for soldiers and their families. My upcoming relocation was not a surprise. Besides, I'd requested the move as part of the six-year contract signed on that flight from Iraq a year earlier.

Autobahn 5 twisted and turned through the state of Hessen like a serpent. My destination was Manheim in the state of Baden-Württemberg, seventy-five miles south of Butzbach. There, I was stationed with the 214th Aviation Regiment on Coleman Barracks.

I rented a placed in the city of Worms. The house on 16 Calvinstraße, tucked away in a dense neighborhood, was isolated from English-speaking Americans. It's not that I didn't want to be around Americans; my goal was simply to force myself to learn to speak German. I figured the best way to make that happen was to surround myself with native speakers and engulf myself in their culture.

I decided not to visit the base commissary, which had all the typical American grocery store items. Instead, I'd explore Lidl or Aldi in Worms, local bakeries, and butcher shops. In this way, I got to practice the language.

Whenever my car needed servicing, I refused to drive to the AAFES auto shop on the base. Instead, I visited the local dealer, where I gladly struggled to explain in German what repairs needed to be done.

I got lost in the seasonal markets and festivals. One Saturday morning, I stepped out my door and took off on a run through the city. I made a quick left on narrow, tree-lined Melanchthonstraße and then a right on the much broader Alzeyerstraße. Off I went throughout the city.

I came to a traffic circle at the intersection of Alzeyerstraße and Kirschgartenweg. There I passed a small group of skinheads. Their arms extended to the sky, fingers together, flashing the heil Hitler sign. They stared at me as I trotted by.

They didn't scowl. Instead, they gazed with intrigue and bewilderment. Likewise, my expression wasn't one of anger but curiosity. I was fascinated by yet another aspect of German history. It's an aspect many would like to forget, yet here I was witnessing part of that past firsthand.

Continuing my run through Worms I passed the monument of the sixteenth-century priest, Martin Luther. In 1521 he'd appeared before the Diet of Worms and was excommunicated by the Pope, declared an outlaw by the Holy Roman Emperor. Eventually, I made my way to the foot of a bridge, the Nibelungenbrücke. It had replaced the Ernst Ludwig Bridge, which was blown up by retreating Wehrmacht—Nazi Germany Armed Forces—during WWII.

In the shade of the Nibelungenbrücke, close to the river banks, I could see the Backfischfest happening. I wandered there for hours, sampling food and drinks while practicing my language skills.

My German continued to improve during my exploration of not only Worms but also the nearby cities of Mannheim and Heidelberg. Before long, I was able to confidently hold short conversations. I'd come a long way from the first few words of German I'd learned over a huge glass of Hefeweizen with Jessica, some time back.

**

Landstuhl Regional Medical Center, where SGT Hall had been transported nearly three years prior, was only about sixty-five miles north of Worms, just past Ramstein Airbase. I was there to see another Army eye doctor. This experience, however, was vastly different from the time in New Orleans.

"What time is displayed on the clock?" the doctor asked, pointing at the wall about fifteen feet away.

There was a round, white office clock with black minute and second hands and bold, black numbers.

"It's just a blur," I said. "All I can see is the round, white clock. I can't make out the numbers." The doctor had informed me after I asked at the start of our appointment that I was technically legally blind.

"Lie back and be still." He placed a clamp beneath one eyelid to hold it open. "Be *very* still."

The machine in the corner hummed as a robotic arm swung over smoothly, suspended above my face. An aperture on the arm twisted and calibrated itself. I lay there with my eyelid held open by the clamp.

And then a laser shot directly into my right eye. I heard a light crackling sound behind my ear. The machine in the corner spoke, counting down five, four, three, two, one. Its voice sounded like something from *Star Trek*.

After the countdown he removed the clamp and placed it on my left eye. The machine repeated the procedure all over again. Altogether, the operation took only a few minutes.

"All right, sit up. What time is displayed on the clock?"

I called out letters on the vision chart beneath the clock. And just like that, my vision went from the 20/300 that he'd estimated at the beginning of the procedure, to about 20/80.

"Over the next few months, your vision should improve to better than 20/20," he said.

They gave me a pair of sunglasses and a big brown bag of medicine. Someone from the unit picked me up. When I got home, I tossed my old glasses in the trash. I closed all the blinds, took some medication, and went to sleep. The next morning, I woke and reflexively reached for the glasses on my nightstand. When they weren't there, I remembered I'd thrown them away.

I walked over to my bedroom window and counted the red tiles on my neighbor's roof. For the first time in my life,

I could see without glasses or contacts. I went into the bathroom and flushed my contacts down the toilet.

You might wonder what I did next, being semi-fluent in German and, now, visually liberated? Well, I did what came naturally. I bought a motorcycle! The autobahn had no speed limit, and I wanted to go fast. I bought a crotch rocket—a black GSX-R750.

The Army and German law mandated that I have a license. Not only did I not have a license, I had never even ridden a motorcycle. Without credentials or experience, I convinced a local dealer to sell me a bike right off the showroom floor.

"Can I borrow your truck?" I asked one of the guys on the base.

"Why do you need it?"

"I bought a motorcycle, and I need to go pick it up from the dealer," I said.

He stared at me with a look of confusion.

"Why don't you just ride it home?"

"Well, for one, I don't have a motorcycle license, and two, I don't know how to ride it," I responded.

He lowered his head and let out a sympathetic exhale. He looked concerned.

"Look, are you gonna help me or not?" I responded.

We hopped in his truck, drove out to the dealership, and with the owner's help, loaded my new motorcycle.

"Be careful out there, bro," he said after we offloaded the bike. "They drive fast over here, and you don't want to end up splattered all over the autobahn."

When he drove off, it was just me and my bike at 16 Calvinstraße. I thought, "How hard can it be to teach myself to ride?"

I'd ridden three-wheelers and four wheelers as a child back in Mississippi. When I was a teenager and had my first girlfriend, I stole Dad's truck and taught myself how to drive a manual transmission to go visit her. I thought, "Well, there you go! I'm practically halfway there. I've already got some experience."

I had purchased a helmet, gloves, and boots a week prior.

From my driveway to the end of the block was maybe five hundred feet—the perfect distance to teach myself to ride, I thought. Not many cars drove down the street, and no one was outside to laugh at me if I fell.

I strapped my helmet on tightly, climbed onto the bike and started the engine. I knew to control the clutch with my left hand and the accelerator with my right. I also realized from riding four wheelers with my cousins that I had to shift the gears with my left foot, and that the rear brake was by my right foot. I was all set.

Clutch tightly squeezed in my left hand, I shifted into first gear. I revved the engine. The sound surprised me and likely woke every sleeping baby on the block. Startled, I allowed the engine to settle before trying it again. I twisted the throttle a tiny bit as the bike vibrated beneath me. I slowly released; the bike inched forward.

"Ha," I thought. "Look at me!"

I made it to the end of the block without incident. Turning around, however, would prove to be tricky. I slightly revved the engine in an effort to get the bike aimed back in the direction of 16 Calvinstraße. I got it turned halfway when things went wrong.

I twisted the throttle just a little bit too much. The engine screamed, and the front wheel shot up off the ground. The bike jumped the curb. I held on like a rag doll while it torpedoed into someone's front yard. Whoever lived on the corner of Calvinstraße and Melanchthonstraße now had a GSX-R750 and a black guy firmly wedged into one of their hedges. Luckily, I hadn't damaged the bike nor myself. For the rest of the day, I continued riding back and forth along Calvinstraße. Eventually, I got the hang of it. I took a local driver's course in addition to the mandatory Army motorcycle course, and then I hit the Autobahn.

I'd wake in the mornings, hop on that bike and not come home until 9:00 or 10:00 at night. All-day long I zipped along the Autobahn, exceeding speeds of 120 mph. On Autobahn 6, between the cities of Grunstadt and Neuleiningen, is a deep curve. Speeding along, much faster than I should have been, I leaned the bike over in that curve. It seemed like I was only inches from the ground; broken white lane dashes turned into a solid white line. At that moment, I wondered, "Would I survive the fall at this speed?" I twisted the throttle a little more. The lines became a blur as the bike propelled through the curve like a rocket. I was in a very dark place inside.

Two years had passed since Madea's death. I was still angry, raging inside. All the screaming I had done the day they'd told me Madea was dead was still going on within me. It echoed around like infinite reflections within a hall of mirrors. I kept it bottled up, my body becoming a pressure cooker. I didn't really care about my own life or anything else's, for that matter.

I had no desire to go back to Mississippi. I didn't want to be around my family if Madea wasn't also there. Everyone who was supposed to be close to me got pushed out of my mind, out of my heart, and out of my life.

I was content existing all alone in the pain and pushing myself to every dangerous limit I could find. I'd ride around Germany on that motorcycle all day long. I'd get angry when the throttle topped out and I couldn't go faster. I knew what I was doing. I lay in bed each night and visualized it. I imagined the moment I'd lose control on the autobahn. I'd see myself lying there motionless in the gravel on the side of the highway, and I didn't care. I'd simply drift off to sleep, wake up the next morning, get on my motorcycle, and do it all over again.

It was early March 2006. My unit had been training in Baumholder—what we called the Rock—for about a week. Rain fell outside as a little Nokia cellphone vibrated in my pocket. I stared at it, at the number, for a moment before I answered. I had a strong feeling about what the call concerned.

"Hello," I answered.

The voice on the other end was hesitant. This confirmed my suspicion, even though we hadn't spoken since the one night we'd shared a few months prior.

"I'm pregnant," she said.

Renee was also stationed at Coleman Barracks, and we were both noncommissioned officers.

"What do you want me to do?" she asked.

Like the destructive path I was on with the motorcycle, my relationship with women during that period of my life was also toxic. I didn't care about my own life, and I certainly didn't care about others who entered my circle.

"We're not going to be in a relationship," I said coldly. "It's your body. If you decide not to have the baby, that's your decision, and I'll support it." I paused. "If you decide to give birth, I will always be there for you and our child."

Over the next several months we shopped for baby items together, went to her medical appointments, and even saw the first images of our child together. For Renee, those months were a roller coaster ride. When she'd call me, I'd pick up, but only out of responsibility to our child. It was cliché and irresponsible for me to say, "It wasn't her. It was me." But it really wasn't her. It was me. I just wasn't right, emotionally, mentally, or spiritually. I was still content with hopping on my motorcycle early each morning and riding it on the Autobahn as fast as it would go, not giving a damn if I fell off. Another jog, run, ride, race through the city of Worms, trying to forget about everything and everybody. That was all I wanted to do.

It was October 10, 2006, when my phone rang.

"I'm going into labor," she said.

A couple of months before Renee was due the Army shipped her off to Ansbach, about a two-hour drive up near Nuremberg. One hundred and forty-five miles, two hours, and twenty minutes later, I arrived. He had already been born when I got there. The moment I held him, all the pain went away. When I looked into my son's eyes, I imagined how it must have felt for Dad the first time he'd gazed into my eyes so many years ago. In that moment, I realized I loved someone else more than I loved myself. My whole life changed. Cradling his tiny body in my arms, I floated along the hospital hallway, emotionally transported to a place I'd never been.

Madea's real name was Josephine. We named him Joseph. I went home and sold the motorcycle. For the first time since that painful day in Iraq, finally, I smiled again.

CHAPTER FIFTEEN:

Her Pink Bandana and Fluorescent Green Scarf

———

My entire world changed the second I saw Joseph's face. Not long after his birth, the Army notified me that I'd been selected to attend Warrant Officer School. The news was bittersweet. It was another moment where the Army said, "Jump!" knowing the response would be, "How high?"

Leaving Joseph at only three months old was one of the most difficult things I have ever had to do. I wanted to be there for him like Dad had been there for me. I didn't want him to have that empty feeling in his chest like the one I had for Otha Lee. The night before I shipped out, I sat in the dark beside his crib. While he slept, I wept. Over the coming years—between deployments and new assignments—missed birthdays and first days at school became the norm.

I'd completed just over two years of the six-year contract I'd signed during the flight from Iraq. The remaining few years didn't matter—the Army's decision to send me to Warrant Officer Candidate School negated the rest of the contract. To my surprise they also informed me that because I'd signed the contract before returning from Iraq, I could keep the $20,000. I guess they estimated that my becoming a Warrant Officer meant I was in for the long haul—a win for the Army and a win for me.

In January 2007, I flew back to the United States to attend Warrant Officer Candidates School at Fort Rucker, Alabama. I was no longer Sergeant First Class Pinkins. I was now Warrant Officer One Pinkins, jokingly referred to as a "One-Dot-Spot" by older Warrant Officers. That September, after a few months at Fort Gordon, Georgia, the Army shipped me back to Germany, this time to Wiesbaden.

That October my universe shifted once again. On the 15th, a crisp autumn day, my daughter was born at St. Joseph's Hospital in downtown Wiesbaden. The moment she stared up at me with those big old beautiful, brown eyes, I fell in love all over again. We named her Rukiya Juanita after Aunt Nita.

Rukiya's mother and I had only been married for a few months when I received orders to deploy again. Just like leaving Joseph the year before, Rukiya was three months old when I boarded a plane to Tikrit, Iraq, in January 2008. Those next eleven months in Tikrit with the 1st Armored Division seemed much longer than the fifteen months of my first deployment.

Sergeant First Class Campbell, one of the coolest guys I've ever known, was from Mobile, Alabama. Once a high stepping drum major at Tuskegee University, SFC Campbell towered at around six feet, three inches tall. You'd often find him somewhere smoking a cigarette. Like me, he'd also welcomed his daughter into the world just before our deployment.

We'd been in Tikrit for several months when, late one evening in October, I finished my shift at the Division Headquarters building. I walked outside and across the large gravel parking lot. "Habari," I said to the Ugandan soldier standing guard at the gated entrance. The Ugandan soldiers had been teaching me to speak Swahili throughout the tour. We'd meet daily at lunch and dinner to practice simple phrases. Early on in the tour, we'd made a deal. In exchange for them teaching me, I'd help them purchase items from the base exchange.

The tour in Tikrit was much different from my first tour in Baghdad with the RuffRyders. This time I wasn't constantly outside the wire. I wasn't conducting patrols, raids, escorts, and QRF missions. My primary duty was that of an Electronics Warfare Officer, trying to help prevent soldiers from getting blown up by Improvised Explosive Devices. I had the night shift, in a cubicle, from six in the evening to six in the morning. Aside from the sluggish pace of the months and constantly missing Rukiya and Joseph, I was fine.

My living quarters consisted of a one-room Containerized Housing Unit. SFC Campbell's CHU was a few rows over. That evening, before heading over to begin my shift, I knocked on his door. Inside, we opened two large white envelopes we'd recently received in the mail. They contained our absentee ballots. Over six thousand miles from home, in the middle of a war, we both voted for Barack Obama to become the next President of the United States.

Several weeks later, on the evening of November 3, I walked through the Division Headquarters security gate at around 6:00 p.m. local time. The Ugandan soldiers who'd taught me Swahili were huddled around a small radio, listening to an election broadcast from halfway around the world back in the US.

"Yes We Can!" yelled one of the Ugandan soldiers as I walked by.

It was only 10:00 a.m. on the East Coast, so people were still voting. I entered the building, settled at my desk, and changed the channel to CNN. It was a slow night; the building was eerily quiet. Only a few people were there. After staying up all night watching the broadcast, I decided to stay on past my shift. The election had not yet been called.

An hour later at around 7:00 a.m. in Iraq, after the Californian result came in, CNN announced that Barack Obama had won the presidency. A few soldiers on duty, both black and white cheered the victory, contrary to the military's supposed nonpartisan nature, and quickly resumed their duties. The few black soldiers on duty, including me, shed tears of joy at such a historic moment in our nation's history.

"Alright, he already done won. Y'all can turn that shit off, now!" came the voice of the Navy officer a couple of cubicles over. It was a stark reminder that even in combat, a political divide existed and sometimes reared its ugly head.

A few weeks later, I returned to Wiesbaden. In the time I'd been deployed Rukiya had started walking, Joseph was running, and the country elected its first black president. I bought Joseph and Rukiya matching tricycles and tied a string to each handlebar. While snowflakes slowly fell, I pulled them around the parking lot of Aukamm military housing. Although it was a cold German winter, their squeals of joy and laughter warmed me like a hot cup of soup. I pulled them round and round that parking lot. Nothing could replace the joy I felt of having them close to me, of hearing their laughter. We lived in a second-floor apartment at 13 Schleswig-straße. Those two little munchkins followed me all over that place. Wherever I went, Joseph and Rukiya weren't far behind. I'd often tie a string around my waist to pull them up and down the hallway along the slick wooden floors. I was their horse. They'd scream with joy every time I took off down the hallway, galloping on my hands and knees with them trailing behind. It is difficult to explain the pleasure of just hearing, smelling, seeing, and holding my babies close. I was trying to get in as much time as I could with them.

Many times, I'd wake in the middle of the night, walk into Rukiya's room, place my ear close to her chest and listen to the quick, soft thump, thump, thump of her heartbeat. Sometimes she would awaken and catch me before I could tiptoe out. She'd grab my finger and pull me back over into her little bed. I'd curl up into a ball, knees tucked beneath my chin, and lie there beside her until I could feel her grip on my finger loosen as she drifted off to sleep. I'd walk out of her bedroom with a full heart, realizing how important it was that she had her dad close to her.

After my second deployment on base in Wiesbaden, Germany. They laughed for hours as I pulled them around the parking lot.

Rukiya's first bike. I didn't realize I'd be so nervous letting her try to learn to ride.

Road trip in Mississippi

Joseph and me floating and having a wonderful time in Okinawa Japan.

Traveling through Charleston, South Carolina.

Rukiya and me hanging out in downtown Wiesbaden after my third deployment.

She'd seen me packing my suit case to go away for work again and begged me to take her with me.

Joseph's first time visiting the Mississippi Delta. I always felt like the little time I had with them would be taken away soon by military responsibilities.

Unfortunately—as many service members can attest—when a war drags on, good times with family often don't last long. Less than a year later, in November 2009, I was deployed again. This time I went back to Baghdad with the 1st Armored Division.

Rukiya was too little to comprehend what was going on. All she knew was that I wasn't there anymore. Each morning when she woke up, she'd walk through the apartment, opening all the doors to see if I was playing hide-and-go-seek. It broke my heart to not be there for her to find me.

Again, the days in Iraq passed slowly, one by one. I took online courses, inching closer and closer to finishing my degree. This time I worked the day shift at the Division Headquarters. At night I occupied my mind by running along the base perimeter. I'd realized that not only was I pretty good at it, but running was also an excellent meditation technique. After a while, I realized I could run an entire fourteen-mile route within Camp Victory's perimeter.

Another dark reality slowly crept into my life. The constant deployments had chipped away at my marriage. I filed for divorce midway through this third deployment. The most painful part was the understanding that I would no longer sleep in the same house as my children. No matter where I was—Iraq, Germany, Georgia—I would now always sort of be "away."

I sat at my desk in the Division Headquarters on Camp Victory. The phone rang; a familiar voice was on the other end of the line.

"What's up, battle?" It was Linc calling from Okinawa, Japan.

He had been stationed on the island for about a year. We discussed what we'd each been up to since last crossing paths in Baghdad years prior.

"This would be a good place for you to take a knee," he said. "Get a break from the constant deployments."

I told him I was fine. "I'm just looking forward to getting home to Joseph and Rukiya."

In December of 2010, I returned to Germany, completing my final tour in Iraq. The only thing I wanted was to see my babies.

I walked through the door of Rukiya's kindergarten in Wiesbaden. I softly called out her name.

"Rukiya… Rukiya," I repeated as a few toddlers ran by in the distance.

"Daddy!" a little voice squealed before I could look down.

That day her class was playing dress-up. She was wearing a pink shirt, black tights, and a black skirt. Her thick black hair peeked from beneath the pink bandana covering her head. A fluorescent green scarf was wrapped around her neck and dangled from her shoulders. I squatted down to reach for her.

It broke my heart when she turned and ran away. I felt like my baby was mad at me. I thought the war had not only destroyed my marriage but had also torn my little girl and me apart. I watched her from the doorway, afraid to get any closer.

As the rest of her classmates ran around and around the room, Rukiya stood just six feet away with her back to me. First, she ripped the pink bandana from her head and tossed it to the floor. Then she unwrapped the florescent green scarf from her neck and dropped it beside her feet.

She then turned around, looked at me from head to toe, screamed, "Daddy," and started running in place like a little cartoon character. She dove into my chest and locked her arms tightly around my neck.

"I love you," I said as tears rolled down my cheeks. With her little cheek pressed tightly next to my ear, she said, "I love you, Daddy." It was one of the best moments of my life.

PART THREE

ROAD TO THE WHITE HOUSE

CHAPTER SIXTEEN:

Across the East China Sea to Tonaki-jima

About 450 miles from mainland Japan, the island of Okinawa sits in the middle of the East China Sea. It's only about seventy miles long and, in some places, only a few miles wide.

In December 2010, I finished my third and final tour of duty in Baghdad. Six months later, in June 2011, after a slight delay because of the Fukushima Daiichi nuclear disaster, four-year-old Joseph and I landed on Okinawa. Rukiya remained in Germany with her mother. Linc had departed the island a few months before I arrived.

I guess the Army had decided I needed a break. A two-year assignment on the island was heaven-sent, and I was excited to spend it with my son. I was assigned to the 10th Regional Support Group, located on the Torii Station Army base in the Yomitan village area.

Our time together as father and son had often been cut short. Having Joseph on the island with me was a dream come true. I went out and bought him a little blue bunk bed, and together we pasted glow-in-the-dark *Toy Story* stickers all over it. We spent our days walking along Gate-Two Street, eating ice cream, watching movies at the theatre in American Village, and snorkeling at Torii Station beach.

After enrolling him in a local Japanese academy, I was up early each morning to pack his lunch and drive him to school. One day while we walked near the base softball field, Joseph stumbled and fell to the ground. Instinctively, I reached to grab his hand. To my surprise, he recoiled. He looked up at me and said, "I'm fine." He got to his feet, brushed the dirt from his hands, and said, "I want to be tough like my daddy."

I stared at him for a moment. Realizing that my son, at that young age, felt that way toward me was incredible. The moment reminded me of when I once mimicked my own dad picking up cans on the side of the highway back in Mississippi. Together on that island was the perfect place for Joseph and me. Surrounded by crystal clear waters, colorful coral reefs, and beautiful beaches, we were more than happy staying there on the island forever. With the constant deployments and pending divorce, all I wanted to do at the moment was decompress.

And just like clockwork, the Army came calling once more. Our time together again came to an end. I was upset at being separated from Joseph again. He cried when I told him I'd have to take him back to the states.

The Army sent me to Williamsburg, Virginia, for temporary duty. With one day remaining in Williamsburg, I met up with an old friend from high school and we decided to take a day trip to Washington, DC, about three hours away.

I'd traveled to thirteen countries and all over the United States, but I'd never visited the nation's capital. I hopped in a rental car and took I-64 through Richmond to I-95 past

Fredericksburg and finally on to I-395 through Alexandria and into Washington.

It was a Saturday and I spent the day among crowds of tourists, traversing the city on foot. From the Lincoln and MLK Memorials to the Capitol building, I walked. I stopped at the White House, peered through the gates, and wondered what was inside. Like a typical tourist, I snapped a few selfies with the White House in the background. I had no idea that in the very near future, I would not only be walking its halls but also sleeping inside.

The next day on the drive back to Williamsburg, I pulled off I-95 and stopped at a random Italian restaurant for lunch. Sitting there, I thought about how I missed Joseph and Rukiya. I finished my meal and returned to the car. Before leaving the restaurant parking lot, I decided to go back inside to use the bathroom. As I passed the bar, I noticed the familiar face of an old friend I hadn't seen in over a decade. It was Linc and he was as surprised to see me as I was to see him. What were the chances that we would run into each other at that time, in that spot?

We chatted for a while. I learned that he was now stationed at the White House Communications Agency and traveling in support of the President of the United States. He'd been living in the area for the past few years and was really enjoying it. I told him I followed his recommendation to get stationed in Okinawa. After a quick embrace, we both promised to stay in touch.

"Call me when you get back to the island," he said. "I want to talk to you about something."

I drove off, back down to Williamsburg. The next morning, I boarded my flight back to Okinawa. Soon after landing, before I could call him, Linc called me. He told me more about his new job and suggested it might be something in which I'd be interested.

"You want to put in an application to get transferred here?" he asked. "You'd love it."

"Nah," I responded. "I'm still enjoying the island, and I have some other things I need to sort out."

He told me to give him a call if I changed my mind and even offered to help with the application.

If anyone in my military circle understood me, it was Linc. He knew I was frustrated that every time I got close to being with Joseph and Rukiya, the Army snatched me away after only a few weeks. At that point, I'd served for just over fifteen years. Long before, I'd calculated that the Army usually moved soldiers every two to three years. If I requested to leave the island too early, they might snatch me away from Joseph and Rukiya again. As painful as it was to be away from them, I needed to be patient. As enticing as it was, I couldn't jump at the first opportunity to work at the White House. I needed to play the waiting game. I needed to ensure I had less than four years remaining in the Army before trying to transition to the capitol. Like my Dad had done for years in Mississippi, I needed to play chess in Japan.

**

I'd run along the Sunabe Sea Wall, watching the breathtaking sunset out over the East China Sea. Some days I'd wake early and run for twenty miles, just because. The island was indescribably tranquil; it had a calming effect that somehow purified the experience of running and amplified my passion for it.

One Saturday morning, I set off on a run not realizing the forecast called for a Typhoon. The weather was beautiful as I departed my housing on Kadena Air Base. Running along Kuko Dori Street, I passed custom tailor shops and clothing stores that catered to the needs of US service members. On the opposite side of the street sat clubs and party joints that often got Marines stationed on the island in trouble with the locals.

As I made my way through the city, the sky began to darken and rain fell lightly. I'd always enjoyed running in the rain, so the drizzle didn't bother me. The cool wetness felt good on my skin and only motivated me to take a longer route. Before I knew it, I was nearing the seventeen-mile mark. The wind and water picked up. Trees started swaying, the sky darkened, and the rain came down in sheets. Tossed from side to side, I trotted along the sidewalk struggling to make it home.

I finally entered Kadena's main gate. I could only imagine the thoughts of the Air Force security guards inside the guard shack as I ran by, flashing my ID card. I had about one mile to go. Unfortunately, it was mostly uphill along the main route past the base entrance. Not until I arrived home after completing the twenty-mile run and switched on the AFN broadcast, did I realize how bad the typhoon was. I still hadn't spoken to Linc since turning down his invitation to apply to the White House Communications Agency. As I sat there, waiting out the storm, I mulled over the opportunity.

* *

Naomi worked on Torii Station, as well. Her office was just down the hallway from mine. She'd grown up on the island

and had attended college on the mainland at Tokai University. As a child, she took piano lessons on an old family piano passed down through generations. When she returned from the university, she'd moved into her own apartment. Unfortunately, the piano was too big to move from her parents' top floor apartment. We talked for hours about that piano and how much it meant to her. I could hear the hurt in her voice at not being able to play it.

Some days we'd grab lunch and walk down to the beach, where she would teach me basic Japanese phrases. Like in Germany with locals and with the Ugandan soldiers in Iraq, I always looked for a way to learn another language.

That Friday morning, Naomi and I decided to do something random. She picked me up in her car, and we drove south on the Okinawa Expressway toward Naha. The goal was to take a random exit and intentionally get lost. I still don't remember which one we took, but we definitely got lost.

Eventually we came upon Tomari Wharf, a port crowded with boats destined for islands throughout the East China Sea. A hotel and shopping center overlooked the clear blue waters of the harbor. The view prompted me to look at Naomi and say, "Let's get on a boat and just go wherever it takes us."

Thinking I was joking, she laughed.

"No, I'm serious," I said. "I do this all the time."

Of course, hopping on a boat and sailing across the sea was a bit more adventurous than the boat rides I'd taken along the River Main in Frankfurt. Here, there were no bordering countries I could simply drive to, no Autobahns extending for hundreds of miles. Okinawa's main expressway ran for only about thirty-five miles. In that sense I was isolated.

That morning, Naomi and I approached a boat captain. She laughed mischievously while urging me to practice my broken Japanese. I jumped at the opportunity. In my broken Japanese, I asked, "How much does it cost?"

He gave us a price in the local currency. We paid and boarded. Before long, the boat undocked and we slowly drifted away, the harbor getting smaller and smaller in the distance.

We climbed to the top level of the ship. It wasn't crowded; we had the outside deck all to ourselves. In my backpack I had a portable speaker along with the iPod I used while running. I switched both on and we listened to jazz and floated for hours across the East China Sea. We sailed past clusters of tiny islands, watched as dolphins leaped from the water. The boat bypassed Tokashiki, Zamami, and Aka islands, and after sailing for more than three hours, we stopped.

Naomi, still nervous, couldn't believe what we had done. As we disembarked, I asked the captain where we were. It was Kumejima, the westernmost island in the Okinawa chain.

Visiting Kumejima was like going back in time. We drove by sugar cane fields, visited laterally growing Goeda Pine trees, and took a short boat ride to the white sandbanks of Hate-no-Hama. Back in the city, I stopped to play basketball with a group of kids using a makeshift hoop. It reminded me of the tire rim my cousins and I used under the old tractor shed on Elmwood.

After walking around the town and eventually parting ways with Naomi, I found a hotel late that evening. I enjoyed dinner grilled outside on the balcony. The next morning, we met back at the ship.

"How long is the ride back to Okinawa island?" I asked the captain.

"Oh! We are not going back to Okinawa just yet," he said. "First, we have to stop at another island."

Naomi was shocked! Her eyes bulged! I could barely contain myself from laughing.

"Where are we going to stay?" she asked, frantic.

"We'll figure it out," I replied, skipping up the steps, excited for another adventure.

An hour and a half after departing Kumejima, we docked at Tonakijima. The ship anchored in front of the main village office. Locals disembarked and embraced their family members; six-feet-tall and black, I knew I stood out like a sore thumb. But I didn't care. I was too excited.

The locals were very friendly. We found a traditional Okinawan red tile-roofed house for our stay. A neighbor brought over fresh fish and rice for dinner on the porch. Luckily, my chopstick skills were up to par. We toured the island for the rest of the day and decided to snorkel later that afternoon. I came face to face with a sea turtle the size of a Volkswagen. I was certainly surprised to see the turtle, but it seemed to view me as just another object as it slowly swam away into the clear blue waters. That night we walked along a tree-lined, candlelit path that extended from the hotel all the way down to Agarihama Beach.

Naomi explained to me the significance of the Agarihama.

"Agari means 'rise' in Japanese. Additionally, in Okinawan dialect we refer to the Eastward direction as 'Agari' because East is where the sun rises. So, Agarihama can be translated to mean both 'East Beach' as well as 'Sunrise Beach.'"

It was humbling to see how important it was for her to ensure Okinawan culture was explained and understood. When I inaccurately brought up bamboo homes, she corrected me, explaining the historical significance of Okinawa's red-tiled roofs and the importance of the Shisa placed there, facing toward the entrance of the house.

The next morning the captain was waiting at the ship, smiling as we boarded. A couple of hours later, we made it back to Okinawa, having completed one of the most amazing trips of my military career.

Several months later, resting on my living room sofa, I watched through the glass doors as rain fell on the patio. I dialed Linc's number, and he answered the phone with a laugh.

"You ready?" he asked.

My decision wasn't really about going to the White House. It was more about Joseph and Rukiya. I missed them a lot. I had just over sixteen years in the Army. I guessed that the application process would take several months, which would put me right at three years remaining. I might not get moved away from Joseph and Rukiya again if I applied.

I said, "Where do we start?"

CHAPTER SEVENTEEN:

The Final Promotion

———

I firmly believe that everything happens exactly when and how it's supposed to happen. The day after I spoke with Linc, the pieces of my long-term plan began falling into place.

"I'm Lieutenant Smith." She was a new lieutenant, fresh out of college.

"Hi, I'm Chief Pinkins," I responded.

She said her husband was a Warrant Officer, as well. He was stationed in South Korea. Unlike me, she was completely miserable on the island. She just wanted to complete her tour and be closer to her family, just like my longing to be reunited with Joseph and Rukiya.

"My next duty station will be my final duty station," I told her. "I've enjoyed serving in the Army, but it's about time for me to hang up my boots."

"What do you want to do when you get out?"

"Law school," I responded.

A few days later, she peeked into my office and handed me a study guide for the Law School Admissions Test.

"Good luck," she said, walking out the door.

**

The application process for assignment to the White House Communications Agency was arduous. In my case, the application and interview period took nearly eight months. And, it turns out, a lot can happen in that time.

On Thursday, November 21, 2012—the day before Thanksgiving—Linc called. It had been a few months since we last spoke. He was on a trip with President Obama in Cambodia. The WHCA team Linc was traveling with was scheduled for a fuel stop the next day at Okinawa's Kadena Air Base.

I lived about five minutes from the flight terminal. My phone rang again while I was enjoying Thanksgiving dinner with a few friends.

"We just landed," he said. "We'll be on the ground for just a few hours."

"I'll be right over."

Coco's Curry House, a Japanese restaurant, was popular on the island. It was only about two miles from the base. I stopped there on my way over and ordered chicken katsu curry with rice. When I arrived at the terminal, Linc was there along with a team of travel-weary presidential support personnel waiting to board their flight back to the states.

"Happy Thanksgiving," I said, handing him the curry plate.

I immediately felt bad because I didn't have anything for the others traveling with him. Linc and I chatted for a while, and he introduced me to some members of the team.

"Ty is coming to WHCA," he told them.

We glanced at each other and he smirked. We both knew my application hadn't even been approved yet.

The next month, December 2012, I graduated from the University of Maryland University College-Asia with a bachelor's degree in political science. On nearly every base I'd been stationed, I'd taken courses through the University of Maryland. When all was said and done, I had completed courses on four different continents. Fifteen years prior, when I left Tougaloo College, I promised Mom I'd finish my degree, and I did. Naomi attended my graduation at the Yomitani-mura Bunka Center and snapped pictures.

Over the next few months I went through several WHCA interviews. One evening, I stood alone in the main conference room just outside my office. Something felt weird; the large video monitor on the wall trembled. I initially didn't know what to think. Then it quickly dawned on me that this was an earthquake. It lasted for a short while and then stopped. We didn't have them back in Mississippi. It was the first time I'd experienced a quake, and I really didn't know what to do. Automobile alarms blared outside, and horns honked at the stoplight across the street. It was a mild quake that didn't cause any damage.

A few minutes after the shaking ceased a pair of federal agents walked through the door for an unscheduled interview. They asked questions about things that had taken place way back in high school. Their initial questioning was followed up a few weeks later by a phone interview with security and intel personnel at WHCA.

I had to submit stacks of written responses answering inquiries about my military career, financial history, and even personal things that no one could have possibly known except a few select people. To say it was extensive and taxing would be an understatement. The whole process felt somewhat like Coach Miller's line drills at basketball team tryouts. It felt like I was still running to make the cut.

Around 2:00 a.m. one morning I drove from my quarters on Kadena Air Base across town to Torii Station. In the darkness, I climbed two flights of stairs on the back of the building leading to my office. I walked past my desk and entered the massive second-floor conference room, switching on the lights. In the far corner of the room was the IT closet, full of servers and video teleconferencing equipment. I wedged my arm behind the server rack and heard the soft buzz of its engine when I switched on the power. It didn't take long for the system to boot up.

When I exited the closet the black and red unit crest representing the 10th Support Group was emblazed on a massive screen that covered nearly the entire far wall. Situated in the middle of the room was a huge, shiny, mahogany conference table. Decked out in full military dress attire—shiny badges, awards, and all—I sat at the far end of the table and waited.

Bright red letters on a digital wall clock displayed six different time zones. I stared at Eastern Standard Time, waiting for it to be one in the afternoon there. The ring signaling an incoming videoconference request startled me. The EST clock read 12:55 p.m. I grabbed the sleek, black remote from the conference room table, aimed it at the massive monitor, and clicked "Answer."

It was like a scene from Star Trek—the Command Conference Room on the other end of the connection quickly came into view. On the screen before me I could see an interior room on Joint Base Anacostia Bolling, over seven thousand miles away in southeast Washington, DC.

I sat at attention. Three representatives of the WHCA walked into the distant conference room. As they casually took their seats around their own shiny table, I was reminded of my first time appearing before an Army promotion board nearly a decade prior. It was 1999 and I was a twenty-five-year-old Specialist stationed in Germany. My unit, the 2nd Battalion, 37th Armored Regiment, had convoyed for over five hours and nearly a hundred miles from Ray Barracks in Friedberg to Grafenwöhr.

After three years in the military, I'd realized the Army intentionally chose the absolute worst, most miserable, and demanding weather in which to train. That old Army saying goes, "If it ain't raining, we ain't training," and it always rang true. If it wasn't extreme heat, pouring rain, bitter cold, or a combination thereof, the Army didn't seem to think it was harsh enough to conduct training.

My squad leader at the time, SGT Zeitz, was a scrawny, bowlegged, Asian guy. Despite his frail appearance, he was surprisingly tough. He and I were out on a retrans mission in our M557 Armored Personnel Carrier. I was scheduled to appear before a field promotion board back at the base camp the next day.

Soldiers often referred to the Armored Personnel Carrier as "the breadbox" because of its square shape. I remember it only as a hard, cold chunk of metal. I enjoyed driving the M577. It was fun. That day SGT Zeitz and I had thoroughly spun around in the mud, digging up an area atop a small hill adjacent to a patch of forest. A group of wild hogs scattered as the Armored Personnel Carrier rumbled to a stop.

SGT Zeitz was adventurous and always wanted to get the most out of every training opportunity. I admired that he never enjoyed taking the easy way out. On this particular mission, we could've slept in the warmth of the heated breadbox. Instead, SGT Zeitz thought it would be an excellent idea to erect tents and sleep outside.

I thought the coziness of the personnel carrier was the most logical approach. Still, however, I was open to the challenge of roughing it. To be honest, I really had no choice. I was just a lowly specialist; Zeitz was a sergeant, as well as my squad leader.

Facing down the bone-chilling Bavarian wilds excited me. I joined the military with a craving for challenges, and working cotton fields had set a high bar for what I considered challenging. In the back of my mind, I'd always quietly believed there couldn't possibly be a job as difficult as chopping cotton in the Mississippi Delta.

On that hill, in the darkness of the Bavarian forest, SGT Zeitz and I erected our forty-foot OE-254 antenna system. The antenna, towering above, allowed the battalion's radio signal to reach other units. We set up our tents, which were the cloth shelter half, ropes, poles, and stakes we'd been issued at Friedberg. By the time we finished that night, the temperature had dropped even further. My fingers felt completely frozen. I crawled into my tiny tent, slid into my bulky green sleeping bag, and zipped it up to my nose. An Army-issued, black balaclava covered my head and face

I eventually drifted off to sleep listening to wild hogs grunting in the distance. The grunts didn't bother me. In fact, they reminded me of the pigs my cousins and I chased around the house back on Elemwood.

I woke a few hours later around 3:00 a.m. The snow had been falling while I slept, and the weight of it had caused my tent to collapse. My sleeping bag had a powdery, white blanket of fresh snow over it. To make matters worse, the radio inside the M577 was blaring command orders to tear down our OE-254, pack everything up, and move to a different location.

It took us about an hour to pack up. With frozen fingers and toes, I slid down into the driver's hatch of the Armored Personnel Carrier. I drove us deeper into the German forest until we found another hill and started all over again. The next day, around noon, we drove back to the main base—Battalion Headquarters. It was my big day. I was to appear before the promotion board. It would be my first time before a committee, bombarding me with random questions, to determine whether I was fit to lead soldiers.

My introverted personality always caused me to overprepare. I tried to think through every scenario, no matter how wild and implausible. Before we'd even departed Ray Barracks on that convoy to Grafenwöhr, I had overly starched and ironed a camouflaged battle dress uniform. I put so much starch on the pants that they could stand upright on their own. I neatly rolled the uniform, just like I'd learned in basic training, and placed it at the bottom of my duffle bag along with a shiny pair of Corcoran black boots.

The day of the interview, starched and spit-shined, I stood outside the door as the snow fell around me. With my right hand, I formed a fist and placed three firm knocks on the door.

The few seconds of silence seemed like hours.

"Enter," a booming voice commanded through the door.

It reminded me of the voice from *The Wizard of Oz* when the Scarecrow, Tinman, and Cowardly Lion requested entrance to the Emerald City. I opened the heavy, white door. Without even acknowledging the loud slam behind me, in rigid military precision, my fingers tightly curled and thumbs pressed firmly against the second knuckle of my index finger, I executed a right face.

Swinging my arms nine inches to the front, and six inches to the rear, I took several steps forward. I then executed a left face. Again, swinging my arms nine inches to the front and six inches to the rear, staring straight ahead with a neutral expression on my face, I took several steps forward. I stopped behind a metal chair, directly across the table from the Command Sergeant Major.

He was flanked by Company First Sergeants, two on his left and two on his right. Their blank stares penetrated like laser beams; I looked to the wall behind them.

"Command Sergeant Major, Specialist Pinkins reporting to the President of the Board as ordered, Command Sergeant Major," I blurted confidently, trying to hide the fact that the introvert inside me was doing backflips at a thousand miles an hour.

"Specialist Pinkins, About-face," Command Sergeant Major barked.

I slid my right foot back and placed the toe of my shiny black boot just outside and behind my left foot and, in one motion, spun my entire body 180 degrees. I now faced away from the board members, staring at the double white doors through which I'd entered. They reminded me of those two double doors at the end of the court during high school basketball tryouts. I also noticed a random administrator sitting along the wall. I was surprised I hadn't seen him when I first walked in.

"Left-face," Command Sergeant Major's voice boomed from behind me.

I shifted my weight to the heel of my left foot and the ball of my right foot. In one motion I rotated my entire body ninety degrees to left. In my peripheral vision, I saw the two First Sergeants sitting to the left of the Command Sergeant Major. Their rank, three chevrons above three rockers with a diamond in the middle, dominated their uniform collars.

"Four steps forward, march!" Command Sergeant Major ordered.

Fist tightly clenched, thumbs beginning to go numb from pressing so firmly against my index finger, I swung my arms nine inches to the front and six inches to the rear and marched four steps forward.

"Half right-face!"

On the ball of my left foot and the heel of my right foot, I pivoted and turned my body forty-five degrees to the right.

"Three steps forward, march!" he shouted.

I took three steps forward. When I stopped, I was in the far corner of the room. My nose was barely an inch from the junction in the wall; I stood there motionless, stiff as a pole. Voices whispered, and papers shifted on the table several feet behind me. What was probably only about thirty seconds seemed like an hour.

And then: "Specialist Pinkins, take your seat," I heard the Command Sergeant Major bark.

Turning back, I about-faced and walked across the room. I stopped directly in front of the Command Sergeant Major, exactly where I had begun. I sat at attention in the metal chair. I stared expressionlessly at the equally blank face of the Command Sergeant Major. The sight of the rank on his collar, three chevrons above three rockers with a five-pointed star within a wreath, was intimidating.

After several rounds of questioning from the Command Sergeant Major as well as the First Sergeants, the Command

Sergeant Major's voice bellowed throughout the room: "Specialist Pinkins, ATTENTION!"

I sprang to my feet, staring straight ahead, frozen at the position of attention.

"Repeat the NCO Creed," Command Sergeant Major ordered.

With my shoulders held high, eyes fixed on the wall just above the Command Sergeant Major's head, I bellowed out loud:

No one is more professional than I. I am a noncommissioned officer, a leader of Soldiers. As a noncommissioned officer, I realize that I am a member of a time-honored corps, which is known as "The Backbone of the Army." I am proud of the Corps of noncommissioned officers and will at all times conduct myself so as to bring credit upon the Corps, the military service and my country regardless of the situation in which I find myself. I will not use my grade or position to attain pleasure, profit, or personal safety.

Competence is my watchword. My two basic responsibilities will always be uppermost in my mind—accomplishment of my mission and the welfare of my Soldiers. I will strive to remain technically and tactically proficient. I am aware of my role as a noncommissioned officer. I will fulfill my responsibilities inherent in that role. All Soldiers are entitled to outstanding leadership; I will provide that leadership. I know my Soldiers and I will always place their needs above my own. I will communicate consistently with my Soldiers and never leave them uninformed. I will be fair and impartial when recommending both rewards and punishment.

Officers of my unit will have maximum time to accomplish their duties; they will not have to accomplish mine. I will earn their respect and confidence as well as that of my fellow Soldiers. I will be loyal to those with whom I serve; seniors, peers, and subordinates alike. I will exercise initiative by taking appropriate actions in the absence of orders. I will not compromise my integrity, nor my moral courage. I will not forget, nor will I allow my comrades to forget that we are professionals, noncommissioned officers, leaders!

A few months later, on a cold and grey winter day back on Ray Barracks, SGT Zeitz and the Company Commander promoted me to the rank of Sergeant in the middle of the parking lot, right outside the base exchange.

** **

"Relax," a voice said over the speakers installed in the conference room ceiling. "This is going to be more of a conversation than your typical interview." I watched the people on the distant end settle themselves into three lush chairs.

"How are you?" one of the voices asked. "And how do you like Okinawa?"

"The island is great. I've really enjoyed my time here thus far," I responded.

"So, tell us why you want to work at the White House Communications Agency, and what do you think you bring to our organization?"

It was definitely more of a conversation than a typical military interview. For about an hour, we spoke on various topics. The final question was perhaps my favorite part of the interview.

"What was the last book you read?" asked one of the interviewers.

"*The Hero with a Thousand Faces* by Joseph Campbell," I responded, perhaps with a bit too much enthusiasm. "My favorite part of the book is when he discusses the hero adventure."

In the book, Campbell writes, "*The adventure may begin as a mere blunder, as did that of the princess of the fairy tale; or still again, one may be only casually strolling, when some passing phenomenon catches the wandering eye and lures one away from the frequented paths of men.*" [4]

Over the past decade and a half serving my country, I felt like I'd been on a similar adventure. From leaving the Mississippi Delta on a bus ride to Kansas to the flight to Germany and being gleefully lost in the Frankfurt Airport, from intentionally getting lost in countries throughout Europe to my time with the RuffRyders in Baghdad to the voyage across the East China Sea, I felt like it had all been a series of amazing adventures.

Several weeks later, I received an email congratulating me on being accepted into the White House Communications Agency.

* *

A few weeks after that, in early May, Colonel Bryant, the Commander of the 10th Support Group, promoted me to the rank of Chief Warrant Officer Three. The promotion took place in the same conference room in which my interview

---

4   Joseph Campbell, The hero with a thousand faces. (Princeton, N.J.: Princeton University Press, 2004), 48.

had taken place several weeks before. My parents watched the promotion ceremony via video-teleconference in what turned out to be the last promotion of my military career. At the end of the ceremony, Colonel Bryant announced to everyone that I was being reassigned to support President Obama at the White House Communications Agency.

I struggled to comprehend what must have been going through my parents' mind—Dad, a sharecropper who had worked so hard for me, and Mom who had dropped out of school to raise me. I wondered what they thought the moment they learned that their son was going to work for the first black President of the United States.

CHAPTER EIGHTEEN:

Welcome Aboard Air Force One

———

After just over two years on the island of Okinawa, I was gone.

First the Potomac River and then Ronald Reagan Washington National Airport came into view as I peered from the plane's tiny, oval window. My assignment at WHCA would turn out to be one of the most memorable adventures of my military career. I figured, much like sailing across the East China Sea or intentionally getting lost in random European cities, traveling in support of the President was bound to present something new and exciting every day.

** **

I'd been at WHCA for more than a year. Although I had seen the President on multiple occasions, I had never met him. Just like most people, I'd witnessed his calm, cool, and collected demeanor from a distance, mainly on television. On Saturday, March 7, 2015, we were in Selma, Alabama. At the foot of the Edmund Pettus Bridge, just outside the doors of the

Selma Times-Journal, a gigantic tent had been constructed in the middle of the street that stretched across Water Avenue. Inside the tent, I stood against the wall. It was a solemn day to honor the sacrifices and bravery of the men and women, who in 1965, had bled on Bloody Sunday in support of voting rights for African Americans.

Having grown up in the Deep South, I had family members who remembered Bloody Sunday. For me, the date was personally significant. The privilege of being there in support of the first black President of the United States was truly humbling.

I was on the trip evaluating another member of the military team of WHCA professionals who, like always, had done a superb job preparing for the President's visit. There was a lot of activity inside the tent that day. The energy in the air was thick. People clearly appreciated the historical significance of the event. In one simple moment, President Obama showed me he was, in fact, that down-to-earth person people saw on television.

I stood along the wall inside the tent when the President and First Lady walked by. As usual, a posse of aides and assistants followed closely behind. Out of nowhere, and as sharply as I'd pivoted when that Command Sergeant Major yelled "right face" at my promotion board in Germany years ago, President Obama turned right and made a beeline for me with his hand extended.

"Who's winning the game?" he asked.

Shocked that the President of the United States was standing in front of me, shaking my hand, "What game?" was the only response I could come up with.

He laughed and walked off. After my head stopped spinning, I remembered it was March. The NCAA basketball tournament was going on. He'd wanted to know the score of a basketball game. "What a fumble on my part," I thought. But that wouldn't be my last interaction with the President.

**

My law school ambitions had drifted from the back of my mind up to the forefront, becoming a constant focus. This was particularly driven by the fact that I grew up in a poor, under-served, and poverty-stricken community—one where people also lacked access to fair, adequate legal representation. This lack of representation, combined with a lack of legal knowledge, often led to friends, family, and other community members getting trampled by the judicial system. It was like poverty was a crime there.

I am usually a very decisive person; however, I'd wrestled for some time with the decision to leave the military. It was tough because I thoroughly enjoyed serving my country. After much thought, though, I committed myself to attend law school so I could go back and continue serving in communities in the Mississippi Delta like my own.

After doing some research, I learned that even before I could apply to law school, I had to take an exam. Even after that, most law schools would still say no if I didn't score high enough. It had been nearly thirty years—way back in high school—since I'd taken a standardized test. I'd also heard horror stories about the Law School Admissions Test. The level of difficulty was one of the reasons Lieutenant Smith decided not to apply. Further, the LSAT is notoriously treacherous because it lasts only a few hours and can determine the fate of your entire legal career. When evaluating applications, most law schools consider the LSAT to be even more important than your entire four-year undergraduate GPA.

In June 2015, a few months after my botched handshake with President Obama, without even studying, I sat for the LSAT on a university campus in DC. It was horrible. The results were even worse than I'd anticipated. I applied anyway, to just one law school, and promptly received a denial letter:

Dear Mr. Pinkins:

Thank you for your application to the . . ....
Law School.

The Admissions Committee has reviewed your application carefully, and unfortunately, decided that it cannot offer you admission at this point.

The Admissions Committee is faced with the arduous task of selecting the most qualified individuals from a highly competitive pool of applicants. Thus, we must deny the admission of a large number of applicants. The unfavorable decisions are difficult to deliver.

The members of the Committee recognize the time you spent and the care you took in completing your application. We wish you success in your future endeavors.

Sincerely,
Committee on Admission

An anxious smile crossed my lips. I slid the letter back into its white envelope. I wasn't surprised, nor was I particularly upset about the rejection. I placed the envelope in plain view in the middle of the kitchen table. If anything, I was motivated—even excited. Viewing the rejection as a temporary obstacle, a minor roadblock, I was thrilled to have begun my next adventure.

From then on, each day after work I attended an LSAT prep class. I understood some of the material the instructor was teaching, but it wasn't coming to me fast enough. I was impatient.

"It shouldn't be this difficult to learn this stuff!" I thought as the LSAT instructor rambled on for hours.

The final straw came one day when I told the instructor I was a retired veteran. A warm, welcoming smile crossed her face as the word "veteran" left my lips. Moments later, though, that smile turned to a dismissive frown when I mentioned growing up in the Mississippi Delta. I'd always found the stigma interesting. Time and time again, when I'd tell someone I was from the Mississippi Delta, there would be a noticeable change in their demeanor. Knowing I'd grown up there automatically contorted some people's views—especially those who'd never visited the state.

This woman's frown and the dismissive expression on her face immediately reminded of the seventh-grade teacher who failed that little boy all those years ago. She had that look that said, "You are not good enough. You can't do this." Even more unfortunate was that her skin color was the same as mine.

I stood up, turned around, and walked out the door with a smile. Like so many times before, when I'd confronted a challenge head-on, I knew I'd already won this one, too. It was just a matter of putting in the time and effort to cross the finish line. Though I'd already paid for the classes, I decided I would no longer attend. I've always believed strongly that I can teach myself anything. I figured, why should the LSAT be any different?

The LSAT became an obsession; my kitchen table became a battleground. I gathered free and hand-me-down study materials and collected practice exams from various online sources. Whatever I could find, I hoarded and put to use. Every day, after work and on the weekends, my nose was buried in LSAT study materials. If I got tired, I'd water Patience, my leafy green ficus tree next to the kitchen table near the patio window.

My goal was to study for the LSAT for an entire year. After which I planned to sit again for the exam in June 2016. Whenever I had a break at work, I studied for the LSAT. While some soldiers took a smoke break, I'd crack open my homemade study guide. Late at night, throughout the WHCA building, I'd sit at empty conference room tables. I even studied in my car, idling in the well-lit parking lot outside the WHCA headquarters.

On days when I had twenty-four-hour duty at the WHCA operations desk, I studied while, at the same time, keeping track of military members traveling the globe in support of President Obama.

** *

On Friday, November 1, 2015, I and sixty military personnel landed at a military base in Kuala Lumpur, Malaysia. The aircraft we flew in on was packed with equipment. Loading, unloading, reloading, cross-loading, and unloading again had become the norm. Often thousands of miles from our initial starting point in Washington, DC, the military men and women of WHCA had perfected the art of moving tens of thousands of pounds of equipment around the world for the President.

This time, after offloading the equipment and reloading it onto local moving trucks, we headed to the JW Marriott in downtown Kuala Lumpur. Sweating and tired, using service elevators, we moved pallets and pallets of equipment from the busy loading dock into the hotel. It always amazed me how oblivious guests were that we had commandeered multiple floors right beneath their noses.

Our job was to replicate the communications capabilities the President and senior White House staff typically had back in Washington. It was a painstaking process that often took weeks to complete. In the weeks leading up to the President's arrival abroad, the military members on each trip would get the job done. It's no surprise that military members and their unique approach to problem-solving, teamwork, and mission accomplishment played such a central role.

A few days later I stood outside the JW Marriott in the early afternoon, waiting to cross busy Bukit Bintang Street. Mopeds, taxi cabs, and luxury cars zipped by; a red cartoonish figure on the "Don't Walk" signal was lit up on a pole across the street. I was lost in thought, trying to recall all the different forms that little red person had taken in the many countries I'd visited.

"Hey, Chief Pinkins! What are you up to?" shouted a voice from behind me.

Dunbar and Ellis were part of the WHCA team that had flown in with us. They were funny, joked around a lot, and reminded me of Jeff Daniels and Jim Carey's characters in the movie *Dumb and Dumber.*

Before I could open my mouth to answer, Dunbar said, "Come with us! We're going to get some drinks and a bite to eat."

My brow furrowed and my teeth clenched.

"Sorry, guys, I can't go."

"Aw, come on! We're in a foreign country, and you haven't hung out with us at all since we've been here," they said, flailing their hands in frustration. "What else do you have to do?"

"I have to study," I said.

"Study for what?" Ellis asked.

"The Law School Admissions Test," I said as the red person on the signal turned green. It began an enthusiastically cartoonish stroll to signal it was safe to cross the street.

"Oh! You're dangerous," Dunbar joked as I waved goodbye, walking across the street to the Pavilion Shopping Center.

It was crowded inside the shopping center. People endlessly entered and exited stores like Tiffany & Co., Mont Blanc, and BOSS. On a lower level, popular American and local fast food restaurants like KFC, Pizza Hut, Chir Chir Fusion Chicken Factory, CoCo ICHIBANYA, and Fuji Sushi neatly lined the mall terminal.

I wasn't interested in any of that. I was searching for something else. Something specific. Before I'd left the JW Marriott, I asked the concierge desk to recommend a printing place. He told me to go across the street to the Pavilion Shopping Center and head downstairs to the basement.

On the lowest level of the mall, tucked away in a corner crowded with boxes, was an old lady sitting behind a desk. She didn't speak English, and I didn't speak Malay. Through hand gestures, I somehow communicated to her that I needed to print several documents from my personal storage device. It took a few minutes, but after hand gestures and laughter, she and I finally understood each other. Afterward, I thanked her and departed the mall with a thick stack of freshly printed, custom-made LSAT study documents.

I returned to my hotel room and compiled the documents neatly into an enormous white three-ring binder. For the rest of the evening I buried my nose in the study materials until late into the night. I fell asleep at the desk.

A few days later, I needed a break from studying. I joined Dunbar and Ellis, the two goofy guys from the street, on a sightseeing trip. We ended up climbing the 272 steps at the entrance of the Batu Caves.

Vendors lined the bottom of the steps, selling snacks. It was hot, so I purchased a bottle of water and a bag of chips. I made it halfway up the steps toward the mouth of the cave when I noticed a fast-moving blur in my peripheral vision. Then I felt two light taps—one on each shoulder. My bag of chips vanished into thin air, and I was left holding only a bottle of water. I was stunned when I turned around to see a macaque monkey reclining against a tree only a few feet away. It stared straight at me as it munched on my chips. I could only laugh.

A couple of weeks later, on November 20, I stood on the tarmac of the Subang Royal Malaysian Air Force Base at 2:30 in the afternoon. Aside from the slight humidity, the weather was beautiful. There wasn't a cloud in the sky, and Air Force One was scheduled to land in less than an hour. This was President Obama's second visit to Malaysia in as many years. I'd attended his previous trip in 2014 as well.

As we waited for the arrival, I helped the WHCA radio technicians whose job it was to outfit the idling motorcade with communications equipment. I was dressed in a slim fit, charcoal grey suit that I'd purchased just outside Kadena Airbase in Okinawa two years earlier. The radio technician and I, slightly behind schedule, rushed to finish installing radios in the vehicles. WHCA's military personnel, especially the radio technicians, had a thankless job, and the President's motorcade sometimes exceeded forty vehicles.

With about fifteen minutes to the President's arrival, I ran from vehicle to vehicle; then, the sky opened up. Instead of the arrival of Air Force One, a torrential downpour commenced. I had no umbrella and was instantly drenched from head to toe.

Ten minutes later, the rain stopped, and the sun peeked from behind the clouds. As if on cue, the unmistakable light blue and white hull of Air Force One—American flag emblazoned on the tail—drifted down from the sky.

Socks, shoes, and suit soaked, I rode along in the motorcade toward the visit's first stop. Never missing a moment to study, I casually flipped through LSAT flashcards as we barreled down the highway. Outside the vehicle window, the bright afternoon sun hovered in the now clear blue sky. It snickered at my soggy misfortune.

Lucky for me, my suit was dark and the sogginess was not readily apparent to others. The first event of the day was the Young South East Asian Leaders Initiative town hall at Taylor's University. I still felt the wetness of the suit on my skin.

Over the next couple of days, the President went on to visit several other locations. He met with the Malaysian Civil Society Group at the Ritz Carlton and attended the ASEAN Summit at the Kuala Lumpur Convention Center. After the whirlwind we finally arrived back at the Subang Royal Malaysian Air Force Base. We watched Air Force One depart, its hull blending into the blue sky, fading bit by bit, before vanishing altogether.

As always, the military men and women of WHCA remained behind while most of the civilian White House Staff departed. The ritual of loading, unloading, reloading, cross-loading, and unloading again tens of thousands of pounds of equipment commenced. Afterward, those selfless Soldiers, Sailors, Airmen, Marines, and Coast Guardsmen made their way, via a military cargo plane, to the President's next destination. Throughout the long and sometimes cold flights, I flipped through LSAT material.

At times I felt as though some—not all—members of the White House staff did not fully understand or appreciate the work that the WHCA military members did to support them. The feeling was particularly acute regarding some of the lower-level staff members. It seemed like, to many of them, WHCA members were invisible, nonexistent, irrelevant—a piece of furniture.

I often thought, "If they only knew the amount of work and long hours these service members put in to support them, they'd view us differently."

**

On March 3, 2016, we were in Milwaukee, Wisconsin. President Obama had just finished a speech at the United Community Center. He applauded the city's victory in the Healthy Communities Challenge, in which the city took first place out of nineteen other cities. They'd signed up thirty-eight thousand people for health coverage through the Affordable Care Act.

My favorite brown satchel hung from my right shoulder as I walked up to a service member standing at the bottom of the steps. Strapped to my back was a massive, black backpack. It was packed with items stuffed into its countless pockets.

"What's your name?" the service member asked as he scanned a white sheet of paper.

"Tyrone Pinkins," I said.

He found the name, smiled, and waved me past.

I struggled to climb the steep stairs with the satchel on my shoulder and bag on my back. Inside the brown satchel was my personal laptop, a few books, and the thick, white LSAT binder. When I reached the top of the stairs and passed through the open door, I didn't know whether to go left or right.

It was my first time aboard Air Force One, and I'd never thought I would find myself lost on an airplane. Yet, there I was. The inside was huge and had multiple compartments. Members of the White House Press Corps were going one way while others headed in the opposite direction.

Clearly, I was just standing in the way. I picked a random person and followed as though I also knew where I was going. Fancy, personalized place cards rested on each seat. As I walked from compartment to compartment, I couldn't find my name. Finally, after what seemed like forever (but was likely only a few minutes), I noticed a brown leather recliner next to the window with a place card that read: "CW3 TYRONE PINKINS, WELCOME ABOARD AIR FORCE ONE."

The satchel slid from my shoulder, and I wrestled the heavy black bag from my back. Relieved and feeling a hundred pounds lighter, I settled into one of the most comfortable recliners ever. At that moment, I wondered, "Could my younger self, that cotton chopping kid back in the Mississippi Delta, ever have imagined this?"

The plane took off fast, seemingly faster than any other commercial flight on which I'd flown. The acceleration and ascent of Air Force One pressed my back and shoulders into the soft, leather seat; I slid on a set of noise-canceling headphones. Thumbing through the options on my phone, I selected my favorite jazz playlist. The smooth sounds of Grover Washington, Hank Jones, Rachelle Farrell, Red Garland, and others danced between my ears.

Out of the right armrest I flipped open the tray table. I reached into my brown shoulder satchel and grabbed the binder and a No. 2 pencil. Then I buried my face in the study manual while Air Force One cruised eastbound at thirty thousand feet toward Joint Base Andrews.

For the next few months, I followed the same ritual each time I boarded Air Force One. Find my seat, drop the satchel, shed the backpack, slip on noise-canceling headphones, and bury my face in my thick, white LSAT study guide.

It was simply wash, rinse, and repeat each time I boarded.

CHAPTER NINETEEN:

Redemption Is a Cheap Wristwatch and a Wooden Pencil

———

A few days later, on Monday, March 7, 2016, I woke up around 5:30 a.m. It was cold outside as I pulled slowly out of my garage for the forty-five-minute commute in early morning traffic. Once in DC, I turned off Constitution Avenue onto the Ellipse, circled halfway around, and parked between the Ellipse Visitor Pavilion and the National Christmas Tree.

I took my satchel from the passenger seat and grabbed a small suitcase from the trunk. After passing what seemed like a hundred checkpoints, I reached the doors of the East Wing. Upon entering I noticed a Secret Service Agent sitting to the right. He glanced up to verify my credentials and then continued with whatever he was doing before I interrupted.

Ahead, on the wall to the left, hung a huge picture of Nancy Reagan in a bright red dress, which matched the red carpet on which I stood. This was the beginning of my first full day and, ultimately, the first of many nights in the White

House. Like a microcosm of black history up until that point, I'd made it from the cotton fields of Mississippi all the way to inside the White House.

It was only about 6:30 in the morning and the place was still quiet. I made my way to our office, where Linc's things were spread neatly across the bed as he packed his bags to leave. I wasn't only replacing him that morning for shift change—I was also replacing him permanently as one of the President's Communications Aides.

Linc had already served for five years in the White House as one of the few people within the President's bubble. I'd spent the past couple of years in Southeast DC at the WHCA Headquarters. I stood by as I was overlooked in favor of others within the agency, some of whom I had outscored on promotion exams. Many of them I had also clearly outperformed on presidential travel missions, and some I'd even trained when they arrived at the agency long after me. Probably one of the more painful realizations was that, even in an agency so closely connected to the first black President of the United States, I still had to work twice as hard to get half as far as some of my white counterparts.

Linc had also had his struggles. Having served for five years as one of the President's Communications Aides, he was nevertheless overlooked in favor of someone who had literally been in the agency for under two months and had less practical experience than many other people in the organization. To add even more sting to the insult, Linc essentially ended up training him to be his superior.

I felt terrible for Linc. He had put in several years, accumulated so much goodwill, and contributed so much hard work. Yet, he still eventually found himself overlooked for the lead position on the four-man Communications Aide team in favor of someone with less than sixty days experience. Like me, he also had to work twice as hard to get half as far.

That morning, Linc and I walked out of the office together and headed across the East Colonnade. A large, bronze bust of Abraham Lincoln stared solemnly as we approached the East Garden Room. Passing through the East Garden Room, two large, white doors opened up to the Ground Floor Corridor. Along the length of the Corridor ran that bright red carpet. On the right, just inside the double doors, sat a bronze statue of four cowboys on galloping horses, revolvers raised to the sky. Directly across the hallway, encased in glass, was a slightly smaller bronze statue of American Indians hunting buffalo on their native land. I couldn't help but think about the violent history represented by those two sculptures and the tension that lay between them.

Ahead on the left were the Vermeil and China Rooms. On the right was one of my favorite places—the library, where, late in the evenings and early some mornings, I'd sneak in and admire the collection of more than two thousand books, as well as the many Native American paintings decorating the walls.

We passed the entrance to the Diplomatic Reception Room. Way up high, perfectly centered over the doorway, was the Seal of the President of the United States. An eagle held in its right talons an olive branch; in its left talons were a bundle of arrows. What was interesting to me, noticing it then, was that *this* eagle's head faced right toward the arrows. The eagle's head on both this, and the Great United States Seal, usually faces left toward the olive branches.

I later researched the discrepancy. In 1945, President Truman signed Executive Order 9646 which, among other things, changed the eagle's direction to face the olive branch.[5] He felt this was symbolic of a nation on the march and dedicated to peace. The East Wing and the Diplomatic Reception Room Seal, with their arrow-facing eagles, were remnants of times long gone.

We continued walking and entered the Palm Room before passing through another set of doors and popping out onto the West Colonnade. The Rose Garden was on our left. Beyond that was the West Lawn and then the White House gate. Outside the gate and across Constitution Avenue, the Washington monument stood tall, dominating the skyline as the morning sun slowly peaked over the eastern horizon.

"You know, this is the path the President walks to work each morning," Linc said.

We stopped and stood in the middle of the Colonnade for a moment. It turns out that before the construction of either the East or West Colonnade, in plain view, precisely where we stood, existed stables, storage, and domestic laundry operations.[6] The Colonnades were built during the Jefferson administration as a means to conceal those day-to-day operations.

I closed my eyes and tried to transport myself back in time, imagining the many African Americans—some free, others enslaved—who played a key role in the construction of this building.

---

5 "Executive Order 9646-Coat of Arms, Seal, and Flag of the President of the United States." The American Presidency Project, October 25, 1945. https://www.presidency.ucsb.edu/documents/executive-order-9646-coat-arms-seal-and-flag-the-president-the-united-states.

6 Fazio, Michael W., and Patrick A. Snadon. The Domestic Architecture of Benjamin Henry Latrobe. Baltimore, MD: Johns Hopkins University Press, 2006.

We continued toward the West Wing. As we approached, I was surprised when the door automatically swung open. The Secret Service Agent at the desk on the other side had apparently activated a switch. We passed the agent, turned left, and went downstairs, passing by endless photos of the President. Eventually, we arrived at the White House Mess and ordered breakfast.

Linc departed and I continued on my adventure, exploring as much as I could without getting in anyone's way. After getting lost a few times, I made my way back to my office. I sat at the desk, glanced over, and noticed my satchel resting on the bed. The LSAT called my name. I unlatched my satchel, grabbed the thick, white binder and, for the rest for the day, buried my face in my study manual.

Several weeks later, on the morning of Monday, June 6, I woke up from another overnight duty in the White House. I hung around longer than usual, in no rush to leave that morning. I dressed, departed the office, and walked past the painting of Nancy Reagan in that bright red dress. Across from Nancy the Secret Service Agent sitting at the desk glanced up momentarily as I exited the East Wing. Walking down the East Wing driveway, I swiped my credentials to exit the large, black, iron gate. On all other mornings I would turn right, walk down East Executive Avenue, find my car parked like usual on the Ellipse, and drive straight home.

On this particular Monday morning, however, I had to take a different route. I turned left and headed up East Executive toward Pennsylvania Avenue. I stopped momentarily to let a member of the White House grounds crew cross the street ahead of me, pushing a cartload of plants. I passed the Department of the Treasury on the right before popping out into the heavy morning foot traffic of Pennsylvania Avenue.

I stood there for a moment before turning right, crossing 15th Street, and heading up New York Avenue. I passed through Chinatown and, after walking another twenty minutes, made a right onto Massachusetts Avenue. Several minutes later, I stood on the corner of F Street & New Jersey Avenue.

The day I'd spent an entire year studying for was finally here. On trains, buses, and in foreign hotels, I had devoted myself to the LSAT. Aboard Air Force One and throughout the White House, I'd studied tirelessly, teaching myself how to take the exam. Now the only thing between me and the exam was New Jersey Avenue and the steps of Georgetown Law School's McDonough Hall.

I hadn't worn a wristwatch in nearly fifteen years. I bought a cheap one at a souvenir shop to use as a timer during the exam. Sitting there surrounded by test takers—some half my age—would have normally made me a bit uncomfortable. That day, though, I felt like I'd poured so much of myself into preparing for the exam that all I could do was go in, sit down, and give it my best shot.

For the next six hours, sitting in that classroom, I ran a psychological and emotional marathon, enduring the most torturous exam I'd ever taken.

When it was complete, I stood up, walked toward the exit, and dropped the wristwatch and my pencils in the trash receptacle next to the wall. I had no idea if studying had paid off, no idea whether I had passed or if I'd wasted twelve months and failed miserably. All I knew was that after preparing for an entire year, I had done my best. I skipped down the main steps outside, took a leisurely twenty-five-minute walk back to my car outside the White House gates, and drove home.

CHAPTER TWENTY:

You Know What, Mr. President? You Look Good, Too!

———

It was September 2016 and I was in Vientiane, Laos. President Obama was flying in to attend the East Asia Summit, making him the first sitting US President to visit the country. I'd already been there for about a week. During our mandatory security briefings at the beginning of each trip abroad, we'd be cautioned about traveling outside the hotel alone. They wanted us to eye everyone with suspicion.

I never really bought into the fear. Over the previous twenty years, I had ventured alone through cities like London, Brussels, and Vienna. I had gone on ten, fifteen, and twenty-mile runs through Germany and Okinawa. I had intentionally resided in European neighborhoods void of other Americans, forcing myself to learn the local language. Rather than fearing the bad in people, I chose to see the good. In my eyes, Laos was no different

We stayed at the Landmark Mekong Riverside Hotel, barely a stone's throw away from the Mekong River. On the drive in from the airport, I spied a nice running trail along the banks. I woke early one morning and stepped out of the hotel into humid, eighty-five-degree weather. Immediately, I thought, "What serious runner could turn down the opportunity to trot along the Mekong simply because of some frivolous security concerns and a little humidity?"

I walked a few blocks, crossed another street, and took off along the Mekong. Just as I suspected, like all the other times I'd allowed myself to get lost in a new culture, no one threatened me, chased me, or ate me. Contrary to the horrors the security personnel spoke of, the locals seemed nice.

Local runners, walkers, and bikers smiled as I passed. Just across the dingy waters of the Mekong River was Thailand, a country I'd never visited. Quaint restaurants, houses, and shacks lined the distant shore. At that moment, mid-run, I knew I'd try to find a way to cross the border and set foot on Thai soil before the President arrived. Later that morning, after breakfast, I walked outside the hotel again. The heat felt like a hundred degrees, and the humidity was out of control. WHCA always commissioned local drivers to help us get around foreign cities; I found one who spoke pretty decent English.

"Good morning," I said. "How are you?"

"Good morning, sir," he responded. "Do you need a ride somewhere?"

"Yes," I said, a mischievous smile on my lips. "I want to go to Thailand."

The driver laughed, clearly not taking me seriously. When he realized the expression on my face hadn't changed, he repeated what I'd said with exasperation, "You want to go to Thailand?"

"Yes. Can you drive me? I'll pay you." I said, retrieving some Laosian kips from my pocket.

The driver looked around nervously.

"Okay. When do you want to go?"

"Now," I said, wide-eyed with excitement.

I hopped into the passenger seat of the small white van, and off we went. We drove past farms, homes, and tiny shacks. We skirted past villages. Some buildings displayed sickle and hammer-stamped communist flags, waving proudly in the wind. We zipped along the highway as the countryside flew by.

After driving for forty-five minutes or so we came to the border crossing. It was snarled with traffic: cars, trucks, mopeds, and motorcycles were bumper to bumper, clogging the road.

"I cannot cross," the driver said, staring nervously.

"Why?" I asked.

"I do not have a Thai visa," he responded.

Staring at the Thai-Lao Friendship Bridge, I could tell this was serious. Trying to cross would likely lead to both of us getting into a lot of trouble. He offered to wait on me to go inside the building to try and convince someone to give me a temporary visa. I decided against it. Even as adventurous as I am, I'd learned over time that it's a good idea to pay attention to how locals react to potential danger. Besides, I would have probably gotten fired from my job. We turned around and drove back down the highway toward the hotel.

"You like my country?" he asked with a curious smile.

"I do," I said. "I enjoy getting to know different cultures."

Either my curiosity about his country made him curious about me, or he felt bad that I didn't get to set foot in Thailand.

"I can show you something." He pulled a tourist brochure from the visor above his head and passed it to me. "Where do you want to go?" he asked.

I flipped through the brochure as we continued zipping back down the highway toward the hotel.

"Wat Si Saket," I said, pointing to a picture.

"Wat Si Saket," he affirmed with a broad smile and a nod.

He turned left off the highway. We continued twisting and turning through the city until we stopped in front of a large white entrance.

"I'll wait here," he said as the van came to a stop. This time the look on his face wasn't one of fear, but one of kindness.

Full of excitement, I walked through the ornate entrance to one of the oldest Buddhist temples in Vientiane. The last king of the Lao Kingdom, King Anouvong, had the temple built around 1818. It was one of the few temples to survive the Siamese Army's destruction of Vientiane during Laotian rebellion from 1826-1828.[7] The temple was surrounded by enormous gold pillars, and the roof was made of dark brown shingles with red and gold trim.

Around the outside of the temple were rows and rows of magnificent bronze Buddha statues. They looked as though they'd sat there forever, legs crossed, left hand in the lap, and righthand fingers slightly touching the ground with

---

7   Suwaphat Sregongsang และผู้แต่งคนอื่นๆ. 2010. A study of Thailand and Laos relations through the perspective of the Vientiane Sisaket Temple and The Rattanakosin emerald Buddha temple. ม.ป.ท.:Silpakorn University

the palm facing inward. The posture was known as "Calling the Earth to Witness." It signified the Buddha's moment of enlightenment. I remembered it being mentioned in Joseph Campbell's, *The Hero with a Thousand Faces*, which I'd read several years prior in Okinawa. Campbell reflected on the Enlightened Buddha:

The god finally challenged [the Buddha's] right to be sitting on the Immovable Spot, flung his razor-sharp discus angrily, and bid the towering host of the army to let fly at him with mountain crags. But the Future Buddha only moved his hand to touch the ground with his fingertips, and thus bid the goddess Earth bear witness to his right to be sitting where he was. She did so with a hundred, a thousand, a hundred thousand roars, so that the elephant of the Antagonist fell upon its knees in obeisance to the Future Buddha.[8]

I was stunned stiff for a moment. It astonished me to realize that a book I'd purchased so many years prior, rushing through the Chicago O'Hare International Airport, had a connection to this moment, in a tiny country along the Mekong River.

After a while, I walked back out of the temple gate and climbed into the van. With enthusiasm, I told the driver about the Buddha statue and its relationship to the book I'd read. The driver smiled and pointed to another point of interest in the brochure.

After winding further through the city, we stopped at an entryway leading to a reddish, honeycombed pavement.

---

8   Joseph Campbell, The hero with a thousand faces. (Princeton, N.J.: Princeton University Press, 2004), 26.

He nodded past me and out the passenger window. I looked where he was pointing to one of the most magnificent structures I'd ever seen. Pha That Luang, a large, gold-covered Buddhist temple in the center of the city, is a national symbol and one of the most important monuments in Laos. Initially a Hindu temple built in the first century, it has since endured several reconstructions after multiple foreign invasions.

I hopped out of the van and followed the pavement. Although the temperature had risen and humidity was in full effect, the sky was a vast sapphire over the gilded temple. Just before I entered the temple grounds, I noticed a long, L-shaped tent in the parking lot. It was a market where locals sold souvenirs.

"How exciting!" I thought.

I entered the tent, passing tables and tables of items: old coins, watches, knives, t-shirts, carpets, and blankets. I stopped every few moments to bargain with vendors before moving on to another table. Behind one of the tables, I saw the cutest kid; it reminded me to purchase t-shirts for Joseph and Rukiya.

I left the market and entered the gate leading to the grounds of Pha That Luang. The view inside was stunning. All along the perimeter were statues that looked centuries old. The richness of the culture expressed—not only in the monument and sculptures but also in how locals treated each other—left me speechless. Again, this contradicted what security personnel had warned us about when we first arrived.

A few days later, Air Force One landed. President Obama was scheduled to be there for three days to attend the East Asia Summit and visit the Presidential Palace, where he would meet with Laotian President Bounnhang Vorachith. He would also speak at the Cooperative Orthotic Prosthetic

Enterprise, where he would announce that the United States would contribute $90 million to clear unexploded ordnance that had been planted by US forces during the Vietnam War. He also visited Wat Xieng Thong temple. At Souphanouvong University, he held a town hall with the Young Southeast Asian Leaders Initiative, much like he had done months earlier in Malaysia.

On the final day of the President's visit, back at the hotel, I stood in the back corner of an elevator. After a few minutes, President Obama stepped in and stood to my right as his Secret Service Agent, his doctor, and a couple more staff members also boarded. As usual, on my back was that big, bulky, black backpack. Across my right shoulder hung my favorite leather satchel. It was quiet as the elevator slowly descended. Without asking, the President suddenly reached into the pouch on my satchel. He pulled out one of my books.

"What's this?" the President asked, jokingly.

It caught me by surprise. But what was I going to say? He was the President of the United States—and I worked for him. Right?

"*Between the World and Me* by Ta-Nehisi Coates," I responded.

Staring curiously, he turned the book over in his hands. The other book in my satchel, the one he didn't remove, was my tan leather journal. I'd purchased it a few years earlier on my flight from Okinawa to DC and used it to document my adventures traveling with the President.

Ever since reading Coates' *The Beautiful Struggle*, I had been enamored with his writings. Whatever he published, I devoured. I'd read *The Case for Reparations* multiple times. I even bought dual copies of his Black Panther comics for Joseph and me to read together. The first time I saw Ta-Nehisi

Coates in person was one morning on the White House South Lawn. He stood next to the driveway as the motorcade awaited President Obama's departure from the Oval Office. I don't remember precisely, but I think it was around the time Coates was interviewing Obama for his forthcoming book, *We Were Eight Years in Power.*

That day, as I was about to approach Coates, I heard over my earpiece that the President was about to leave his office to get into the limousine. It actually annoyed me that he didn't stay in the oval office a few minutes longer. At that moment, I wanted to meet Ta-Nehisi Coates much more than I wanted to take off in the motorcade. Moments later, we were exiting the White House gates, off to some event in DC.

Standing in that elevator back in Laos, as he slid the novel back into my shoulder satchel, President Obama curiously looked me up and down—head to toe. I was wearing that same slim fit, dark grey suit that had been drenched in a Malaysian monsoon.

"You look good!" he said jokingly.

There were a few seconds of awkward silence. I then looked the President up and down back—from head to toe and said, "You know what, Mr. President? You look good, too!" Everyone in the elevator, including the President, exploded in laughter.

With a toothy smile, he quipped, "I got nothing. I can't follow that. What can I say?"

I had already missed my opportunity to engage with the President when he walked up to me in Selma, Alabama, more than a year earlier. Long before that moment in the elevator, I'd decided I would never miss my opportunity again.

The elevator stopped, and everyone disembarked and headed to the motorcade outside. A little while later, Air

Force One sped down the runway and slowly lifted into the air, disappearing behind the clouds as it headed back to the states.

For a while it really bothered me that the President had foiled my opportunity to meet one of my favorite authors. But the shortcoming was about to be rectified on October 11, 2016, when Air Force One touched down at Piedmont Triad International Airport in Greensboro. The President was there to visit North Carolina A&T State University, where ESPN's The Undefeated hosted a student forum with the President, centered around sports, race, and achievement. Guess who was traveling along with the president this time? Ta-Nehisi Coates! Ha!

Sometime after the President entered the Alumni Foundation Event Center and was deep into the forum discussion, I walked into the lobby. Across the room, I immediately recognized Ta-Nehisi Coates standing alone next to the wall. Usually, military personnel working at the White House are expected to keep our heads low and stay out of the way. We were expected to blend in as much as we could and, if at all possible, only interact with elected officials and their guests only when absolutely necessary for work responsibilities. When I saw Ta-Nehisi, all the rules went out the window. I made a beeline toward him, much like President Obama had done with me when I stood next to the wall of the tent back in Selma.

"Hi, Mr. Coates, how are you?" I said, extending my hand.

"Please call me Ta-Nehisi," he said with a warm, welcoming smile.

"I absolutely love your writings," I said as we shook hands. "I just finished *Between the World and Me*."

"I'm glad you like them. Thank you for your support."

I was about to ask Ta-Nehisi what was he working on next when, over my earpiece, I heard that President Obama was "wrapping up." My conversation with Ta-Nehisi Coates was foiled again by the President. I grimaced slightly, sighed internally, said, "It's a pleasure to meet you." Then I headed out the building to the motorcade.

CHAPTER TWENTY-ONE:

Inside the Oval: Hey! That's My Guy!

———

On Monday, November 14, 2016, my American Airlines flight sat idling until departure. The destination? Lima, Peru. I was traveling ahead of the President, who was scheduled to arrive a few days later on the eighteenth. As the Boeing 737 rumbled I slouched in my seat, pondering the previous Tuesday's election results.

Like many other Americans going into election night, I was fairly confident that Hillary Clinton would win. We were going to follow up on the historic election of the first African American President of the United States with the equally historic election of the first woman President.

I felt that not only would she win, but she was going to win by a landslide. Sabrina and I had made popcorn with extra butter, gone downstairs, and snuggled on our cushiony sofa to watch the results. I joked with her about the remote possibility that Donald Trump would actually win. We both laughed.

When one of the major networks announced that Florida was too early to call, I shrugged nonchalantly. I thought, "Before the night is over, Florida will go for Hillary by a small margin. We got this."

When Virginia and Michigan became competitive, I became slightly concerned. When Trump took Florida and CNN announced that Michigan, New Hampshire, Pennsylvania, and Wisconsin were too close to call, the alarm bells began to ring; Sabrina and I stared intently at the television.

"How in the world could Trump be this competitive in places like Pennsylvania and Michigan?" I said to no one in particular.

At that point, it was late in the game. While MSNBC and CNN frantically worked through counties on their magic board, trying to explain how Hillary still had a chance, I knew it was already over. The writing was on the wall. Shortly after midnight, Dana Bash announced that Hillary Clinton had called Trump to concede the election.

I was in shock at the realization that America—the America I love, the America for which I wore the uniform, the America whose freedom I had fought for in three wars—had elected one of the vilest, most vicious, dishonest, and unqualified candidates to the highest office in the land. Because of the Electoral College, a group of just 538 individual electors, Donald Trump had just been made President of the United States—contrary to the popular vote and the will of a majority of the American people.

A half-eaten tub of popcorn sat on the floor beside our couch. Sabrina and I were both stunned. I walked upstairs in a daze, took a hot shower, climbed into bed.

I woke the next morning around 5:30, grabbed my cell phone, and scrolled through various news articles to confirm that it had really happened.

On my way to the White House, I kept asking myself, "Is this really real? Did Donald Trump just win the presidency?" I drove along Suitland Parkway, searching through Sirius XM radio stations, and heard the same disbelief in the voices of news anchors on CNN, MSNBC, and Joe Madison's show.

I parked my car on the Ellipse, as usual, grabbed my small suitcase from the trunk, and then made my way through the security checkpoints. Interested in the mood within the White House, I stopped by the office of the President's Military Aides. All five of them were there. That alone was unusual since they typically rotated out each day just like us.

I was the lone Communications Aide in the office that day, and the only one of color at all. I felt the upcoming presidential transition would be very interesting, especially given the discriminatory statements Trump had made about people of color during his campaign.

I walked out of the Military Aides' Office, overcome by a feeling that my remaining time in the White House might evolve into something I hadn't previously contemplated. I had wrongly anticipated working for the first woman President of the United States. I was in no way prepared for a person with such questionable temperament to be sworn in. Still, I fully understood, appreciated, and accepted that the military members of the White House Communications Agency served the office of the President, not the person.

On the one hand, as a voter, I disagreed with basically every principle and policy Trump stood for. However, on the other hand, I thought it would be fascinating to see—from the inside—this transition, this process, this approach to governing. It was, after all, likely to differ from anything witnessed in modern US politics. Above all, I was honored to continue serving as I had and fully intended to work with the incoming administration's staff just as professionally as I'd worked with the outgoing Obama administration.

Throughout that day, I wandered the halls of the White House. I sensed the thickness of sorrow and surprise wafting all around.

Outside the Eisenhower Executive Office Building, on West Executive Avenue, I sat at a picnic table having lunch with an intern from Vice President Biden's office. I'd recently learned that she was also from the Delta and that we'd actually attended the same high school. As I munched on a black bean burger, our whispered conversation discussed the outcome of the election. I could see the emotion of the electoral loss all over her face.

"Let's walk over to the Rose Garden," I suggested. "President Obama's about to hold a press conference."

We crossed the street and walked past the James Brady Press Room. On the way I reminded the intern to keep her chin up. The security agent sitting in the booth next to the rear entrance to the Palm Room looked up to check our credentials and waved as we passed by. We exited the room and stood next to one of the white pillars on the West Colonnade, overlooking the Rose Garden. About five feet to the right of us stood Valerie Jarret, Susan Rice, and several other members of the White House Staff.

As President Obama popped out of the Oval Office to speak, some of his staff hugged, cried, and consoled each other. I imagined the slaves and indentured servants whose footprints we were standing in at that moment and how they had, centuries ago, toiled in an outdoor laundry and stable on that very spot.

* *

After idling for what seemed like forever, the Boeing 737 had finally taken off. Now at thirty thousand feet, I was well on the way to Lima, Peru in advance of Obama's final international trip as President. He was traveling to the APEC Economic Leaders Meeting. It was a bittersweet trip. However, it was also one I got to share with my longtime friend Linc.

A few days later, I was back at the White House on Thanksgiving Day. I felt especially privileged to be working that day because the President was scheduled to conduct his annual Thanksgiving calls to service members stationed around the world. And I was going to assist.

It was a quiet day. I wandered from room to room, slowly making my way toward the West Wing. Walking past the security agents posted throughout the building, I still marveled at how much like a museum the place really was. As I made my way along the bright red carpet, I passed the Diplomatic Reception room on the left. I waved at a Secret Service Agent standing there in the grand foyer. Passing through the Palm Room, I popped out onto the West Colonnade, where I noticed an old black gentleman whom I'd seen on several previous occasions, although we'd never spoken.

"Happy Thanksgiving," I greeted.

"Hi, and Happy Thanksgiving to you," he responded, removing a work glove from his hand and extending it to shake mine.

"I've seen you around here a lot," he said.

I felt an intimate connection to him, to the easiness of his smile. The President wasn't due to the Oval Office for another hour. So, I stood there leaning against one of the white pillars and we chatted for a while. His name was Edward, and he was sixty years old. He reminded me of Freddy, the BBQ joint owner played by Reg E. Cathey on the TV series *House of Cards.*

"I've been working here forty-three years," he said in a low, raspy tone. It reminded me of the slow, southern Delta drawl. "I don't know if I can stay on."

The election results had even Edward considering leaving the White House.

We chatted for a short while longer and then I continued on my walk. I exited the West Wing. Standing in the middle of the street between the White House and the Eisenhower Executive Office building, I cocked my head back and peered up at the morning sky. Out across the Ellipse, the Washington Monument pierced the sky. The recently opened Smithsonian National Museum of African American History and Culture stood proudly nearby.

I felt relaxed, inhaling the morning air and smiling at the fact that I'd taken part in such an amazing moment in history. I had worked for the first black President of the United States.

When I looked right, toward Pennsylvania Avenue, I was slapped back into reality. It was only November and they'd already started building the inauguration stage. I turned around, walked back into the West Wing, and met up with the on-duty Military Aide. We made our way to the Oval Office to await the President's arrival.

I stood in the President's secretary's office right outside the Oval, looking over the list of service members who would receive a call. Out the window, I saw President Obama's relaxed stride as he made his way across the West Colonnade. He was carrying what must have been the thickest white binder I had ever seen. It reminded me of the LSAT study binder I'd previously lugged along on many of my flights on Air Force One. The President entered and maneuvered around the secretary's desk before plopping the binder down with a thud.

"Hey, guys," he said with a smile and then continued into the Oval office.

The Military Aid and I worked together to connect each caller. I listened on a separate line to each conversation, to ensure sound quality and make sure the call didn't get disconnected. It was interesting to hear the President connect and communicate thoughtfully with total strangers. He had this way of making people feel as though everything was okay. That must have been particularly helpful to the service members on the other end of the line, some of whom were, at that moment, deployed away from their family to dangerous places.

After he completed the calls, the President told us he was pleased they'd gone smoothly. The Military Aide and I departed, heading back toward the East Wing. After we'd entered the Palm Room, I realized I had left my journal on the President's secretary's desk.

As I made my way back across the West Colonnade, President Obama popped out of the Oval Office on his way back to the residence.

"Thanks, man," he said with a smile extending his hand.

**

It was mid-December, and Obama's tenure as President was quickly coming to an end. He had only a few weeks left. I stood outside the Oval Office decked out in my formal-dress blue Army Service Uniform—shiny ribbons and all. Today was the day I was scheduled to take my official departure photo. Through the corner of the door, I could see the bust of Dr. Martin Luther King, Jr. on a table next to the fireplace. I had pointed it out several times while facilitating West Wing tours with family and friends.

One of the unique privileges of working for the President was that I had the opportunity to give private tours of the White House. Facilitating West Wing tours was hands down one of my favorite things to do. When I was first assigned to WHCA, I told myself I would help as many people as I could, especially people from poor and underserved communities. They deserved to gain access and exposure to that place. By the time I finished, I had escorted over two hundred people, including more than a hundred youth, on private tours through the West Wing.

More than riding in the motorcade, more than meeting the President, more than flying on Air Force One, more than sleeping in the White House, and, yes, even more than meeting Ta-Nehisi Coates, the opportunity to provide access to people who otherwise would not have seen that place meant everything.

I walked into the Oval Office that day, decked out in my military dress uniform.

"Hey! That's my guy!" Obama said with excitement as he shook my hand and gave me a firm slap on the shoulder.

We posed for a few photos in front of the Resolute Desk.

"You're leaving! So, what's next for you?" he asked.

"I'm retiring. I've served over twenty years," I said.

"What are you gonna do next?" he repeated.

Months earlier, I had received the results of the LSAT exam I'd taken in June. My score was much better than the first abysmal one I'd received in 2015. The studying had paid off. In fact, I had already received acceptance letters from twelve different law schools—including the lone law school that had denied me before. I guess they'd had a change of mind.

"Actually, I'm heading to law school."

"Well, let me know if you need anybody to look over your papers—because, you know, I went to law school, too," he said jokingly.

We both laughed.

CHAPTER TWENTY-TWO:

Hello. Will You? I Do.

HELLO

Some people meet online, others through friends, and others while attending university. Then there is Sabrina and me. Ours was a chance encounter that almost didn't happen.

Dr. Henry A. Wise, Jr. High School is only a ten-minute drive from the house I'd recently purchased in Upper Marlboro, Maryland. I wasn't even supposed to be there that day. However, I'd gotten a last-minute call from WHCA to see if I could attend a meeting since it was close to my house.

It was much larger and nicer than the high school I'd attended back in Mississippi. The parking lot was wide, the black pavement smooth and void of potholes. I noticed Sabrina before I even got out of my car. Something about her immediately caught my eye and would not let go.

Sabrina, along with two of her White House colleagues and I, walked into the school together. I listened as she spoke; we made our way along the hallway, past empty classrooms. Each word that escaped her lips was laced with an intoxicating melody that drew me in even more.

When we arrived at the gym, the hardwood basketball court glistened as if just waxed and buffed. From windows way up high, rays of light bounced off the walls, illuminating the blue and gold bleachers that rose from the floor to the rafters. Sabrina sat alone on the bottom row.

"Hello, I'm Ty," I said, extending my hand.

"Good morning. I'm Sabrina."

"Are you from Maryland?" I asked.

"No, I'm from New Mexico," she said. "I've been in this area for about two years now. I have family here."

"I just moved into town a few weeks ago," I told her. "I'm still getting to know the area."

After the meeting, I sat outside, alone in my car. Her voice echoed and danced between my ears while images of her smile tiptoed through my mind. Her eyes unlocked secret doors that had been shut in me for so long. I thought about what I'd say to her the next time we met. I was surprised at myself. I wasn't looking to meet anyone at that time, and it wasn't typical of me to so quickly become interested in getting to know someone. But there I was, sitting in my car, thinking intensely about a person I barely knew.

What I didn't realize was that a few rows over, Sabrina was sitting in her car as well. She was on her phone, debating with one of her best friends about whether she should come over and offer to show the new guy around town.

I was startled by the tap, tap, tap.

Sabrina was standing outside my car. I rolled down my window.

"Hi, I'd be happy to show you around town sometime," she said as she nervously flung a piece of paper into my car. Before I could open my mouth to say anything, she was gone, hurrying back to the safety of her own car. I smiled as I watched her drive from the parking lot, disappearing around the corner.

I went home, made dinner, and sat at the kitchen table with my back to the glass patio doors. I had purchased that table a few years back in Okinawa. It was dark brown, rich mahogany, and it had been in military storage for a year until I found the house. For dinner, I enjoyed a salad with spinach, tomato, scallions, and olives, with ranch and some sunflower seeds sprinkled on top. Mid-bite, I stopped chewing and looked up from my plate. The realization I'd just come to shocked me. I sat there in awe.

I smiled, laid down my fork, picked up my phone, and dialed Cousin Lenora's number.

"I met my wife today," I told her.

I could hear Lenora smiling through the phone.

Over the next several weeks, Sabrina and I went in opposite directions. We talked on the phone a few times, but I was never in town long enough for us to go on a date. She was transitioning from teaching at Howard University to working at the Department of Justice. I was hopping from state to state with President Obama. Before we knew it, months had passed and the new year had come and gone. All we'd had was the initial introduction back on that shiny basketball court and a few phone calls.

It was the first week of February. We hadn't spoken since December. I'd just returned from a three-week trip to New Delhi, India, and I finally had some empty space on my calendar.

"What are you doing on February 14th?" I asked when she finally answered the phone.

"I'm not busy," she responded.

I arrived at her cousin's house in my best suit with not one but two dozen roses. I rang the doorbell. Unbeknownst to me, her cousin was peering down from the upstairs window laughing, tickled at my southern chivalry.

Sabrina seemed surprised by the flowers as we walked down the driveway and that I opened the car door for her. Mom taught me to treat women kindly, and I really liked Sabrina even though we hadn't spoken much since the first hello.

I'd been planning our date for some weeks. Because I wanted everything to go well, my military instinct had created backup plans to the backup plan. In case something went wrong with the first restaurant, I made reservations at two additional restaurants. I bought tickets for an after-dinner play at the Baltimore Center Stage theatre. Just in case that didn't work out, I made reservations to sit and listen to live jazz.

Despite all my arrangements, everything that could go wrong *did* go wrong. Along the drive from Upper Marlboro to Baltimore a light, romantic snow fell. I'd already identified the perfect garage to park, which was right around the corner from restaurant option one.

We arrived on time for our reservation. The hostess told us to have a seat while they prepared our table. After about ten minutes, we were told they were overbooked because of Valentine's Day. It would be an additional forty-five minutes before we could be seated.

No sweat, I had a backup plan. Call an Uber and go to restaurant option two. Luckily for us, an Uber was in the vicinity. When we walked outside to the curb, snow fell heavier than before though still romantic, as long as we didn't get stuck out for too long.

The Uber approached and drove right on past us while the driver stared directly in my eyes. We walked around the corner to meet him when Sabrina's heel got stuck in the sidewalk; the snowfall had tipped well past romanticism. The Uber driver got impatient and pulled off just as we made it.

Red heels ruined, we waited in the snow on another driver. We never made it to restaurant two because the second driver dropped us off on the wrong street. By the time I'd realized it was wrong, he too had driven off. The snow was falling even harder as the Uber's tail lights disappeared around the corner.

With my plans going up in smoke, I tried to maintain a positive appearance. Inside, I was freaking out. I thought, "I've planned combat missions, been all around the world, and intentionally gotten lost in foreign cities, yet, I can't execute a perfectly planned date."

Along the sidewalk, in the cold, wet snow, we walked. Stopping beneath a store overhang, I turned around and peered through the square windows to find soft glowing candles. There were people inside.

"It's worth a try," I thought. "The night couldn't possibly get any worse, so what do we have to lose?"

I opened the door, Sabrina walked inside, and the hostess looked up with a smile.

"A table for two?" the hostess offered.

Sabrina and I looked at each other and smiled.

"Yes, please," I said.

The name of the restaurant was Soto Sopra. We sat and ate and laughed the night away, especially at everything that had gone wrong thus far. I admired her sense of humor. She thought I was charming and admitted that the suit and flowers were cute. After dinner, we enjoyed the play *One Night in Miami* at the Baltimore Center Stage.

On the drive back home, we talked the entire way. I walked her to the front door and we kissed on the stoop.

The moment reminded me of Nia Long and Lorenz Tate in the 90's classic *Love Jones.*

**

WILL YOU

Sabrina values her time and knows her worth.

"If there is one thing you want me to know, what is it?" I asked one night at a friend's house party.

"Don't waste my time," she said.

Sabrina and I were still traveling a lot, and our busy schedules kept us apart. Sometimes we were lucky enough to be in the same city. When I was in Selma for the 50th Anniversary of Bloody Sunday, she was there too. Before the President had arrived, we snuck away from everyone and went on a dinner date.

Afterward, we held hands and walked through the city, talking about everything. She told me about her family's long history of military service and about growing up in New Mexico. I told her about growing up in Mississippi and my travels while serving in the Army. I shared my plans to attend law school; she said she wanted to get her Ph.D.

Over the next several months whenever one of us was in town the other was gone. We resorted to seeing which of us could find the most unique gift as we hopped around the globe. No matter how far apart we were, she constantly tiptoed through my mind. There she continued to unlock doors that had for so long been shut tight. And I liked it. In Kuala Lumpur, the day after the macaque stole my chips, I found myself crossing that busy street again in the rain. I remembered a bracelet I'd passed on my way to get copies of LSAT materials printed in the shopping center basement.

The bracelet was a mixture of turquoise marble and wood and reminded me of Sabrina. I purchased it. When I returned to DC and we had our next dinner date, I gave it to her.

I felt at peace when I was with her. Years ago, I had left the comfort of the Mississippi Delta, traveled the globe, fought in war, and experienced cultures that I once only dreamed of. None of it could compare to being with Sabrina. Her smile was warmer than the Mississippi sun. When I looked in her eyes, what I saw was more beautiful than an Okinawa sunset over the East China Sea. Her conversation was more exhilarating than a high school slam dunk, and her intellect seemed as vast as those cotton fields that stretched out forever. Her mere presence motivated me.

* *

It was Friday, June 23, 2017. At that point Sabrina and I had been together for more than three years. For the past twelve months we'd talked off and on about marriage. I could tell it bothered her that I usually either avoided the subject or dismissed it out of hand. She'd even threatened to leave and had her bag packed. I talked her into staying.

My parents had flown from Mississippi to Washington, DC, to attend my retirement ceremony at the White House Communications Agency's headquarters. I'd proudly served my country for twenty-one years, mostly overseas, and my parents had never physically attended a promotion or award ceremony. It was a difficult decision to walk away from the Army. I enjoyed serving and felt it was an honor to wear the uniform. However, I knew I wanted to do other things, namely attend law school and give back to my community, which had given me so much.

My retirement speech was all about Mom and Dad—the impact they'd had on my life and career.

The ceremony was bittersweet for Sabrina, though. She was there as my girlfriend—not fiancée or spouse. She had to sit through the entire ceremony while the military not only recognized me but also my parents and even Joseph and Rukiya. There was no protocol to recognize a girlfriend.

What Sabrina *didn't* know was the entire thing had been planned to surprise her. For twelve months, I, along with a few of my closest friends—Linc, Lydell, and Burnadette—had coordinated this very day.

At the end of the hour-long ceremony, I stood at the podium. I called Sabrina up to receive flowers from the ceremonial usher. The flower presentation was intentionally squeezed in at the end of the ceremony to appear somewhat tacky. By that point the three-hundred-person audience were simply waiting to stand and leave.

In front of everyone Sabrina walked to the stage, as a girlfriend. She received her flowers, not realizing I was behind her on bended knee, in full military dress uniform, holding an engagement ring.

As the audience let out an audible gasp, confusion crossed Sabrina's face. That is, until she turned around and heard me say, "Sabrina Curtis, will you marry me?"

* *

I DO

Just over a year later, in Santa Fe, New Mexico, in front of family and friends, not far from where Sabrina was born, we both said, "I do."

We stayed in the park for a long time that day just talking and laughing. We were both happy and excited about where our relationship was heading.

Sabrina had no idea I would propose to her at the end of my retirement ceremony. It took an entire year of planning.

We walked along the Georgetown Waterfront looking forward to our future together.

My entire retirement speech recognized my parents for instilling in me a resilient attitude and for all the hard work and sacrifices they made to raise me to be the man I am today.

Final salute! I thoroughly enjoyed serving my country and will forever be grateful for the many memories and friendships made.

PART FOUR

STILL RUNNINNG

CHAPTER TWENTY-THREE:

The 23rd Mile

———

For the past three years, since I began law school, some version of the same dream has filled each of my nights. That dream is the twenty-third mile. The race always begins the same: startled awake, I sit, legs dangling over the side of my bed. I drag myself to the bathroom and splash water on my face.

When I open my eyes, my face is dry and I'm no longer inside. The early morning darkness is interrupted by dull yellow streetlamps casting my shadow onto the concrete driveway. I stand motionless, for a moment, with tight-laced shoes, a fluorescent green shirt, and the pair of grey shorts I've owned since Germany.

For as long as I can remember, I've been running either from something, for something, or to something. Running from poverty, running for that little boy who so many years ago shared his story with me, and running to what was beyond that twenty-third mile.

Trotting along the smoothly paved street as the neat line of lampposts illuminated Congresbury Place, I make a right on Tewkesbury and then a left on Lake Forest Drive.

"Where Would I Be" by Kindred the Family Soul thumps in my headphones as my pace quickens.

In a flash, the lampposts are gone, the yellow light no more, and I find myself running alone in the darkness along Highway 4, straining to make out the path ahead. I glance at the iPhone strapped to my left bicep. "Only six miles completed…" Staring back over my shoulder, I think, "I still have a long way to go."

With each stride, the rhythmic crunch of gravel echoes through the forest. An aluminum can ricochets off the side of my shoe. The metallic clang pierces the darkness, awakening old memories of Dad collecting cans along Mississippi highways on cold winter days to feed our family.

I'd been running from poverty for a long time, determined to ensure that Mom and Dad's sacrifices for me were not in vain. Poverty, racism, and limited education made it difficult for them. But they always found a way to make ends meet and they gave me the tools to keep running this race our ancestors started so long ago. Many fell behind, sacrificing themselves so the rest could keep running. That understanding, ever-present in my mind, was the reason I kept running there alone in the dark, reaching for that twenty-third mile.

As the sun creeps through the trees lining Highway 4, I think about all the things I'd been lucky enough to be exposed to over the past twenty-three years. Learning new languages, exploring a vast array of cultures at home and abroad, finishing my final tour of duty, back home, at The White House, and developing new diplomacy skills while meeting presidents, heads of state, and most importantly, getting to know the everyday people in those countries. They, I suppose, are just trying to make it like most of us back home—all of this, and so much more, contributed to where I am at this moment.

As the morning traffic races by on my left, thoughts of Joseph and the day he'd come into this world tiptoe through my mind. I remember floating through the hospital halls with him cradled safely in my arms. When he stared up at me and our eyes met, everything changed. I imagined myself staring up at Dad when he walked into my life so many years ago, and changed everything for my mom and me. Drifting through the hospital with Joseph in my arms, all I could think was, "You are my son, I am your dad, and my heart is full." When I was at my lowest, Joseph came along and filled the void that Madea's departure left in my heart.

I keep running. The birds in the trees harmonize, an orchestral choir, reminding me of Rukiya's first sounds on the night she was born. That night when she cried, I wept tears of joy, my heart exploding in a supernova of love.

Joseph and Rukiya both gave me the feeling of loving someone more than I loved myself. I make a left onto Suitland Parkway. Trotting past Andrews Air Force Base, I'd already run fourteen miles. "Nine miles to go," I whisper to myself.

Thoughts of Sabrina wander through my mind, as I make a left onto Firth Sterling Avenue. Passing Joint Base Anacostia Bolling, I remember the day I'd proposed. The moment we met I knew Sabrina was the best thing to ever walk into my life. From her stunning intellect to her thirst for knowledge, her undying compassion for others to the ease with which she loved not just me, but both our kids. She was everything I needed, and more than I deserved.

Mom and Dad taught me the importance of taking care of my children, cherishing my wife, and protecting my family.

They'd given me so many examples of what it looked like to truly love someone.

At the twenty-mile mark, I cross the Fredrick Douglass bridge. Looking down, I notice that instead of the murky waters of the Anacostia River below, I saw visions of fluffy, white rows and rows of cotton. I remember sitting on that old, dusty porch on Elemwood, Madea setting a bowl of pinto beans in front of me, my mom and her sisters passing by the back of the house working in the field. I hear my cousin's laughter and the pitter-patter of little feet as we ran around and around that old house, chasing chickens beneath that huge weeping willow tree. All of these things are a part of me and make me who I am today.

I make my way down South Capitol Street. I go left on Washington Avenue and right on Independence before passing the Rayburn House Office Building. I'd run twenty-two miles.

"Less than a mile remaining," I think, sprinting across the Capitol lawn. A few more blocks and I pass E Street and then F Street before stopping on the corner of First Street and New Jersey Avenue. Breathing heavily, I bend over at the waist, tugging at the hem of my shorts, just as I'd done years earlier in basketball. Only this time, instead of a blaring whistle bouncing off gym walls, I hear the soulful tunes of Frankie Beverly's "We Are One," thumping in my headphones.

I'd made it to the twenty-third mile. It was the same place where I'd started nearly three years ago. It was the same place where I first sat waiting in my car as the miniature African drum dangled from my rearview window while, in the mirror's reflection, the US Capitol building gazed intently, only a few blocks away.

At this point in the dream, I pause to reflect. Standing on that intersection in my mind's eye, I have the same thoughts I'd had waiting in my car, anticipating my first day at Georgetown three years prior. I think about how Dad left school in sixth grade, how Mom left in the ninth. I think about how they sacrificed their education, and so much more, to get me here. I think about what they've given me, even though they had no bootstraps or boots. I think about the little boy from Mississippi in the shack by the fast-flowing creek. I envision him standing there, shoeless, on the sidewalk next to me, both of us staring intently at the building across the street.

I've had some version of this dream every night for the last three years.

**

Twenty-three years have passed since that little boy shared his story with me. A few years ago, on a trip back down to the Delta, I drove out to that old shack, nestled between that cotton field and that dirt road. The little boy was no longer there. The shack was barely standing—now dark and unoccupied. The rickety mailbox was gone; the grass had grown tall along the creek. No little dog was running around.

I stared at the spot in the middle of that dirt road where he fell to his knees and sobbed after realizing he had failed math class. I wondered, "How did life turn out for him?"

About three years ago, on a cold December day, I walked out of my front door and down my driveway. Snowflakes fell, melting on the back of my neck. I crossed the street and stood next to a set of mailboxes. I opened my mailbox and found an acceptance letter inside. I read it, smiled, and closed my eyes. I thought about deciding long ago not to give up and subsequently finding myself on an amazing journey around the world.

Since that day, the many experiences I've had brought me what I never thought possible. My insights and world-view had been broadened by new communities of people, strengthened by an education that lifted my family toward new directions.

You see, if you've not already come to it, the little boy in the story at the beginning of this book is me. When I opened the Georgetown acceptance letter on that cold winter day nearly three years ago, I could not help but wonder if my twelve-year-old self could've even dreamt of graduating from a major law school. I'll at least be able to tell my younger self, under the Mississippi sun in the middle of that dirt road, that his parents sacrificing their education wasn't in vain. That his community and the social, cultural, and economic capital he'll be exposed to will help him to overcome. I can assure him that Madea and Daddy-Eck's garden grown and homemade meals, Val's talent shows, Sensei Duckworth's Kumite, Mom's soft brown eyes, Dad's puhkhans, and Coach Miller's mentorship, among so many other things, will all help propel him forward. The love he'll receive from Joseph, Rukiya, and Sabrina will help to keep him on track. I can tell him that one day he'll travel the globe, work for the first black president, and attend one of the best law schools in the country. As long as he never gives up.

**

For the past three years, I've driven twenty-three miles each way to attend law school at the Georgetown University Law Center. However, today, I decided to run to class. As I began running I reflected on my life—just like I've done nightly in my recurring dream for years.

I was born across the street from a cotton field on January 23, 1974. Now, as I reach the twenty-third mile mark across from McDonough Hall, I've geared up to keep running. I'm hoping I can eventually pass the baton on to others, just as it was passed on to me by my parents, grandparents, and ancestors. If my experience has taught me anything it's that you can work hard, but achievement is near impossible without help. I can never fully express how thankful I am for all the help I've received in my life, for all the sacrifices that were made on my behalf.

Today, I'm running the twenty-three miles to class in my final year of law school. As my sneakers hit the well-manicured DC pavement, I can look down and see that little country boy's bare feet hitting the dirt road while he runs alongside that fast-flowing creek. I see his family, community, and ancestors behind him, cheering him on. I see that my story, his story, is their story. I see him smiling as we approach the finish line together.

Acknowledgments

___

Thank you, Sabrina, my wonderful partner and wife. You, Joseph, and Rukiya, are my everyday inspirations. Your continued love, support, and encouragement were essential for completing this book. Thank you, Mom and Dad. Without your sacrifices and your belief in me, this story would not even be possible. Thank you for encouraging me to reach beyond the stars and for teaching me to see the good in others.

Thank you to my publisher, New Degree Press, for making this book possible. Thank you to Jordan Waterwash, Eric Koester, Brian Bies, Kristy Carter, Michelle Felich and everyone on the New Degree Press team who helped me along this journey. A special thanks to my good friend Jason Kise for your invaluable support, and keen editing eye.

Last, but certainly not least, thank you to everyone who supported me from the beginning of this process by purchasing my book early. The initial contributors include Abraham Medina, Ahmad Murrar, Alan Bray, Alison Buehler, Angela Brown, Angela Grayson, Anthony Gordon, Anthony Houzah, Anthony Brownlow, Bernie Miller, Beverly Fortune, Bobbi King-Warren, Brandale Mills Cox, Brian Miller, Brittany

Pinkins, Burnadette Faison, Cathey Lewis Bell, Chad
Raduege, Charles Lindsey, Christopher Carmack, Cierra
Dennis, Claretta Hite, Corey Antley, Cynthia Walker, Daniel Davenport, Danielle Robinette, Darius Johnson, Darlene
Becton, Darryl Christmon, David Gerlach, David Kolokolo,
David McCallum, Debi Huff, DeEtte Henderson, Delano Gibson, Demetria Jackson, Demetrick Banks, Denisha Jackson,
Don Crawford, Donnell Green, Lanita Jackson, Lura Danley, Edricque Tolbert, Elaine Clay, Elgin Funches, Ellen Watlington, Eric Coleman, Eric Koester, Everett Bellamy, Felicia
Brown, Fernando Tomlinson, Fredirick Conner, Gary Bovee,
Gary Dorsey, Gilberto Perez, Glen Jackson, Gloria Porter,
Gregory Miller, Gustella Williams, Gwendolyn Douglas,
Jady Chen, Jameca Falconer, James Williams, Janae Staicer,
Janice Galloway, Jason Kise, Jenise Davis, Jennifer Pinkins,
Jessica Berdley, Jimmie Townsend, John Atwell, Jonathan
Smith, Josh Aultman, Josiah Hughes, Juanita Jackson, Julie
Yelle, Justin Gentry, Justin Rattey, James Young, Katie Buys,
David Buys, Keith Vanyo, Kenneth Crawford, Kris Everson,
Lakeitha Alexander, Laketric Allen, LaMonte Westbrook,
LaQuita Cameron, Larry Babb, Lashanda Feazell, Lenora
Winn, Leon Brown, Linc McCoy, Linh Vo, Lionel Scatliffe,
Lorenzo Lewis, Luella Brown, Lydell Faison, Malcolm Morse,
Marcus Cooley, Marilyn Edwards, Marty Kibiswa, Marvin
Brown, Maura DeMouy, Maurice Dunn, Michael Fisher,
Michael Franklin, Michael Kinsey, Michele Poole, Monica
Jackson, Morgan McClure, Myron Byrd, Naomi Taka, Norielys Bonilla, Owen Agho, Patricia Pie, Paul McKnight, Robert
Ellis Screws, Ramona Brock, Ravan Austin, Rebecca Jackson, Reginald Anderson, Remesh Adams, Reshma Baig, Riah
Kim, Robert Golightly, Robert Stephens, Roderick Fisher,
Ronald Scott Novack, Rosie Jackson, Roy Rucker, Sabrina

Bernadel, Saibatu Mansaray, Samuel Grayson, Sarah Jones, Scott Enfield Berry, Scott Gray, Shandrick Taylor, Sheldon Jones, Sonya Poole, Stacey Green, Stephanie Booker-Wynn, Stephen Hall, Suprina Hite, Sylvester Pinkins, Tamia Hall, Tanya Hardy, Temesgen Woldezion, Thomas Mayfield, Tim Sander, Tobias Jenkins, Toyce Small, Tracy Flewellen, Tristin Brown, Uchenna Osagiede, Val Tanner, Valencia Richardson, Valencia Sherman-Greenup, Wade Grayson, Walter Clay, Wylie Clough.

To all those I missed, thank you.

CPSIA information can be obtained
at www.ICGtesting.com
Printed in the USA
BVHW040049280920
589743BV00008B/50/J

9 781641 374965